THE EDGE OF
EVIL

BOOKS BY JERRY JOHNSTON:

Why Suicide?
Going All the Way
The Edge of Evil

THE EDGE OF

EVIL

The Rise of Satanism in North America

JERRY JOHNSTON

WORD PUBLISHING
Dallas · London · Sydney · Singapore

The author wishes to express appreciation to the following publishers for permission to quote from their books:

Material on "The Doctrine of Satan" from the Ryrie Study Bible, copyright 1976, 1978 by the Moody Bible Institute of Chicago, and Moody Press. Used by permission.

Jay's Journal, © 1979 by Beatrice Sparks. Reprinted by permission of Pocket Books, a division of Simon and Schuster, Inc.

Library of Congress Cataloging-in-Publication Data

Johnston, Jerry, 1959–
   The edge of evil.
     1. Satanism—United States. 2. Satanism—Canada.
I. Title.
BF1548.J64 1989   133.4'22'0973   88-33897
ISBN 0-8499-0668-7

Printed in the United States of America
9 8 0 1 2 3 9 MP 9 8 7 6 5 4 3

To

SEAN SELLERS

who, as the youngest man on death row in Oklahoma, for the murder of his parents, is climbing out of the black world of satanism. My time one on one with Sean convinced me that something had to be said to the thousands of other young satanists who want to escape before they too drop over the edge of evil. You *can* get out.

Acknowledgments

A project of this magnitude is not accomplished alone. My thanks go to several key people.

To Chris, my best friend, wife, and closest associate, who knowing the risk in an assignment like this, encouraged me on for the sake of people everywhere, who needed to know the truth, particularly young teenage satanists who think there is no way out.

To Geraldo Rivera, a media personality with true guts. Regardless if certain critics want to censor him into a "trash T.V." category, I, millions of other genuine people who want reality, and the ratings themselves, will be there cheering him on.

To the daring, brave people of the Investigative News Group whose "Devil Worship: Exposing Satan's Underground" T.V. special registered the highest audience rating of *any* documentary in prime time.

To my research associate who helped me plow through the mountains of information we dug up. To Donna Monroe, my assistant, who organized and orchestrated the flights, hotels, faxes, federal expresses, computer discs, modems, and my ever disheveled desk.

And finally to Ernie Owen, Kip Jordon, and Jim Black at Word who believe in me and my dreams . . . thank you.

Jerry Johnston's message is regularly heard by thousands of people in civic centers from coast-to-coast.

Contents

x ◀ Contents

Foreword

Whether Satan exists is a matter of belief. But we are certain that satanism exists. To some it's a religion. To others it's the practice of evil in the devil's name. It exists and it's flourishing.

It is teenagers who are most likely to fall under the spell of this jumble of dark, violent emotions called satanism. And in some cases, they are driven into committing terrible deeds.

Satanism is more than a hodgepodge of mysticism and fantasy, more than a Halloween motif. It's a violent impulse that preys on the emotionally vulnerable, especially teenagers, who are often lonely and lost. It attracts the angry and the powerless, who often sink into secret lives—possessed by an obsessive fascination with sex, drugs, and heavy metal rock-and-roll.

Often satanism seems to be a personal psychodrama, a kind of license for strange, sometimes violent behavior. Sometimes it is just half-baked mumbo-jumbo and scrawled symbols. But other times it goes deeper and is far more deadly. Satanism goes far beyond teenage obsession.

All of us know that life is not safe. Every day we face the possibility of crime, disease, accidents, and disasters. So here comes satanism which most of us would like to write off as harmless antics by some lunatic fringe. A few years ago, but not now. We have seen that satanism can be linked to dope and pornography, child abuse, and murder. It has led seemingly normal teenagers into monstrous behavior. Some merely preach mysticism. Others, however, practice the most horrifying kinds of evil.

Jerry Johnston takes the lid off satanism in North America. He has criss-crossed the United States and Canada in search of the truth about satanism. This informed and readable report is the result of that research.

GERALDO RIVERA

Investigative reporter Geraldo Rivera. The Bettman Archive.

Introduction

Saturday Night Live's Church Chat Lady is in her all too familiar behind-the-desk seated pose. Her hands are sanctimoniously folded with the mock stained glass windows positioned perfectly behind her. Reflecting on the demise of a crying Christian leader to her right, with an awry smile, she asks the audience, "And who shall we blame this on?" She suggests "SAAAAATAN?" And the crowd howls with laughter.

But is this satan someone to be laughing about? Although occultic practices are as ancient as man, there is a fast-growing developing subculture movement in the teenage community, namely satanism. Unlike the temporarily mimicked dress style of rock idols, satanism among the young is here to stay. But to where will it lead? I predict this will become the most hideous and horrendous reality for educators, parents, and teens themselves to deal with in the next decade as we enter the Twenty-first Century.

Throughout North America I have stood on the platforms of auditoriums and gymnasiums and met head on, wall to wall, hundreds of thousands of the young generation. Some time ago I started noticing a distinctive new category of kids attending my talks who did not fit the norm.

These young people glared with a fascination that was dark and deadly. The very word "occult" means "hidden things." And with these curious looking teens there was just the sign-posts that they were involved. In all those audiences I kept noticing more and more teens with homemade pentagram tattoos and symbols carved into the web between their thumb and index finger. Too many notebooks scrawled with "666" and "NATAS"—satan spelled backwards or "LIVE"—evil spelled backwards. Satanism plays with opposite, with mirror-images, with the reverse of anything good: satanists memorize the Lord's Prayer backwards. Teachers are asking what to do about students turning in essays about satanism and death.

1

More than one parent stands shocked upon the discovery of materials left behind in the room of a son or daughter who has committed suicide. A skull, a pentagram drawn on the floor under the rug, or behind a picture, and a notebook called a Book of Shadows with entries that are horrifying.

It is so bizarre, it almost blows the mind. In quiet, small towns along with the booming metropolis, there are innumerable incognito, covert satanic groups. They blend in so inconspicuously with society, they go as unnoticed as a bland wallpaper stretching across a wall.

Noted authority Arthur Lyons states that the United States harbors the fastest growing and most organized body of satanists in the world. Sounds unbelievable, doesn't it?

Occasionally there are those unmistakable "accidents" that remind us that satanists are in our city working secretly and seductively to lure more in. What was it that possessed fourteen-year-old Tommy Sullivan to tackle his mother to the floor in the basement of his New Jersey home? Possessed by an uncontrollable frenzy, Tommy stabbed his mother fourteen times, slit her throat, slashed most of her face away, and set the house on fire. This likeable teenager, known in the community because of his paper route, slit his own wrists and throat with such force that he almost cut his head off.

The descriptive mandate from his Book of Shadows revealed that he had seen a vision of Satan. In his trance he was ordered to kill his family and preach satanism to his friends.

How I wish Tommy's situation was an isolated event. But it is not. In every state and across the provinces, satanism among the young with its bizarre, violent behavior is growing like a prairie fire. Georgia's Melissa Ernest, seventeen, shrieks as the judge sentences her to life in prison. Teamed with her coven friends, Melissa participated in the human sacrifice of her friend, Theresa Simmons.

And from the hall of satanic infamy there is more. Richard Rameriz, noted Night-Stalker, blurts out "Hail Satan" in a Los Angeles courtroom. His pentagram tattoo is noticeable on his raised palm. Jim Hardy, Ron Clements, and Pete Roland, all from the obscure Carl Junction, Missouri, and charged with first-degree murder, dump the battered body of Steven Newberry in their "Well of Hell." Why? According to Ron, "Because it's fun." My interview with Jim Hardy in chapter 4 reflects the acute depravity of the satanic philosophy on a young mind.

As I spent nearly two hours behind bars with Sean Sellers, I was reminded of the horror of it all. At nineteen, Sean is the youngest man on death row in the state of Oklahoma. I, along with our T.V. crew, was frozen as Sean carefully described how he murdered his parents as they slept in their bed. Sean said he stood at the bed laughing hysterically immediately following his crime. Again, my immediate response, Why, Sean? "Because I loved them," was his reply.

Instead of settling for what has been reported and receiving the accompanying bias, I have gone to the experts, the law enforcement personnel, satanists themselves and the teenage killers, and in this book they detail their own viewpoints. It was an eerie mobile saga that had me criss-crossing the United States and Canada viewing firsthand the stark reality.

How are the kids recruited? What are their personal stories? And how can we protect our own children from falling prey is carefully and meticulously set forth. It is no ghost and goblin story. Jerry Simandl, veteran expert of the Chicago Police Department's Gang Crime Unit, shared with me that there are four distinct levels of the satanic movement coast-to-coast. They are:

1. **The teenage dabblers.** These are young people who take up a preoccupation with the occult through such over involvement with fantasy role-playing games, suggestive heavy metal music, drugs, seances, and a quest for power. The teenage dabbler faithfully studies the *Satanic Bible* and has made it one of the best selling paperbacks for the past twenty years. (According to Avon Books of New York as of February 1989 the Satanic Bible is in its twenty-seventh printing with 618,000 copies sold!) He or she is usually above average in intelligence and generally a loner. Occasionally there may be a small sect of friends (i.e., a coven). The dabbler practices chants, incantations, and reads numerous occultic books, including *Satanic Rituals* and *The Complete Witch*, by Anton LaVey, among many others.

2. **Self-styled satanic groups or covens.** Teens are recruited through free drugs and sex parties where they are told only a select few may enter a special room. During the party the person is photographed or videotaped in a "compromising" situation. Then, if invited into the special room, candidates are gradually told about a contract with Satan. If they hesitate to join, they are told the photo or videotape will be used against them. Who are the recruiters? Stereo-typical normal adults employed in every vocation in a community, but in reality, undercover satanists. Sounds fantastic, doesn't it? And if it weren't so frequently reported and verified, it would have to be untrue.

3. **Public religious satanists.** Whether theatrical or truly intellectual adherents, these people attend your "First Satan Church," etc. (Michael Aquino and Anton LaVey are two of the prominent people in this category.) Their number is growing. There are hundreds of similar religious satanic groups in cities everywhere. Since they are incorporated as non-profit religious organizations they enjoy a tax-exempt status similar to a church or synagogue. The United States military even recognizes the Church of Satan. The most damaging contribution of this group is that their writings sell in the millions.

Debra Winger's gripping portrayal of the devastating shock learning of the intricate organization and high level members of the Ku Klux Klan in the movie, "Betrayed," mirrors what could certainly take our breath away if we only knew the full scope of this particular satanic group.

④ **The Hardcore Satanic Cults.** This group has always been with us. They are internationally located throughout the world. Perhaps more organized than the mafia, they are known to kill, abduct and brainwash ever so secretly. Dr. Al Carlisle of the Utah State Prison System has estimated that between forty and sixty thousand human beings are killed through ritual homicides in the United States each year. This statistic is based upon an estimated number of satanists at the level where they commit ritual human sacrifices times the frequency with which these would be done during a satanic calendar year. Dr. Carlisle estimated that in the Las Vegas metropolitan area alone six hundred people meet their deaths during satanic ceremonies each year!

The new category of "ritualistic oriented" crime is quickly establishing itself in police bureaus everywhere.

The buzz word is "power." The consuming, continuing drive of the satanist is to gain greater power. Parents, educators, and teenagers themselves need to know what is happening on the high school and university campus. This has been my domain in hundreds of cities. In this book I have presented the facts with very little of my own opinion interjected.

Call it the phenomenon of the '90s. And take it one step at a time as you learn about *The Edge of Evil;* more importantly, see what prevention and information steps you can take to protect yourself and the ones you love.

JERRY JOHNSTON
Kansas City

Part One

◆▶

Satan's New Children: The Young Sorcerers

 There are two ways to be fooled:
One is to believe what isn't so;
the other is to refuse to believe
what is so.

—Kierkegaard

Anton S. LaVey, whose theatrical brand of Satanism has nonetheless seriously influenced thousands of his young readers. The Bettman Archive.

▶ 1 ◀

In the Beginning

I readily admit I'm a little dazed after months of hearing stories about sacrificed chickens and babies and talking to a priest who participated in the exorcisms on which "The Exorcist" was based. I have interrogated the chief of the Los Angeles Police Department on how to handle evil; I've looked into demonic eyes, listened to therapists and counselors and cops with stories and opinions I don't want to think about. I've read too many books, listened to too many tapes, pored through stashes of my own notes scrawled on parking ticket backs or business cards as I searched for the last name of Matt the witch who works at Dari D-Lux or the address of the minister-satanist who runs the camp in Indiana or Geraldo Rivera's phone number. Earlier tonight I Federal Expressed a plane ticket to Lynn, who was promised she'd not live through this highest of black holidays because she'd renounced the satanic cult she'd been born into—the Brotherhood of the Flame. I tried getting law enforcement to put a man on her at least till tomorrow morning, but I don't know if I was believed any more than she has been with her bizarre stories of satanic terrorism. If she lives through the weekend, the plane ticket will at least get her out of the area.

There seems to be no end to these satanic stories; but it's time to start sharing this wild mass of material with you.

Occultism: Fad for the 1990s

So our investigation into Satan's new children culminated with the fear. But it started with the suicides.

Over an eight-year period, I have stood on the peeling varnish of gym floors and the stages of multipurpose rooms in more than 3,000 schools and in hundreds of convention center auditoriums. I have looked into the faces

7

of 3,000,000 teenagers and tried to convince them life was worth it. I have admitted that I had been one of the teenage statistics who try suicide now at a rate of 1,000 a day (National Center for Health Statistics).

Imagine those 1,000 teenagers lining up every day, block after block, all wishing they were dead. Look at the line. Pick out the eighteen who succeed every day. Imagine the eighteen funerals every Monday and every Tuesday and every day, month in and month out. Think of the faces of the parents, of all those teenage friends left behind.

After the assemblies, ninth graders with blue hair would cry about friends lost to depression and intentional drug overdoses. Senior lettermen would mumble about girlfriends' abortions and Dad's beatings and depression. And sophomores would whisper about the suicidal thoughts that haunted them after flunking English 101.

It was during the '87–'88 school year that I finally began to notice: There were too many of them with homemade pentagram tattoos and symbols carved into the web between their thumb and index finger. Too many notebooks scrawled with "666" and "NATAS"—Satan spelled backwards. Too many teachers mentioning kids' occult preoccupation with death in essays. And too many parents contacting me with "We couldn't believe the stuff we found in his room after the suicide. A skull, a pentagram under the rug, black candles, a notebook with entries we don't want to think about . . . ."

I'd known for some time that several of the publicized suicide pacts made among high schoolers were occult-related. On January 6, 1988, popular Vermont sophomore Michelle Kimball killed herself in a suicide pact with her boyfriend. He survived. Her suicide note said that she worshiped Satan and knew her parents wouldn't understand.

In Roy City, Utah, a youth's satanic oath was found in his billfold after he died of intentional carbon-monoxide poisoning. The handwritten note said: "In the name of Satan, Lucifer, Belial, Leviathan, and all the demons, named and nameless, walkers in the velvet darkness, harken to us, O dim and shadowy things, wraith-like, twisted, half-seen creatures. Welcome a new and worthy brother."

Sixteen-year-old Steve Loyacano left a note in Colorado that said he was "caught between a hatred for this world and a thirst for blood," that he couldn't handle it. He died of carbon-monoxide poisoning in the family garage.

But I wasn't prepared for the deluge of satanic crime and pain that hit the high schools of the United States and Canada this past year. There has always been interest in the occult on junior high, high school and college campuses. But in the last few years, the interest has slid to the dark end of the occult spectrum. Satanism is in vogue.

Here's what's happening; here's what we'll be exploring in *The Edge of Evil*:

Teenagers are dabbling their way into satanism. It's a fad, just as bobbie sox and hula hoops and pet rocks were fads. But it's a fad that's incredibly dangerous, since on the teenage level satanism invariably includes drugs, sex and mindbending states of altered consciousness. Somehow hula hoops just didn't have the same punch.

Another phenomenon is rumbling from our culture's underground: organized satanic cults. They've always been there in some form; but today they're protected as religious organizations. And for various reasons they're getting blatant in their activities; they're actively recruiting teenagers to join their drug or pornography operations, to exult in their revels.

The combination is volatile: teenage dabblers, warped by drugs and experiments to conjure demons, get in over their heads in crime—arson, vandalism, grave desecration, animal mutilation. And some don't stop there. Some go on to murder. Some join their cultic elders in a lifetime of devotion to the lord of death.

How many kids are involved? Who are these organized satanists? Is today's satanism actually dangerous or just a sensationalist topic for melodramatic talk shows, fuming preachers and cheap books?

I don't know. I'm no occult expert. Which is why I have dug into the issue, asked the experts and developed some rational strategies to deal with satanized kids and to prevent teenagers from dabbling their way to other worlds.

The Satanic Quest

At a window table dangling out over the green-blue Pacific, I leaf through a set of notes I've been jotting on teenagers and satanism. I've asked a California-based friend to gather up some information on the topic and to meet me at Stagnaro's in Santa Cruz.

Santa Cruz is the perfect beach town—a wonderful setting for the best times a teenager could have surfing, backpacking in the coastal hills, scuba diving, screaming on the roller coaster, hanging out sitting on car hoods along Beach Street to watch the girls or the guys cruise.

It's tough to imagine any teenager in a town like this having to turn for new kicks to the old black arts of satanism.

Yet Santa Cruz is one of the hottest spots in California for satanism. The early '70s saw a rash of mysterious occult murders and the presence of hardcore satanic cults in the redwood-and-pine hills surrounding this town which is named, in Spanish, "Holy Cross." And today, high school kids here are in on the satanism fad like they are all over the continent. What a waste.

Just then my friend, Tom, appears and I greet him. He is eager to start our discussion.

"I don't know about this topic. So far we have your dozen or so dead babies, massive group orgies and rapes whenever there's a Bride of Satan ceremony. We have hysterical grandmothers with kidnaped grandkids sold as slaves to satanic cults, three appropriately solemn women appearing on talk shows to describe how they were breeders for the devil. We've got demons, we've got your demon possessed, demon oppressed, demon depressed and demon obsessed. These demons do everything to you—you can get blood-baptized, pentagram-sanitized, sanforized, Martinized—"

"All right, all right." I notice people starting to squint into the sun to see just who's mumbling such obscenities over by the window. "Let me guess. You don't like the topic."

Tom shrugs. "It's a nasty subject, Jerry. These are nasty people. The minute this sensational stuff is mentioned, defense mechanisms are set up to avoid it."

The waiter takes Tom's order while I explain. "I'm not going for the sleazy stuff. I'm not going to do some heroic exposé of the hardcore criminal satanic cults. That's for the cops."

"Good. Otherwise you'll get your yard strewn with dead chickens. If they go easy on you."

"My point is, I'm tired of adults looking at this satanism fad teenagers are into as just a silly passing phase. Once the fad has come and gone, they'll still be sex-drug-demon fiends; which is not a happy situation when they'll be the adults of the next century. When they get into it, they go straight to Hell. They do not pass 'Go,' and they do not collect $200."

The waiter looks alarmed as he serves my salad.

"Monopoly game talk," smiles Tom at him. The waiter nods, leaves, and Tom says, "Long as you keep it on that level—that kids can't shock their '60s parents with drugs or sex since Mom and Dad knew all about it. So they zap them with Satan."

"And instantly drop into a world of sex as worship, drugs to make it easier to cut up the family cat, and warped, warped minds."

"And spirits," adds Tom. "Going to stay away from the mystical end of it all?"

"Sort of. But it's bound to come up since that's what it's really all about. What have you got for me?"

Tom flops his briefcase flat on the carpet and opens it to reveal a stack of huge manila envelopes. "Some of it's so crazy. How do you express it: 'Man Cuts Off Own Head with Chainsaw As Satanic Sacrifice—And Lives!' But everything is annotated with a source. I know you have had a good time chatting with some of these characters." He picks up a packet and a slip of paper twirls away on a draft from the doorway.

I leap to grab it midair, realizing that not only the waiter but the entire Stagnaro Seafood Restaurant now knows we must be hopelessly drugged or deranged spies. The scrap reads: "Arthur Lyons writes in his book, *The Second Coming: Satanism in America*, that 'the United States probably harbors the fastest growing and most highly organized body of satanists in the world.'"

Tom picks up another loose scrap. "Well, most of them are annotated. At least we know it came from Lyons' book. It'll be listed in the bibliography envelope. This scrap from somewhere says, 'Satanic cult survivors have reported names of cult members who are law enforcement officials, judges, politicians and other government leaders, medical doctors, ministers, entertainers, teachers and psychologists.'

"Listen," he continues, "We have copied off thousands of microfiched news clippings about teenagers and satanism. There are probably a hundred more that could be copied, but at least here's a representative stack." I reach over and set a packet of photocopies on the table. "Maybe I could run them alongside the narrative or something like starting in chapter two. Each account is nothing in itself, but the sheer attrition of story after story from all over starts to suggest that there's definitely something going on between kids and Satan these days."

Between bites I ask, "So we have a list of contacts? Teenagers, satanists, anti-satanists?"

"Right. Some of them are professionals, some just kids. I think the way we'd better present it is Studs Terkel-like. Let's just let them talk. So the feeling will be more human interest than industrial-strength crime. There is also a hodge-podge of general info; let me read a few overview pieces while you are eating.

"Here's one," he says, "from a John Frattarola article in a 1986 *Passport* magazine." He mimics Paul Harvey with, "Page two: Blah, blah . . . referring to what she and other authorities—I take it she's a therapist." He reads:

Dr. Gould is referring to what she and many other authorities are calling an epidemic of ritual abuse which is sweeping our nation and our world at a frightening pace. And children from infants to teenagers are the primary targets.

In every state in the nation there are reports and investigations of satanic crimes. Two million children a year are reported missing, many of them runaways. Five thousand unidentifiable bodies of children are found each year in the U.S. Hundreds of teenagers are committing suicide, or attempting it after attending satanic heavy metal concerts or listening to black heavy metal music. Thousands of children from neighborhoods, preschools and daycare centers around the country are telling strikingly similar stories of human and animal sacrifices in connection with strange devil rituals. Satanic graffiti can be found on highway overpasses, walls . . . . Cemeteries are being desecrated and graves robbed. Bodies of mutilated animals are reported being found in connection with occultic rituals.

In California alone reports have been staggering. In the Los Angeles area there have been 64 preschools and 27 neighborhoods with reported satanic activity over the past two years. In Orange County there have been at least six murders with satanic ties in the last year and a half. Ten straight-A teenagers in an Ontario, California, high school recently put together a two-page step-by-step plan on how to get rid of their parents. Step number ten was the "ultimate sacrifice"—cutting up the bodies of the parents and feeding them to dogs, then sacrificing the dogs. In Fremont a Japanese high school exchange student was beaten and stabbed to death by a teenage couple with satanist backgrounds. In Mendocino County several children claim to have been raped at a preschool while being forced to chant, "Baby Jesus is dead." Twelve boys in Pico Rivera said they were sodomized by four neighborhood men during satanic rituals. In San Francisco an eight-year-old girl reported to police that she was made to stab a baby by her father in a candle-lit room with an upside-down cross. Seventy children in Bakersfield were removed from their homes because they were claimed to be used in satanic rituals by their parents. Also under investigation in Southern California are charges of satanic ritual abuse in an institution for deaf children. Similar—

"True stuff?" I interrupt.

"True stuff," he says. "Here's a blurb from a crime briefing called the Criminal Intelligence Report out of Bethesda, Maryland. In one of the February '88 articles on 'Satanism and Crime' they say, 'There is increasing evidence that the United States and Canada are facing a rapidly expanding area of criminal activity that some experts claim could be the most difficult to detect of any that law enforcement agencies have had to deal with.'

"Here's a California Council on Criminal Justice report of the State Task Force on Youth Gang Violence. Finding 8 says that among other types of gangs —punk, heavy metal—satanic gangs have emerged as a new phenomenon. It says satanic gangs 'differ greatly from the more traditional street gangs. Most of their activities are secretive and therefore are hard to identify. . . . Members are mostly white and of a middle-class socio-economic status . . . ; their behavior is violent—they enjoy shock value . . . , believe in anarchy; and their goal is to destroy, not protect territory as usual in street gangs. These groups' activities include drawing graffiti, using illegal drugs, abusing children and assaulting parents. Grave robbing, desecration of animals and human remains—' Actually, we call them stoners."

"I wonder if what we are finding is just happening in California? I know it seems like everything starts out here and then seeps through the rest of the western hemisphere, but—"

"Nope. West Coast, East Coast, Midwest, South, Southeast, the Northwest, British Columbia. Remember, we dredged up some contacts in the Toronto area; I figure you'll hit that satanic hotspot just about Halloween. There'll be a full moon on October 25th—perfect timing for you to get abducted by devil worshipers."

"Right," I say.

"One last thought, then I'll leave you to your own devices. This is the intro to an article I've been working on. Thought it might give you some tidbits to ponder as you head back to MidAmerica."

So he reads:

There are a million of them in the United States alone. They're sometimes community leaders, daycare directors. But most of them are younger, ages 13 to 22. They're the kid down the block.

Some of them are simply practicing their religion. But others kill dogs; according to one in junior high school: "We threw it off the balcony and stomped on its head." They cut themselves and dig up graves. They steal babies and commit human sacrifices. Most are just dabblers, interested in heightening their sex-and-drug thrills. But dabblers often fall into deeper levels of involvement in a raging subculture we don't like to think about.

The underground, primary practitioners are well organized, networking through drug and porno rings, through computerized bulletin boards to schedule ceremonies and target victims. They're the new satanic underground.

A Trend for the 1990s

No, I'm not one of those alarmists who snivel about clandestine groups conspiring to rule the world. I'm an author and specialist who's talked nose-to-nose with kids who are tough, happy, depressed, romantic, outrageous, nice, dangerous. I'm not easily fazed anymore by foulmouths, by rebellion and delinquency, by teenagers who love to shock adults.

But the young of today's satanic subculture scare me.

The new twists to the ancient arts are goosebump material:

—Fourteen-year-old Tommy Sullivan murders his mother, tries to burn his father and brother to death, then slits his throat and wrists with his Boy Scout knife. Newark, New Jersey, police who find Sullivan dead in the snow in a neighbor's yard conclude the youth was "entranced by the occult."

—Animal mutilations increase among occult groups. "The animal is decapitated and left in a ritual position," says Orange County, California, Animal Control chief Ron Hudson. "Usually officers will find the front feet cut off because they're used by Satan to walk the earth."

—Fifteen-year-old runaway Theresa Simmons is ritually strangled by three Georgia ninth graders in what Douglas County sheriff Earl Lee describes as a killing of "sex, satanic devil worship and witchcraft."

—Lauren Stratford admits on a nationally televised talk show: "As a teenager I was used as a breeder to have children, and two of them were killed in snuff films."

—Seventeen-year-old Theron Roland of Carl's Junction, Missouri, thinks Satan will appear and bless him with power after he and two other teenagers beat a friend to death with baseball bats.

—A small group of Northport Harbor, New York, teenagers force student Gary Lauwers to say, "I love you, Satan" while stabbing him; then they drag him into the woods, gouge out his eyes and leave him to die. Investigator Bill Keahon, head of Long Island Major Offense Bureau, tells the *New York Times*, "You take a mixture of some very disturbed young people with antisocial behavior in their background, and you have a daily intake of drugs, angel dust, mescaline and the like. From there you go to kids who sacrifice animals, who cut animals up, and the next step is murder."

The list goes on, and the list is getting longer. There's no doubt the topic of satanism is sensational. The media often capitalizes on the public's morbid curiosity about the bizarre.

Believe It or Not?

What do you think? Can we be rational about this topic when we're hearing about babies tortured or teenagers lured to drugs-and-sex satanic parties or that prominent members of communities are practicing satanists?

Perhaps the best advice to keep our investigation sane is to follow Grandma's old admonition not to believe everything we hear. Or read.

For example, in no less than five decently credible sources on satanism, I ran across a document which was in every case presented as factual.

Law enforcement officials confiscated a letter which purportedly contains the protocols of the Witches International Coven Council or WICCA—not to be confused with the wiccan school of "white" witchcraft. Apparently the WICCA group met at a conclave in Mexico in 1981, and San Diego police obtained a copy of their resolutions:

1. To bring about the covens, both black and white magic, into one and have the arctess to govern all.
2. To bring about personal debts causing discord and disharmony within families.
3. To remove or educate the new age youth by:
   a. infiltrating boys/girls clubs and big sister/big brother programs
   b. infiltrating schools, having prayers removed, having teachers teach about drugs, sex, freedoms
   c. instigating and promoting rebellion against parents and all authority
   d. promoting equal rights for youth.
4. To gain access to all people's backgrounds and vital information by:
   a. use of computers
   b. convenience
   c. infiltration
5. To have laws changed to benefit our ways, such as:
   a. removing children from the home environment and placing them in our foster homes
   b. mandatory placement of children in our daycare centers
   c. increased taxes
   d. open drug and pornography market to everyone
6. To destroy government agencies by:
   a. overspending
   b. public opinion

Now, I'm no textual critic, but this alleged document is as genuine as a three dollar bill. Much as the "Protocols of the Learned Elders of Zion" was a fake document on how the Jews of the world were plotting to overthrow everybody, this letter is either a not-too-clever rendition of the fears of an enemy of the black arts or a twelfth grader's civics doodling.

The only lexical hint that the author knows anything about the occult is the single word "arctress." Other than that, the vocabulary is that of any English-speaking adult. Avoiding the use of any other secretive witchcraft/satanic jargon in a supposedly top secret witchcraft/black arts manifesto is fishy.

The grammar is inconsistent. If satanic witches gathered from all corners of the globe in Mexico for an international fest, surely someone in the mob would have balked at the phrasing "To bring about the covens . . . into one." Now, the witches and wizards and satanists I've run into so far are intelligent people. Some of the teenage dabblers are a little fuzzy from their drug-induced highs, but adults who are dedicated to the dark side appear to me to be generally well-read, usually well-educated. They'd never write as the ultimate document's opening line anything like "bring about the covens into one."

Finally, the content of the letter is nearly ridiculous. And again, these people are not airheads. If a satanist group were plotting to overthrow the world, would they enumerate items that only applied to the US or Canadian social structure? Not too many countries are blessed with boys or girls clubs, daycare centers, or schools in which prayers can be "removed." So the American ethnocentricity of the WICCA letter suggests it comes from a group or an individual from North America with absolutely no insight into establishing a world-class satanic religion.

The content also is simply ludicrous. Does "having teachers teach about drugs, sex, freedoms" mean anything? Or if the manifesto were serious about such a goal, wouldn't it at least mention in what way these items were to be taught: Should the teachers, in order to establish satanism as the world religion, teach pro or con "freedoms"? WICCA satanists are going to "gain access to all people's backgrounds" by "convenience"? They're going to "bring about personal debts"?

Now, how much would you believe? The seventh goal wasn't formulated at the 1981 conference; it was to be revealed at the celebration of the summer solstice in 1986. In that revelation, also confiscated by friendly contacts, covens are authorized to abduct and sacrifice adults or children on the twenty-fourth of each month for the following 11 years, until 1997. At that time the satanists expect to be in complete control.

This seventh goal, according to a minister who is an expert on the occult and heavy metal music, has been announced formally to the public through unsuspecting record companies. By piecing together bits of information from various Ozzy Osbourne heavy metal album covers, the minister says that the final plan is a blatant increase in satanic activity right up till June 21, 1999, when Satan himself will establish a physical reign on earth.

Now, from biblical prophecy, we know that such an ultimate twist of fate is certainly predicted. But to set dates by flaky documents and heavy metal album jackets hardly coincides with the Bible's statement that "no man knows the day nor the hour" of these events.

But let me step out of my cynical critic robe. We need to get something straight as we embark on this search for satanism in North America. We're not going to believe everything, okay?

There is virtually no hard evidence regarding the wiles of the devil. It's impossible to empirically prove experiences. But it is possible to gain evidence through testimony, the basis of legal proof.

So we'll be listening to plenty of bizarre stories. Some of them are not true. They're nothing but druggie tales or total hoaxes—after all, who can believe a satanist if he worships an entity with a nickname like the "father of lies"? Some of these testimonies have been doctored by the storytellers or by the story reporters to heighten our interest in the threat of satanism. Perhaps some of the stories were entirely true in their first telling, but as in the game of passing on a complicated message which differs with every telling, they've been diluted with interpretations and embellished with editing. And, flatly, some of the bizarre stories are true.

But let's be critical. Not cynically critical, but critical. Let's keep a sense of humor as we delve into this unhappy topic. And I'll keep in mind our goal if you will: to learn enough about satanism to protect and advise our kids.

▶ 2 ◀

Satan Loves Me

McAlester, Oklahoma, is a combination of old and new: antique dark-brick stores and glassy fast-food restaurants. The prison is old. It looks like a college campus behind the steel fences, guard towers and spiraling rolls of barbed wire that glint in the hot Oklahoma sunshine. The buildings are dark brown brick with white colonial-style trim.

The All-American Kid

Sean Sellers, called down from his death row cell, sits jumpsuited behind a double-paned glass in a visiting booth. I sit on a slippery steel stool, nod through the finger-printed, smeared glass, and ask on the phone intercom, "They treating you right?"

He's a good-looking kid. He should be going to movies, showing off on a skateboard, working out at a fitness center, getting ready for college, managing the pizza joint he worked at back in Oklahoma City before all this happened.

Colorado Connections

Greeley, Colorado, has satanic groups that meet weekly on Friday or Saturday nights in abandoned schools, churches or farmhouses deep in the rugged countryside. According to the local media, participants range in age from 12 to 30 and are directed by six northern Colorado coven leaders who "meet Sunday mornings in a local restaurant to discuss the groups' activities," according to Mike Peters who writes for the *Greeley Tribune*. Mike says the overall head of the covens is a Denver man who calls himself "Lucifer."

Sean Sellers' parents were long-haul truckers when the family lived in Greeley. Sean filled the empty hours when both parents were on the road

17

with the occult. He excelled in a local kids' Dungeons and Dragons fantasy roleplaying group, so he was made Dungeon Master. The responsibility prompted the junior higher to pore through every book he could find on witchcraft, satanism, sorcery, wizards and black magic. He regularly stole the most interesting books from the Greeley Public Library.

And he found his way into a self-styled satanic coven. "We used to have baptism ceremonies," he remembers. "The leaders would be in black robes, but the new person would be in a white robe. We would stand in front of an altar that had black candles and a silver chalice on it. They made the new person strip, kneel before the altar; then we'd cut his hand and let the blood drip into the chalice. Then we would pass the cup around, drinking the blood and dedicating ourselves to Satan."

During Sean's 1984 sophomore year the Sellers moved to Oklahoma, where Sean's interest in the occult brought him to the attention of another satanic coven practicing in the Oklahoma City area. A witch gave Sean a special incantation, a powerful new prayer to the devil.

Up till now Sean had painted a protective pentagram on his chest before invoking the spirits. Now he removed the pentagram; he wanted Satan to possess him. Before his altar, black candle burning, Sean intoned the prayer and, in his words, "something happened. I felt a power there. The temperature in the room dropped about ten degrees. I got a shot of adrenalin and I felt my blood pressure go up. There was an erotic sensation, a lifting sensation in my whole body. And sharp claws—fingers—touched me. I opened my eyes and saw bright spots dancing around the room. There was this mist, and I saw demons flying.

"And then there was this voice. A whisper. It said, 'I love you.' I knew that God didn't love me; but Satan did."

As his sophomore year progressed, Sean formed a club called "Elimination" to recruit new followers to Satan. The grades of his self-styled group were: White Beginners, Red Masters and Blue Leaders. As usual in satanic recruitment technique, the beginners were to know nothing about the satanic belief system until they were gradually pulled into the camaraderie and loyalty of the group.

Sean wrote back to a friend in Greeley, helping him start his own "Eliminators" club. Sean sometimes included with the letters vials of his own blood to, in his words, "write with, drink, do whatever with."

Sean knew he was getting in deep during his junior year; he mentioned to several adults that he thought he might be going crazy. Indications of his obsession with satanism surfaced in some of his school writing, such as an essay that reads: "I love my friends, I love my family, but I am free. I can kill without remorse and I feel no regret or sorrow."

Just after school had started in September 1985 Sean played out his prediction. It was time for a sacrifice to Satan.

Sean sneaked his dad's .44 pistol and with his buddy Richard drove late to the convenience store where the clerk had earlier refused to sell him beer and had embarrassed his girlfriend. The murder was slow-motion: Richard asks the man outside to look at his car while Sean watches; Sean loses his nerve. They all go back inside. The clerk is behind the counter. Richard begins walking from the restroom. Sean raises the pistol; the clerk shrinks back to open the cash register. Sean fires and misses. The clerk runs for the back of the store but is stopped by Richard. Sean fires again and the clerk goes down. He fires again. And again.

The police never solved the homicide; and six months later Sean was deeper still into his own Hell. He called himself Ezurate after the name of the demon he was sure possessed him. Sean prayed at his bedroom altar to Satan, and Ezurate dressed in black underwear and pulled out the .44. In the middle of the night, he stepped down the hall to his parents' room. It was so dark Sean/ Ezurate could scarcely make out the two forms sleeping on the waterbed. He aimed at the first form's head and fired. His mother raised up on the other side of the bed and looked to see her son aiming at her forehead. He fired.

The prosecution at Sean's trial said Sean killed "just to watch somebody die."

Radical Teens

Now he answers my "They treating you right?" as his voice buzzes through the intercom-phone: "Not bad. Hey, thanks for the book; I saw you on TBN on TV a couple weeks ago."

"Ah, fame," I say. We talk like friends for about a half an hour and I eventually ask Sean what he would say to teenagers if he had a good soapbox to stand on.

"I'd say something like 'I woke up this morning like I do every morning in a cell that's six by 15 feet and I see cement blocks and steel and bars and concrete. And I'm reminded every day of the past; it won't leave me alone. I can't get away from it. I can't escape the reasons why I'm here. Every day it's there.

"'And every morning I wake up wishing that when I reached out saying I want out of satanism, someone would have been there.' So if any teenager wants to get involved in it, call me. I can't even express in words how I feel about how serious it all is.

"If there's anything to say about getting involved in satanism, it's: 'Don't!' Don't get involved. Get out of it. It's not worth it 'cause it's going to destroy your life. That's all there is to it: It will destroy your life. And I'm living proof that that's true."

I ask, "What would you say to parents?"

"I'd say there's gonna come a time if your child is involved in the occult— there's gonna be a time your child reaches out and asks for help. Maybe just one time. And if you're not there to see what's going on, if you're not there when that child reaches out, he might never do it again. I reached out one time—but there was nobody there for me."

"When was that?"

Sean goes on. "And I destroyed my life, the lives of my family, the lives of other people."

"Is that trying to put the blame on somebody else? On your parents?"

"No, I don't mean it that way. I just mean it's an important thing for parents to know what's going on and be there to stop a kid from going as far as I did."

"When did you feel you reached out for help?" I ask.

"It got to where I knew Satan was really fouling things up. My mom was always crying, my dad was wanting to kill me. I'd open my eyes and think, 'This is not what I want to be doing; this is not what I want to be like. I want out of this mess.' And I called different Christian ministries and talked with them and they didn't tell me anything. I went to a priest; and he told my mom to give me back my satanic books. She'd taken them away and he says, 'They're not your books; they're his books. Give them back to him.' And so that didn't work. I went to a prayer group thing and they quoted a lot of Scripture to me but they didn't tell me what I now know I needed to hear."

"Which was . . . ?"

"You don't have to be involved in the occult to be somebody. You don't have to be like that. I got involved in the occult in a way because of seeing a lot of hypocritical Christians, you know. They were doing the same things I was doing. So I thought if that's what Christianity is all about, I don't want to be Christian 'cause I don't want to be a hypocrite. Then when I found satanism, I said, 'Yeah, this is what I want to do.' I was told I could be different. I didn't have to be like Christians; I could strive to be above all that. The Christians at my school didn't say anything about the way Jesus loves me; it was just: 'That's the guy that drinks blood; that's the guy that ate a live frog over there. Don't mess with him.' I'd go 'Hi' and they'd go 'Bye.'

"So it felt like no one was ever there. And I got so mad, I got so frustrated with all these 'good' people around me that I said, 'Fine. Forget it. I can't get out.' And that's what I was always told: Once you're involved in satanism you can't get out. So that's when I really got into it. I dove into it with everything I had. Because I figured, 'Well, if I can't get out of it, then I'm going to do the best I can in it.' That's when I jumped in with both feet and got in over my head and started drowning."

"If parents will just watch and not blow it off—like my parents did. My mom walked in on me one time while I was calling a counseling hotline from a Christian ministry and she didn't like the fact that I was doing it."

"Sometimes," I say, "parents feel threatened by the fact that their kid needs help because it might suggest they're not doing a good job as parents."

"She didn't seem to think I needed any help. I remember asking a couple of times, hinting around that, 'I think I'd really like to talk to someone; sometimes I think I'm going crazy.' But she'd say, 'Well, if you think you're going crazy, that's a good sign you're not.' I went to a teacher and asked her, 'I need to really talk to you.' And this teacher was really close to me—and I don't know what happened but we never really got together to talk. I think I was really reaching out but there just didn't seem to be anybody there.

"Teachers really have to watch because a lot of kids who won't talk to their parents will reach out to teachers, to people they feel they can trust. Every day teenagers commit suicide because they think that there's nobody there, that nobody cares."

We talked further about Sean's newfound faith in Christ—who he says isn't the wimpy Jesus of the hypocritical Christians he knew in school. From his cell and the collect-calls-only phone on his cellblock, Sean is actively counseling kids dabbling in satanism, has appeared via satellite on a Fall, 1988, Geraldo Rivera special on satanism, corresponds with Christian crusader Bob Larson with whom he's done a tape called "The Devil and Death Row," and is forming an organization by teenagers for teenagers called "Radical Teens for Christ."

"RTC, huh?" I say.

"Yeah. I had all the materials written this last year for starting groups against satanism on campuses, but, uh, it all got sort of taken from me. It was a very weird deal. So I have to start all over again. But that's cool; I've got plenty of time."

But Sean doesn't have plenty of time. His attempted defense of "satanic influence" didn't fly. At the trial, he said that he'd held rituals "every night and invited demons into my body. There was a persona—not a person but a persona—of another, created by demons and completely evil . . . . They made a separate person in me, someone I called Ezurate. It was him who committed the murders and not Sean Sellers."

But it's Sean Sellers who's on death row now, scheduled to die by lethal injection for sacrificing three people to Satan.

▶ 3 ◀

Parties and Drugs and Power

Kansas City. The Lighthouse is in an area of Kansas City where huge old trees grace huge old houses. It's a sunny autumn afternoon as I drive along a picturesque creek with stone banks and up the driveway to the salmon-colored brick building that looks like a massive church. Set on a hill, The Lighthouse is a home for unwed mothers.

In front is a carefully groomed garden area with a stone plaque dedicating the place to the millions of unborn babies whose mothers chose to abort rather than give them up for adoption. The white walls of the entry and gleaming stone floor reflect on a plastic sign: "220 Babies Saved So Far."

Becky Abbott, a pretty counselor at The Lighthouse, lets me in, and explains that the building used to be a convent. "Other people say they are uneasy here; I don't. I don't even feel that way down in the basement, where the bishop used to be buried." Becky introduces me to Danielle and Anna, who, I take it, volunteers as a sort of chaplain to the girls.

Danielle is probably eighteen, with clear, pretty eyes and blond hair cut about chin length. She's in pants and a dark blue sweater with red, yellow and white stripes. And she's pregnant. Very pregnant.

"Going to be a boy," I say.

She scowls, then smiles. "Four weeks. I'm due in four weeks. I'm excited."

The small, white room is a visitors' lounge; it's bright with windows that take in the rush hour traffic on Meyer Boulevard and the Kansas City autumn sky. An old-fashioned metal crib is lined with blue quilts and crocheted pillows.

Danielle adjusts herself to sit on the couch.

I explain the project: teenagers are buying into satanism like crazy, and they don't seem to be aware of the price they're going to pay.

"Paying the price, yes. I paid a high price. I wish I could take it all back and say it never happened, but it did," Danielle says.

22

"It started when I was younger. I was abused by a mother that was abused and had a bad family situation. I would cry when I was little and then I decided that when I was older I would control them, myself, my feelings, their feelings, and no one would ever hurt me. I'd control the situation."

"Do you remember thinking that? How old were you?"

"I was six the first time I started thinking that. I had sat on my bed with my wet swimming suit on, and it left a mark on the bed. So my mother gave me a beating for it, and said I was stupid and irresponsible and I could have ruined the bed. And I remember after she left that's when I decided—the anger and the hurt and the pain. The physical beating was nothing. It just wasn't anything compared to the mental abuse."

"How many six-year-olds go through that?"

"I'm beginning to think quite a few of them," Danielle says.

"What happened then?"

"My parents divorced when I was nine. And I was sent to live with my mother. And at that time we still did not get along and I still wanted to get her back for everything she had done. So I would sit there and think—I wish I could just make this lamp fly across the room and hit her, just hit her and shut her up. And things like that. I remember thinking that really strongly."

"When did you get into the occult?"

"I was about 13. I would get anything I could get my hands on to read at old used book stores, public libraries. I had boxes of books. I would just get more and more into reading about it and then I actually got involved."

"Any special books?"

"The Witch's Bible, Satanist Bible—I read that. Spells and just all that type of book. There was one called, I can't remember what it was called. There was just all kinds of them. *How to Use Your ESP, How to Develop Mind Control, How to Play Games,* everything. Some of it was parapsychology, it all deals with the same thing."

"You had money to buy books?"

"I wouldn't eat lunch or anything. I would save all my lunch money and go buy books. And then my friends, of course, lent some of it and if you went to auctions and stuff you could get real cheap books. They came in big piles and you could always find some good ones."

"Do you remember your first incantation or spell?"

"I remember practicing around with stuff like that. You know, reciting them. And I didn't really start getting into casting spells, casting hexes and doing other things until I had entered into the group."

"How did you first come into contact with a group? Did you seek somebody out or did they seek you out?"

"This guy was always hanging around the school grounds; he was not in school. It was an older man, not old-old. He was 24 or 25. I was 14. I knew from his eyes, I mean I just looked at him and I know that he was. And then the way he would talk. Like he would hear some kids talking about—like I wish I could do that—or, I wish I could do something—or something like that. And he would say, well, are you willing to pay to do this? And he would bring in kids like that. I observed him for a while, I would listen to him."

"Did you do any of the 'I wish' things with him?"

"No. I had gone up to him and asked him what he wanted in exchange. He just looked at me and smiled and from then on he would talk to me every day. He was on the school grounds. He would act like he was picking up trash and the authorities never said anything to him—of course they didn't know what he was talking about. Things like that. I got to know him. He would in fact —he was the first one that I'd ever had a link with. He's the first person I ever heard in my mind. Like, I'm talking to you this way—we talked without speaking. He's the first person I ever heard do that. The first time he just said my name in my mind in his own voice. He disappeared and I've never seen him since. He did not introduce me to a group, he would just talk.

"My next contact was just with friends. Well, people and kids that I would meet and I remember we were at a party one night and the guys were going out to do a seance. There was a special one going on out in a field and so they asked if I would like to go. So I went with them; there were four guys and three girls. Another group was holding the seance, a big group. I don't remember who it was but after that we just started going. We went out there and they had slaughtered a cow. They ripped its heart out. It was just standing there and they just ripped—while it was still alive—they just ripped its heart out.

"This was not a new group. The guys I went with were most likely recruiters. Before you could see it they did an incantation over you. The other two girls passed out. It's out in Blue Springs, Missouri, and we went in a truck and a car. We had to walk behind property lines and there were barbed wire fences we went through. There were trees all around. It was well hidden. As I walked up they were waiting and I met a lady and they were in black robes with red trim, that's what most of them wear most of the time. They stood up and they had their heads covered until they drank the blood and then they took their hoods off.

"Well, I was really uneasy because I didn't really know what was going on and there was no place to run to. I couldn't have found my way back to the car if I wanted to. So one of the guys was on one side of me and one of the other ones was on the other side of me and then were walking around and one of the girls came up to me and just stood there and looked at me . . . . She touched my forehead and then ran her hand down my forehead and she started an incantation that I did not recognize. I later found that part of the words that she used—but I am still not sure to this day exactly what she said. She did not do this to the other girls because they had passed out. They were in the back seat so wasted from the party that they never made it up to the field.

"The male stood up and as he raised his hands they all got in the group in a circle. I didn't get in at first. The girl that had put her hand on me came and got me and stood me beside her and he made the chalk circle with powdered chalk. Made a pentagram in the big rocks set in the ground. The ground was cleaned of grass from certain places—it was so dark I couldn't see very far out. It seemed like it was just dirt because afterwards when they were taking me away I looked back and they were covering the pentagram over and they were cleaning up blood and they were covering everything. He made the pentagram just so he could call up demons, it was a special one with all the writing in it. He made the pentagram and then the writing with his finger.

"The people were still standing up and he said something and they kneeled and then they got back up and that's when they started—he raised his hands again and was saying some things. I don't remember everything he said. And he said a lot of things. The other people were dressed in regular clothes, but all in dark clothes. These were all people that I did not know, even the guys from the party I did not know very well. Everything goes at a party. Then he stepped out without breaking the circle and everyone was still kneeling and then he threw something. And there was smoke.

"Then he had gone to the cow. It was standing in the back on a rope tied to a tree so it couldn't get away. He walked over to the cow and he just pulled it apart. He shoved his hand in under the rib cage and said something before he did it. Everyone was watching him do this. I don't remember him having a knife then. I know he had one after because he slit the throat to drink the blood. He walked up to the cow and ripped out its heart. And it looked like he did it with his bare hands. It was still beating when it came out."

"There was a Hells Angel back in the '60s and that was his specialty," I say. "He would use his hand. He would jam it underneath up under the rib cage and pull out a person's heart and show it to them before they fell over. Not the kind of guy you want at your birthday party."

Becky Abbot rolls her eyes and Danielle continues: "Well, I turned around and threw up. I knew it was a heart. There was blood everywhere. There was a vein and there was blood coming from it. I got really ill. It was the first time I had ever—I mean I had read about it—but I had never seen someone actually do it. The cow fell over. The priest handed the heart to the woman and I don't know what they did with it after that—he got an open wound that was still leaking and just stuck a goblet—a chalice under it and drained the blood right into the cup. And then he put something else in it and he prayed over it and then he drank of it and she drank of it and then he passed it around to everyone in the group.

"I drank it and it was disgusting. I got real sick. Of course that was my first experience with that though. Not much happened after they passed it around. They went into chanting and he went into talking and was going to speak and they nodded and him and her both looked at each other and nodded and the guys that I came with got me and left and I don't know what happened from that point on. But as we were leaving when I turned around they were covering up that pentagram."

"What was your next episode after that?"

"Just going to seances with different people. One of the same guys though. His name was Aaron. He came with two other girls that I don't know who they are. One is named Stacy but I don't remember much about her. Everything always first branched from a party, then we just got together with girls, I with Vicky, another friend of mine. She was really into it, too, just thinking about doing things like that. Even when we were little. She got interested at the same time I did. And we got involved in it with a group in Oak Grove, Missouri, a small group. We had seances at parties."

"Did you do drugs at these parties?"

"A few of them."

"Is there any way that what you experienced so far was just drugs? And how do you know?"

"Because I just grew from that. I steadily got worse. I grew—the evil in me grew—the hatred and the wanting. I grew. The wanting of power—control —domination. It was a different sort of feeling instead of just drugs and I didn't need drugs soon. I didn't need liquor or drugs. I like them, but they weren't a necessary part. Soon we would never drink anything because you needed to concentrate with your full potential."

"When did you first run into what you would call a demon presence?" I ask. "Or were you told about spirit guides as you got into an altered state of consciousness? Was there a time when you had an experience of seeing something—someone?"

"After I got into it, after a while I would continually talk with demons— I could call them up—at first I had to call them up. I didn't call the first time. The first time that I talked to them was in my room and I was alone and I was angry. And I had wanted to hurt a girl and I wasn't exactly sure how I was going to do it. So I would sit there and boil over and, if I could, just do something. Then all of a sudden I heard, 'You Can.' At that point I was not sure if it came from inside or outside my head. It was probably coming from inside because of the things I had done up to there. I'd probably already opened the door at the ritual—I had already opened the door. I was thinking real hard 'like how?' That's when I messed around but I didn't actually do everything it told me; I was just hoping for short cuts. You have to do quite a lot.

"The next time was when I called one up. I had read a necromancy book. I had read that you could call them up for protection. At that point I was wanting to hurt somebody else—physically though. I mean I was going after a girl. So I had made a circle outside in my backyard and no one was home. There was a fence and it was very secluded. I drew the circle with a stick: it was daytime because I could still see what I was doing. I got the book out and stood at the side and did what the book told me. I know that in one I had to recite the name three times to call it up. And I thought—*I don't know any names*. Then I had a name. It was Orkan; it later turned out to be my guide. Thank God I got rid of him. I had called up this demon."

"Can you be specific, Danielle?" I ask. "You chant the name, you go through the incantation—what actually happened? Is it dark by this time?"

"Yes, it is. It's not pitch black but it is dark. Like evening and he appeared. Most of the body was smoke. All I saw was the eyes. It just appeared or manifested there. I could see his eyes and they were red. I didn't see the head, it was dark, it was just like it was a void. That was the first time I saw him. At first I was scared. I called this dude up and I had to flip to the back pages to see how to get rid of him. Because I was stupid and I didn't think; now that he was here, what do I do? I know it would work but I was not prepared for exactly what popped out. He asked me what I wanted and I told him and he laughed. That is when he said I'll teach you. He just stood there.

"I ran for the light that was on the back porch and I was reading through there. He was just waiting for me I guess. He didn't make any move or anything, he just stood there. Of course he couldn't get out of the circle. I can't remember the words right now, but there were three separate words and it was gone. But after that I no longer needed the circle to call him up. I would just say his name three times.

"The next time I did it was when I had gone to fight the girl and I had been thinking about it but I wasn't sure I was going to do it. Anyway, I'm a strong girl, I've always been physically strong. And he appeared. Just to me. Now if there had been another witch present or if there had been another satanist they would have known he was there, felt him. He is one of the major thrones. And he has many other names. He could have thousands of other names, but that is the name he used with me. Orkan."

"At that time were you considering yourself as a witch or a satanist or what?"

"I considered myself as just me. I was getting what I wanted at that point. He showed me that through him I could do more things physically, be stronger. Of course there is that word stronger—power. So we went on with it that way. He taught me and he eventually entered me. And he was right. I was very much stronger. I could physically pick up people a lot heavier than me and throw them around."

"So far, hearing what you are talking about, some eighth grade guy can think, 'Gosh, I wish I could have some power. I might just check into this.' What is the downside to this? What did you pay? When was the very first time that you realized you were in over your head?"

"I realized that, I would say, when I was sixteen. No, I just was fifteen because I had not turned sixteen yet and we were driving down the road and we were listening to Black Sabbath. Vick, Katy—Katy had gotten really strong at that point. The boy driving, he was Shannon's boyfriend and I can't think of his name but he wasn't in it. He was really fried out on the way up there.

"We were in a small truck; I was sitting on Jerry's lap. None of us had seat belts on. And this dude passed out driving. No one could get to the wheel, no one could get to the brakes. No one could get to anything. And the wheel was turning on its own. I mean his hands were fallen. His feet were on the accelerator. You could see his feet moving toward the brakes or the accelerator. It wasn't him driving—there was just no way. I thought I was going to die. Right then I thought, *Goodbye everybody*. Because we were on a road that was like this and going around corners. Either side of the road, if you went off, you just went down. And we would have died. We never came close to wrecking. I was driving and we got there and I grabbed the truck keys. I wasn't about to get back in that truck unless I was driving. But then on the way back the fried kid got the keys and he was driving.

"We went through the house and there were pentagrams, writing—ancient writings all over the walls. There was blood in one room on one of the beds. Well, it wasn't on a bed it was just a mattress on the floor. There was fresh blood and we got out of there when we saw that. Something was killed there. There was lots of blood."

"So what are the downsides?" I smile to her, thinking what bizarre recollections she has of her fifteenth year. "What did you pay?"

"I paid—there is just so much that you pay. I mean it's not just one thing. You pay with your mind. You are no longer in control even though you think you are. At any time they could use you as a sacrifice. You don't understand that. At any time they could take whatever they want. They are there to take anything that they can get and if they can use you up in the process, well that is just even better because you are going to Hell with them. You will give them more power. You just pay so much and soon you are going to pay your soul. They will ask for your soul."

"Did you do that?"

"I signed a piece of paper but I don't remember exactly what was on the paper. At that time I was out of it but I remember signing it in blood because I had to cut my hand to do it. I had to deny Christ and I'll tell you what, I'd never do it again, not for anything.

"It's like kids think they can be happy—they think they can find happiness and love and a feeling of being wanted in those groups."

"You said that one of the ways you paid was with your mind, thinking you were in control of things but then realizing that they controlled your mind?"

"And in fact I didn't realize how much they were in control of me until I came here because I thought I had gotten out. I paid. The years have eaten away at me. I can't get those years back. The things I have done wrong I can't go back and change. But I can change it for somebody else. Maybe I can stop them from doing what I did and they won't have to pay the price."

"How about the feeling of that eighth-grader still thinking about all that power?" I ask. "Thinking I'm not going to let anybody control my mind, and I don't care if I throw away a few years because that's what being a kid is for? What's going to keep him from messing around with satanism and trying it anyway?"

"I would tell him to think about the future." Danielle pats her basketball-tummy, her baby. "I mean, even if he had children those children aren't his. They are the group's. I mean, that child can be molested, killed as a sacrifice at any point. And there is nothing you can do about it because if you try they are going to kill you.

"I would ask him if he would like to burn in Hell forever. If he wants to pay that high a price, because that's exactly what he's doing. For a few years he's going to have strength, power and maybe money and maybe things beyond imagination.

"But it doesn't take long to feel the horror."

I hug Danielle as I leave.

▶4◀

Because It's Fun

From the Lighthouse Home for Unwed Mothers, Becky drives me through a maze of downtown and suburban streets. I stop to call my secretary, who tells me about the phone calls she's been receiving.

"It's just such weird stuff," Tricia says. "Apparently this woman has come out of some kind of satanic cult and got our number and I never know what to say. She won't leave her number or tell me who or where she is. She's sort of hysterical sometimes and says they break into her house and beat her and rape her. And her husband's a minister of some kind and the cops won't do anything until they get some evidence other than her word like catching them in the act of attacking her. She's terrified. She calls about every two weeks and I never know what to say."

"Could be wacko," I say, "trying to get attention. But from what you're telling me her story sounds similar to a couple of others', people who've tried to shake a satanic cult group." I wish I knew what to suggest to Tricia. "I don't know beans—yet—about what to do when she calls. Maybe suggest seeing a counselor—"

"She is."

"Good. Maybe suggest that she and her husband make a specific list of what they know as facts and of what they can only guess at; maybe the police have just been dismissing her as a hysterical crackpot and she needs to document what's happening to her for credibility. And then just listen. They need somebody to listen, to reassure them that no matter how bizarre the tale, they're still worth caring about."

I tell Tricia to not worry that everything she's hearing is absolutely accurate. "From the people I'm talking to, I gather that satanism is about like the druggie culture—they have their own reality, they're trained to lie. And about 80 percent of what's said is baloney, even if they sincerely believe it."

30

"But the other 20 percent may be true?" Tricia says as she hangs up.

"May be true," I say. "Some of it just may be true. Goodnight."

And I fall into a fitful sleep wondering—even with the facts documented in court—how much of James Hardy's story is true.

Jim Hardy

Jefferson City. Up near Kansas City, Leawood police chief Craig Hill had told me the Steve Newberry case was probably the quintessential story of teenage satanic dabblers falling over the edge into madness, into murder.

Missouri is deep green under a clear sun and as I drive through Sedalia I again am struck by how we make our own hells. I remember how ugly life felt when I attempted suicide as a teenager; my hometown was like a bad taste in my mouth. And yet I now know I grew up in one of the most beautiful sections of the country. James Hardy, Theron "Pete" Roland and Ron Clements made their hells out of these rolling hills, lush maple and oak stands of forest patched by slabs of new-mown alfalfa and soybeans. The land of southwest and central Missouri is heaven compared to the sweaty, cement insides of the state prison visitors' center.

The walls are gray and pockmarked. And when I meet James Hardy, I reluctantly decide that he fits. He belongs inside this concrete maze in the middle of green, clear Missouri.

"Thanks for talking with me," I begin.

He sits at a stainless steel table, folds his hands with arms straight out in front of him and says nothing. His hair has grown out brown; he had always worn it bleached-blond in school. His face is lean and angular with muddy blue eyes; a face that would be called attractive in a teenager who'd be tanned, working hauling hay, taking girlfriends to movies these warm summer nights. Now he's serving life without parole. His jumpsuit is a frayed and faded gray.

"They treating you all right?"

"Yeah," he says.

I ask several more questions to in some way break through the concrete veneer of James' shell. There aren't many cracks in the walls.

The Sacrifice

Steve Newberry was 5'9" and 210 pounds; he was fat and slow. He'd started school a year late because of medical problems and flunked the seventh grade; so he was a senior at 19. Steve was one of those kids who's so out of the main mob of teenagers that he'll do anything to be in. He regularly bought drugs for the Jim Hardy crowd with his earnings from a restaurant job, and was initially rejected as a good victim for a satanic sacrifice since the kids would be missing out on Steve's free dope. Steve was into drugs along with the rest of the crowd that gathered around Jim Hardy and his chief sidekicks Pete Roland and Ron Clements. They did pot, barbituates, cocaine, amphetamines and whatever they could get in the little town near Joplin.

Jim remembers last October Ron turning to him in psych class and asking him if he'd ever been serious about killing a person. Jim says, "I told him 'Yeah,' you know. We talked about it a lot. Then he says, 'Well, let's kill Steve.'"

After killing and torturing more animals than they can remember, Jim, Ron and Pete eagerly planned their ultimate sign of dedication to Satan for Halloween night. But Steve's mother foiled the plan by taking her family out of town for the weekend.

Thanksgiving weekend they tried again. Across from Jim's house, on land owned by the Farmer's Chemical Plant, the boys had found an abandoned well and had often thrown mutilated animals in it. They called it the Well of Hell. Jim told Steve there were some stray dogs running around near the well and maybe they could catch one and kill it.

"The thing is," says Jim, "Steve knew we were going to kill him before we ever brought him out there. Just the look in his eyes, like 'I know that you're going to kill me but I'm not going to believe it.'" Lance Owens joined Ron, Pete and Steve at Jim's house: "That day for sure he knew we were going to kill him," says Jim. "There were four baseball bats and five of us. I threw one to Pete, one to Ron, one to Lance, and I could tell by his look Steve was really wanting one. So I grabbed a little hatchet from my garage and told him, 'Here, you carry this ball bat and I'll carry this ax.' He knew something was going on."

Jim's derision of the teenager he beat to death is obvious even now; he's saying in so many words: "Steve was so stupid, no wonder he's dead."

The boys hiked in the late afternoon to the well site. Pete had offered to strike the first blow, but as they stood around the well, with no stray dogs in sight, Pete lost his nerve. They kicked around the edges of the Well of Hell for a half hour; then walked back in the dark to Jim's house.

"Every time we failed," Jim says, "I don't know what drove us. But we wanted that experience. Pete and me from killing animals, I think, and Ron just from talking about it. We just had to have that experience. I know it had to spring from Satan."

The next weekend was set for the final attempt. Jim, elected as almost a joke to be president of the student council, served turkey dinners to the elderly with the rest of the student government officers. That night he and Pete rented the video of the sequel to "The Texas Chainsaw Massacre."

Sunday, December 6, was clear and cold. Jim says, "I went over to Pete's and helped him rake some leaves; we were burning them and this little cat comes running up to me—so we took it along. We drove over to Steve's and I went in to get him, told him we were going to go out to the well to kill a cat; his mom acted really suspicious."

Pete, Steve, Ron and Jim hiked the half-mile through the brush to the Well of Hell. Pete tied the kitten up in a tree and they took turns swinging at it with their baseball bats. Jim's account of the final events are: Steve spoke after the dead kitten had been cut down: "I wish we had something bigger to kill." Ron said, "What're we going to do now, Jim?"

Jim said, "I don't know." Pete suggested they smoke some dope, and Steve began fumbling through his pockets to see if he'd brought a pipe.

Then the voice inside Jim's head said, "Do it now!" and he swung the first blow. They chased Steve who stumbled in the dark brush saying, "Why me, you guys? Why me?" Jim remembers Ron saying, "Because it's fun, Steve."

Before tying Steve's body to a boulder and dumping it into the Well of Hell, Jim poked Steve with a broken bat and said simply, "Sacrifice to Satan."

The Beginnings

And now I wonder how it all started. "When did you first get the idea to worship Satan?" I ask Jim.

"About junior high. Before then I got into drugs and I'd get kicks with thinking about death. I always had this obsession about killing—like I'd shoot a bird and then get real excited about tearing it up. Then in junior high we moved to Carl Junction and I'd sort of pray to both God and Satan to see if anybody would answer. Then I figured Satan liked more what I liked to do so I sort of fell away from praying to God."

"Satan answer any prayers?" I ask.

"Sure. I had money and drugs—I'd get them in real surprising ways. We were always praying for demons but they never came."

"I thought Ron once said he thought he was demon possessed," I say.

"Well, yeah. I think I was too—lots of times. I'd tell stories to kids at school about torturing somebody and they always thought I was joking; and I sort of was. But there was something in me that meant it; there was definitely something inside me. I'd hear a voice."

"Still hear it?"

He didn't answer for a few seconds. "No. But it would—Actually I thought I saw it sometimes. It would tell me to do things."

"Like to be the first to hit Steve with the baseball bat?"

"Yeah. 'Do it now,' it said."

"Any final words to other kids wanting to dabble out there?" I ask.

"You can't just mess around," Jim finally says. "It sucks you in."

I say, "You hang in there" to Jim as I gather up my notebook. All the while I can't get out of my head Ron Clements' words to the dying Steven Newberry: "Because it's fun, Steve."

I call for the guard.

▶ 5 ◀

Your Every Dream

Pat Metoyer is fit in his late forties and is used to questions on the occult; nearly every inquiry that comes into the Los Angeles P.D. about occult crime winds up on his desk. I sit beside it in the Criminal Conspiracy Section while two other cops investigate Pat's drawer for a missing payroll check.

"Some detective," one says of the other as he pulls out the missing check from the stack.

Between phone calls Pat tells me about a case he consulted on, a textbook case of a lone teenager dabbling in satanism:

The Power of Satan

Phil Gamble was fifteen in 1985 when he leafed through a pamphlet he'd been handed at a Motley Crue concert. It was called "The Power of Satan":

Dear Member:

Welcome to the good times ahead!

First off, Satan and his organization would like to thank you for showing faith and solidarity. We are sure that through our mutual help of one another we will defeat the diseased minds of the priests of the churches and temples of the world that seek to slander our mighty lord Lucifer. Eventually, our mighty leader Satan will regain his position of prominence. Those who help in our crusade will be rewarded handsomely; your every dream will be fulfilled. Those who work against our master will be punished!

In all our years of research of the different ways to make contact with the mighty Satan, our experience has taught us that the most effective way is as follows:

First you must get yourself a table which will serve as an altar. Next you need a sword to lay on the altar. Use a long knife if no sword is available. Next you need a chalice or goblet filled with wine. Next you need a parchment or piece of brown paper if commercial parchment is unavailable. Do not kill an animal if none is available. [An odd entry!]

Next you need a black candle. As far as clothing is concerned, it is definitely preferable to wear a black robe. If black is unavailable simply get any color and dye it black.

The pamphlet goes on, giving a specific incantation for summoning the demon Lucifuge Rofocale with the help of Prince Beelzebub and the count Astaroth: "Make it possible for the great Lucifuge to appear to me in human form and force, without bad odour, and that he grant me by the agreement which I am ready to sign with him all the riches I need."

Obviously of Canadian authorship from the spellings, the booklet proceeds to suggest invocations to the spirits for the destruction of enemies:

"I call upon the messengers of doom to slash with grim delight this victim I have chosen. Silent is that voiceless bird that feeds upon the brain pulp of him who hath tormented me and the agony of this shall sustain itself in shrieks of pain, only to serve as signals of warning to those who would resent my being."

The *Monroe County Evening News* in Carlton, Michigan, reported on February 3, 1986, that the day before—on February 2, the occult holyday of Candlemas—"Lloyd Harold Gamble, 17, was shot and killed in his home at 10600 Otter Creek Road about 11:30 A.M. Sunday Monroe County Sheriff's deputies took a 15-year-old boy into custody at the scene of the shooting. Sheriff's Department chief investigator Lt. Michael Davison said the youth had called the department to report the shooting and was still on the phone with dispatcher Carolyn Pitcher when the detectives arrived at the house."

The 15-year-old was Phil, the victim's brother. As he talked with the police dispatcher, Phil said he expected his parents home at any minute and he would kill them if the police didn't arrive to stop him.

Three days after the incident, the parents called the police to report some items they had found hidden in a green vinyl sack in Phil's closet. The bag contained a dark blue candle, a long black robe and hood, a silver chalice, a glass bottle of red liquid, white parchment paper, and 11 Motley Crue, Black Sabbath and other heavy metal groups' cassettes.

Under a rug in Phil's room the parents had found the "power of Satan" pamphlet, a sword and a paper pentagram cutout.

Goat's Head Artwork

I remember reading about the case in Larry Kahaner's book *Cults That Kill* put out by Warner Books in 1988. I dig the book out of my bookbag in the car and leaf through Kahaner's account. On page 189 he interviews Larry Clock, a juvenile probation officer in Monroe County:

"Prior to this incident, we had started to get some undertones of things going on. There was the case of a boy who lived with his very elderly grandmother. He went around the house and took down all of her religious pictures. He took her crucifix and turned it upside down, then beat her up. At the same time school officials were finding all kinds of satanic symbols in his locker. He was making a big deal about letting everyone know that he was involved with satanism."

Clock continues, "About two days prior to the Gamble homicide, I told Mike [Davison] we really have the makings of a problem in one of the school districts. We had a kid stomp another kid . . . and then jump on the table in the cafeteria—in front of all the other kids—and start flashing the devil sign [made by holding the two middle fingers with the thumb so the two fingers point up like horns].

"At some of the schools, kids were hanging up their artwork of goat's heads and baphomets along with the other students' drawings. The teachers didn't know what it meant. We were getting all this scattered stuff, but you figure it's just kids doing kid things."

Kahaner also interviewed retired police captain Dale Griffis who consulted on the case. "I think this kid crossed over from the dabbler stage to the self-styled satanist stage," said Griffis. "Here's a kid who's a loner, not doing great in school, into drugs and so on. Kids who are having problems sometimes think, if I just had these magical powers, I could solve them. Satanism is about power.

"This wasn't a spur-of-the-moment murder," said Griffis. "It was cold and calculated. I believe he thought he felt he was doing his brother a favor by killing him. He was elevating him to a higher consciousness. He had mentioned those exact words to the police dispatcher."

Phil Gamble was declared mentally unfit to stand trial and was confined to a mental health facility.

The Kingdom of Hell

A letter confiscated at a Southern California school seems to say something about what dedication to the lord of death can do to a young mind. The letter is reproduced in John Frattarola's article on "America's Best Kept Secret" in the special 1986 *Passport* magazine.

The following is an edited letter, confiscated from a high school student by his principal and turned over to a police officer investigating satanic crime in his area:

At the Kingdom of Hell Satan gazes at humanity—a wide smirk on his evil face, his eyes glaring, staring, thoughts of supreme wickedness resounding throughout his head . . . . for them (humanity) there is no hope, no saviour to lead them into a promised land of milk and honey. For them, there is only death and pestilence forever more . . . . Satan looks favorably upon his followers—the ones who worship him, kill for him, sacrifice virgin blood for him. The ones who dedicate their ceremonies and pleasures to his infernal name. It is they who shall rule the earth—the strong, the mighty all others shall be trodden under cloven hooves—the swords of the Satanists will fall heavy upon the necks of the holy, the pure, the humble, the sanctified, the god-lovers . . . . Millions will suffer and die—all their hopes shattered because of a "god" who doesn't care whether they live or die—to God, all his children are nothing more than heaps of extrement [sic]—not worth half a penny . . . . All the god believers will all become the slaves of their new masters. Since they are slaves, then Kryst [sic] is the King of Slaves—the shackels [sic] and chains are tight on the torn hands of the bearded faggot. Who will behead him in front of all his quivering followers—all who have done good in his name? Satan sits on the throne of God—he raises his blood-sprayed sword and proclaims himself the new ruler of the universe. The royal crown of Heaven is now placed on his head by his chief demons. All his children praise him and a large banquet is now prepared for the great victory of the new ruler . . . .

A banner flutters in the distance with the symbol of Baphomet enscribed on it with the words written: "Satan, the ruler, king and Lord of all the Universe, the one who conquered the mighty Jehovah Yahweh and hearled [sic] him back into infamy never to be heard from again. Hail Satan! Luciferi Excelsi! Diabholus Supremus! So Be It." A new world is then formed in the names of Satan, Lucifer, Belial, and Leviathan. A world with perfect creatures to inhabit the new earth. Creatures that will worship the Black Lord forever more. Creatures that will once again take pleasure in performing all the "sinful" actions of man . . . . Take heed all ye who read these God-forsaken blasphemies. If you be a God-believer, prepare to suffer and serve—if ye be a Satanist, prepare to rule over the sons of God. For they will eat the crumbs which fall from your table. Satan spits on the children of light. If you be one, Satan watches you in the shadows, he dwells within your nightmares and dark thoughts. Satan watches you at this very moment—your every move, thought, and action are seen by him from the pit of Hell. The fiery abyss is ready to open up for you. Beware.

A writer in Los Angeles who lives for this sort of cultural dregs asserts that 30 percent of the hundreds of multiple or serial killers he's studied have had backgrounds in satanism.

Richard Ramirez is one alleged serial killer I'm interested in on this fine Balboa day, since he bought into satanism back in his hometown of El Paso, a Texas hotspot of satanic activity. The trial of Ramirez—the "Night Stalker"—is now revving up in Los Angeles. I've stopped by the courthouse in downtown L.A. to nose around, but nobody's talking. Anyone having to do with the Ramirez defense doesn't want further incriminating rumors to jeopardize his case; and everyone interested in his prosecution doesn't want to pollute their "airtight" case against this dabbling satanist.

The court action is incredibly boring: A seemingly endless queue of more than 2,000 prospective jurors is being interviewed by both sides as to their knowledge and prejudices in the case. Nobody seems to want to serve as a juror, particularly since the case is predicted to be a two- or three-year affair. Most of the time I've spent in the muffled, carpeted courtroom has been a litany of sick pets needing care or travel plans or school schedules or other reasons a prospective juror could not serve. All the while, Ramirez sits, almost nattily suited in black, with none of the demonic chutzpa shown in his 1985 arraignment when he shouted, "Hail Satan!"

During 1985 Southern Californians were terrorized with the news accounts of a "Night Stalker" killer who murdered at least 13 women and raped, sodomized, robbed and terrorized many more. His victims more often than not lived in yellow houses—usually near freeways. He would attack late at night and usually leave satanic pentagrams at the scene. He'd kill the husbands; then rape the wives, forcing them to "swear to Satan."

The Night Stalker, who took his moniker from an AC/DC heavy metal song, was captured in true Hollywood fashion in August 1985. Ramirez' composite portrait was drawn from surviving witnesses' descriptions, and his photo was eventually publicized. As the Night Stalker attempted to step into a car near an East Los Angeles market, a woman began shrieking, "El matador!" —"The killer!" Her husband and brother responded and the footrace was on. Eventually they caught the slim suspect and with a growing crowd beat him senseless before police arrived.

More than a decade earlier, Charles Manson was probably the most publicized of the satanic wackos convicted of multiple homicides. His successor in the helter-skelter of satanic serial killing was the enigmatic figure of David Berkowitz—the "Son of Sam." In a book titled *The Ultimate Evil,* author Maury Terry has followed a dangerous, incredible trail of clues suggesting that Berkowitz and Manson were both members of a sophisticated satanic cult called The Process. Terry warns that, although pushed further underground by publicity such as his gripping book, The Process is alive and well and operating in such areas as New York and Houston. And its aim is terror.

▶ 6 ◀

The Exorcism

Marriage and family counselor Kay Meeuwse sits in with me on an interview with a young lady she's known. Tammy clenches her hands on the lace tablecloth in the suburban La Mirada home in Southern California. She's eager to help keep other kids from getting sucked into the dreams she still has of demons and regret. She's pretty in a white blouse and blue skirt, eyes heavily made up.

Kay and I chat with her for a few minutes; then I ask, "Tammy, were you in a family that has a history of occult involvement?"

Trying to Find Something

"No," she says. "It has a lot to do with trying to find something. My family wasn't involved with it. My mom wasn't religious, my stepdad wasn't religious, and I was searching for something—My life was, I just felt like a lot of kids: I felt depressed all the time, all alone like I was trapped. I was an abused child by my stepfather; he's alcoholic. My mom was like a subservient wife to him and she would do anything for him but she would leave him and then go back."

"And drag you along with her?"

"Yes. And my little sister. We always had a lot of verbal abuse. I never did good in school. I was always lonely in school and I didn't have many friends. I was more like a loner. The first time I ever came in contact with dabbling in witchcraft was when I was a little kid and I was really angry, I was around nine years old, and I was angry at my stepdad. I was just angry at the world. And I went in his fish tank, and he loves fishes, and I took a fish out and I cut it. I made a little ceremony of it and then I put it back into the tank like that and let him find it like that.

"I prayed as I got older because—I mean I'm overweight now, but I used to

39

be *really* overweight. I was huge, okay. And I started praying to the devil: 'Oh, I'll serve you if you'll help me be thin,' and stupid little prayers like that, you know. But that was opening the door. I keep saying 'you know.'"

"That's okay. Did you actually pray out loud, or was it just something you kind of thought?" I ask.

"No, I prayed out loud. I got on my knees and prayed. I knew there was a devil and I knew there was a God because my aunt was a Christian and all the time when I was a kid she would take me in a room and teach me about God and the devil and all this stuff. And how God was more powerful. But I kind of withdrew from believing in God for a while because the way my life was going I was thinking *Well, if God is real, how can he make my life be like this? I'm just a kid.* And I kind of withdrew from my family and I started running away.

"Before I ran away my friend Stephanie babysat for this lady who was a high priestess of some satanical group. I don't know which one it was, but— Then I started staying there and she had like different colored candles in her house for different things. Like red was for love, and white was purity, and black was death, and green was jealousy. And she would say incantations with these candles and something was supposed to happen. I've seen things levitate and stuff and it was—I felt a presence in there that was powerful, but it was evil; you know what I mean, it wasn't good. And one time I asked her if I could get into it and she said, 'Well, it's really hard, but we go to this club. It's nothing but a club where people who practice witchcraft and warlocks go.' And I never went to the club because I ran away. But still she taught me things; I learned by watching her, like prayers and all this stuff. But I didn't know what I was doing. I remember being so excited to see like horror movies about demons and witchcraft. I was so intrigued by and fascinated by satanic movies and how much power. . . ."

"The movies got you more curious, you mean?" asks Kay.

"Yes. And I used to listen to music that had a lot of death stuff in it—like heavy metal. Like right now there is a guy out; he's a heavy metal singer; he's called King Diamond, you've heard of him?"

"Yes," I say. "He seems to be one of the few who are fairly serious about satanism. A lot of the groups are just in it for the shock. It gets them publicity. But did you dabble any further into the occult?"

"I started reading a lot of books and stuff. I didn't buy any satanic books, but, well they were satanic but they didn't have prayers or rituals in them but I would kind of like pray in my mind bad against somebody and it would just happen. It's because I was so open and vulnerable to receive anything because I just wanted something that would fill me up, you know, make me feel like a whole person. So I think I was open to receiving whatever the devil had to give me. Or God or whatever; it didn't matter to me."

The Devil Is Wild and Crazy, You Know

I ask, "Did the devil ever answer?"

"I thought so. When I would be hurt or something from somebody doing something to me—maybe I was just feeling hurt about my family, okay—and I would sit there and I would think about the devil and all these people that would pray to him and I would pray and say I believe in you and then this weird language would start coming out of my mouth and I didn't know what it was. You know, like tongues, okay.

"And then when I really got demon possessed was when I got more rebellious. I went into a foster home when I turned sixteen. I took my mom and my dad to court because when I ran away and my dad picked me up from the house where they were training me to be a prostitute he hit me really hard and gave me a black eye. And then my mom started hitting on me after that. And I took them to court and declared child abuse and verbal abuse and I said I didn't want to live there any more. And I would keep running away unless they put me in a foster home or until someone killed me. And so they put me in an all black foster home in Compton where a lot of drugs are dealt. There's a lot of satanic worship in Compton."

Tammy stands, stretches and asks for a glass of water. When I switch the recorder back on, Tammy is saying, "The devil is weird; he's wild and he's crazy. And I was weird, wild and crazy. I would do anything for a thrill. Anything. And I think that's what made me summon up demons to possess me because I would receive or accept anything. I would do anything, and that's what he was looking for—someone who'll do anything wild and crazy.

"Well, I started going to a continuation school and I met the secretary there; she was a Christian. She started telling me about God. And everybody at the school would always tell me, 'Tammy, every time Ms. Jackson tells you that there is a God, there is Jesus, you turn bright red in the face like you're as angry as the devil himself.' I would start thinking about God; then I'd start getting a lot of fear. I'd walk outside and I'd hear voices talking to me. You know, little whispers. And I wasn't on drugs at the time. I had quit drugs for a year and a half.

"And I would walk like into the garage and I would feel something pulling at my legs like they were crawling on the ground trying to pull me down. And my foster sisters would tell me I'd wake up every night screaming 'Bloody Mary, Bloody Mary' and then I'd lay back down. There are always all those old stories about demons coming into girls' bedrooms; and sometimes I'd sort of be dreaming of something like that and I'd sort of—I'd like wake up afterwards and it would be—It would be like the act had really happened to me. I don't know how to say that.

"And then every other night or so I'd wake up sitting in the living room in a lotus position praying in some weird language that I didn't even know what I was praying. And I'd always get out of the bathtub or something and I'd look in the mirror and my face had this weird color to it. I would always feel someone or something always standing beside me, like it wouldn't leave me and it was like a dead weight on my shoulders. It was just like hanging on me, you know. I could tell it was evil. You know when something is good and when something is evil. I just felt it."

By this time in interviewing people from the occult, I've grown fairly inured to demonic stories; but as I glance over at Kay I realize this may be the first time she's heard one of the bizarre tales. She's white as a ghost.

Tammy goes on: "And then one night he was saying, 'Kill yourself; kill yourself.' I had never tried suicide in my life, but I ran to this house that I had went to, okay, to buy some PCP, and there was a school yard in the back. And I ran out there and my friend was running after me, one of my foster sisters and she was a white girl. And she was saying, 'Tammy, Tammy,' and I was saying, 'I just want to die!' And I picked up a Pepsi bottle. I looked at it just for a second, and I broke it on the ground and I slit my wrist. And then I saw the blood coming out and I heard this voice saying, 'You're going to die,' and it was laughing. I heard it just like you would be talking to me, and I kept telling my sisters, 'Can you hear that voice, can you hear that voice?' And they looked at me like I was crazy, but I heard it.

"The next thing I knew I woke up and someone was slapping me; I guess they were trying to keep me from being unconscious. Then they took me to my foster parents' house and the paramedics came."

Kay asks, "Did you ever hear those voices before or after that time?"

"Yes. Sometimes. Then they put me in a mental ward for about two weeks. It was awful."

"Did they have you on some kind of medication at that time?" Kay asks.

"Yes, but that was the only time I had to take something. Well, I got out and stayed at Ms. Jackson's house that night and I couldn't sleep. I was tossing and turning and I was having dreams about horrible things like going to Hell and being in a sea of fire and that's even recorded in the Bible. And I went to church with her the next day but when they started like praising the Lord, I couldn't take it. Something in me just rose up and was angry. I was so angry and it tried, it was like pulling me out of my seat, like someone was sitting there in back of me pushing me: 'Get up; go up there and choke that woman pastor.' I was actually going to go up there and put my hands around her throat and choke her. That is how much rage was inside of my body and I didn't even know the woman. Just because everybody was praising the Lord, and being all happy. And I would go, 'No, No,' you know.

"Just Let Them Have Me"

"So I ran into the back room because I couldn't control myself and I started getting all the chairs and throwing them against the wall. It took me over; and I was throwing all the chairs against the wall and everything and I was rolling around and this man's voice came out of my mouth and it's like I saw everything that was happening outside of my body. It's like . . . ."

"But you knew what was going on?" I ask.

"Yes. It was—it was like I was huddled in the corner; I was all afraid. And the thing, it was just like a man inside of my body; I was just raging, and the pastor—I was tearing everything up—the pastor had to send two men to the back to hold my arms down because I was just tearing everything up. And they came back there and they were like 200 pounds each, big men. And the thing that was in me threw them against the wall, across the room, just threw them like if you took a doll and just threw it. I couldn't believe it and everybody I saw standing in the doorway was like 'Oh my God, it's a real demon-possessed person.'

"And then I fell on the floor when the pastor came in there and it started writhing and I was like a snake and everything. And I felt my eyes go to the back of my head as she started applying what she said was holy oil. When she put oil on my skin it burned like someone took a lighter and went s-s-s-s-s-s-s! I even have marks on my skin from the oil.

"But anyway, as she called everybody in there to start praying over me and then I bit the pastor's daughter. See these teeth right here? They've always been kind of weird. I bit the pastor's daughter on the face. I didn't get much but she was bleeding. And then they started saying 'Name of Jesus.' And they started saying all these scriptures in the Bible about by the authority of Jesus Christ and then this man's voice just went [aaaaaaaah] and he went, 'This is my house; this is my domain. Leave her alone!'

"And then it was quiet. And like from a distance I heard everybody saying, 'It's gone; it's gone.' But the pastor looked at me and she said, 'No, it's not gone; it's hiding. That's why her eyes rolled into the back of her head. Keep praying over her.'"

"I Know How Evil Feels"

"It took an hour and a half and finally she took ahold of me, like she laid on top of me—I was like this on the ground on my stomach, and she laid over me sideways and she said, 'I'm praying for her and I'm going into battle with this spirit so intercede for me so I can come back.' To this day I don't know what it means but I felt something. It was like I had something in my stomach and it was battling with something else. It was weird.

"And finally I heard her say, 'Tammy, Tammy, come on. You can fight it.' And I go, 'I can't. I'm tired; I can't. Just let them have me. I can't.' She said, 'Come on, you can do it; you can do it.' So I was trying to hide—It's really _____, I can't explain it. But I felt something like a lead weight lift, like slide inside from the top of my feet and go all the way up to my head and then it just burst out. It finally left me, okay. And I was like crying like a baby and was all exhausted. I was soaked with sweat. My hair was soaked. I was just—I mean this thing really had me, okay. It had me.

"And she said, 'Okay, now, Tammy, you need to ask the Lord to come in now to replace what has left. You need to ask His Holy Spirit to come in and just fill your life and change you.' And at first I couldn't talk. I could just kind of moan. Then somehow I said, 'God, come in and be my Savior.' And I passed out and I woke up and I had this joy. So I knew God was real—You don't mind my saying this do you?"

"No."

"Okay. I know God is real for the fact that I felt His presence come in. All the good I felt come inside of me—nothing evil because I know the difference between how good and evil feel. I know how evil feels."

▶ 7 ◀

The Devil in the Southwest

I'm driving, air conditioner finally off, windows open and papers flapping in whirlwinds in the back seat in the coolness of mile-high northern Arizona. It's a sunny afternoon and Flagstaff folks are friendly, directing me to the modern suite of offices of the Coconino County Sheriff's Department. I've come to check out the beginning of a story of a satanized kid whose story is now unraveling in Midlothian, Texas.

"Ninety Thousand People Would Think I'm Nuts"

Detective Jeff Greene is young, tall and friendly. He can spend a few minutes with me even though he has mounds of paperwork stacked on his desk to be finished this afternoon. "We haven't had much that's really serious around here," he says. "Just animal mutilations. Mainly just teenagers doing dogs and cats. We had a girl that was 16 that was cutting her cat's throat when her grandmother walked in."

"Do you think I could talk with the girl?"

"Well," says Jeff, "the reason we heard the story is she's been involved in some criminal activity and is in a juvenile facility."

"There's always something else," I say.

"Yeah, she's a very troubled girl. Probably the serious occult stuff going on around here is the groups that meet over at the university. I don't know much about them, but there have been mutilated dogs found around the campus.

"There's some satanic activity—teenagers—active around Platte and some of the smaller communities. In Williams there are about ten or 12 kids involved who meet at an old train depot that's covered with satanic symbols. There are fire marks on the floors; they're just kids.

"Just like that kid in Texas; he carried it as far as he could. He had a friend

45

who left town to join the Job Corps in Reno. He came back for Christmas vacation and I talked with him. I mean, he gave me all the details of what he and this Texas kid were involved in, the kid who killed the undercover officer. And it was just bizarre. We sat and talked for hours—"

"Did you happen to tape the conversation?" I ask.

"No, he said he wouldn't talk if I taped it. And he wouldn't let anybody else be present. It was really just for my own information. He said that 90 percent of the Job Corps kids in Nevada are into satanism and he loved it."

Nevada—particularly Las Vegas—is where bored northern Arizona youth find bright lights and big cities. I'd been running into bits and pieces of scary information about Nevada's battle with faddish satanism. Roger Young of the Las Vegas FBI office and Las Vegas Metropolitan Police detective Bob Luke were profiled as antisatanism crusaders by the Carson City, Nevada, *Appeal*. An April 1986 story had quoted them saying that, even then, "satanic worship is growing, particularly among upper and middle-class white teenagers who are indulging in satanic music, sex, in drugs, and violence in growing numbers." They said the worst thing would be "for the public to not believe that satanic rituals exist in Nevada and throughout the nation. Episodes are frequently not placed in police reports because people are afraid they'll be mocked." The article mentioned that Luke displayed invitations to teenage parties. One such party drew 30–35 vehicles painted with occult symbols to Sunrise Mountain outside Las Vegas.

I also remember that Dr. Al Carlisle of the Utah State Prison system estimated that in the Las Vegas metropolitan area alone, nearly 600 victims are killed in satanic rituals every year.

Back in Flagstaff, I ask Jeff about the kid from the Nevada Job Corps: "What sort of stuff did he tell you?"

"The mutilations, the animal sacrifices they would do. He told me about his goal. He has a goal of making a deal with the devil, making a pact for what he wants. Just sitting here talking about it sounds really bizarre. Ninety thousand people would think I was nuts to spend time worrying about this stuff."

"Listen," I say. "I've been in L.A. for two weeks, and it's all very worth worrying about."

"He wanted to make a deal, and he explained how taking someone's life would be necessary to make that pact. It'd be the ultimate gift, to take their own life or someone else's. And the younger, the better. He explained how it would be easy to get away with it because nobody expects it. He said, 'If I was going to do it right now, I'd just befriend somebody that's living in the woods, somebody who's got no family. I'd get to know him really well, make sure there's nobody gonna be looking for him, and then sacrifice him.'

"I mean," Jeff continued, "this kid was serious as anybody. It was really scary. He believes in it."

"Yes, they do," I say. "How about this Midlothian case? What's the kid's name?" I'm referring to a case in Midlothian, Texas, in which a satanic dabbler group of teenagers is charged in the slaying of undercover police officer George Raffe, who had posed as a high school student to infiltrate the little dope-dealing band of devil worshipers.

"Can't give the kid's name," says Jeff. "He's still a juvenile and the trial is ongoing. We had no idea what was going on in the beginning. We had two juveniles brought in with a third in the hospital—he'd been beaten with a baseball bat. Of course, that's not what they first told us. Then the younger one, the kid that's in trouble in Texas, cries and gives this amazingly convincing story about how the older brother had done it. We searched the family's trailer and found lots of occult stuff we didn't think much of and tons of heavy metal music albums and tapes."

"The older brother is still incarcerated here?"

"Right. And the younger one moved with relatives to Midlothian a few months later. So when the case broke down there, they called up here to try to piece it together and see what this kid was pulling. All this satanism stuff was new to them; the girl who instigated it claims to be a witch. And he was doing the same thing down there in the murder of George Raffe as he had done up here—making a tearful confession that somebody else had done it. The kid is good, I tell you. He had me fooled completely."

We'll see how good the kid is with a jury.

The Other Side

Albuquerque. I had driven across the high desert country of California with its grotesque Joshua trees, across the Colorado River into northern Arizona pines and surprising volcanic peaks. Late in the desert night I had arrived in Albuquerque: gold-colored lights spread north and south along a wide, flat valley.

Today I'm meeting Gino Gerachi down at the Sunset Grill, a glitzy, fun restaurant of laughing, dressed-to-the-teeth, young upwardly mobile professionals. Neither Gino nor I seem to fit; we are, we remind each other, at least laughing. We glide up the escalator in the middle of the place and ask for as quiet a booth as possible. The waitress introduces herself as Ellen as we sit and hustles off for iced tea while Gino launches into his occultic experiences.

He's not tall. He's probably in his late twenties. He has an elastic face that wraps around wide smiles and crumples into concerned frowns within milliseconds. And he's smart—as are most dabblers who get serious about the black arts.

We're talking about how difficult it is to believe in the existence of "another side," of a spiritual dimension. "The thing that is the veil," says Gino, "that keeps us, the people at large, from not being in contact with demonic spirits is this mindset or state of consciousness that doesn't allow entrance. But when you alter your state of consciousness, you allow supernatural spirits to come and inhabit you."

I ask, "Can you remember the first time you made contact with some kind of spirit?"

"It was a life-changing experience; of course I remember it. The first time that I thought I'd made contact was when I altered my state of consciousness. I went into kind of a trancelike state and I began to have visions of spirits talking with me."

"What'd they look like—ugly, beautiful?"

Gino smiles even now at the recollection: "Beautiful, loving, kind, warm, gentle, generous. I had real good feelings and it started off with like female spirits. Because I had a tendency to trust females more than I trusted males. In my involvement with the occult, I discovered that spirits usually manifest themselves as the most gentle and trusting person the individual can imagine.

"I talked with a lady on the phone this morning who is involved in automatic writing, who said that when she started automatic writing the spirit claimed to be her dead father who had been dead for 23 years. Apparently the longing of her life had been to have a loving, generous, real relationship with her father. And so immediately, the spirit said, 'I love you and I'm your dad.' And she goes, 'Oh, I love you too, Dad.'

"And so as in my case and hers, you can see how the emotions will open up and you're willing to believe anything and do things you normally wouldn't because you love and you trust this spirit guide."

I say, "In your initial experience, then, you were in an altered state and you started seeing beings?"

"I started seeing beautiful beings and they would just talk to me, teach me."

"About—?"

"About how we're all manifestations of the one Life Force—basically the stuff I now know as Hinduism, pantheism, New Age teachings."

"Did you think you were going crazy at that point?"

"No," Gino says. "I really didn't. You know what's amazing? When you're—"

Ellen the Sunset Grill waitress sets down Gino's chef's salad and says, "Excuse me. Is that going to be okay for you?" Then she asks me, "Are you interviewing him?"

"I'm interviewing you, too," I say.

"Really? What for?"

I ask Ellen, "Do you know anything about satanism?"

"No, I don't."

Gino shakes his head as if thoroughly disappointed: "She doesn't know."

"I know about metaphysics. Is that one and the same?" she asks.

I say, "No, but—Well, metaphysics is anything beyond the physical; it's like a continuum. And way down at the deep end is satanism. But people often at least start thinking in that direction by just dabbling in the paranormal area of the continuum. And it's amazing—"

She turns to Gino. "Are you an authority on this? Why are you being interviewed?"

"As a teenager I was involved in witchcraft and ritual magic," he says.

"My girlfriend and I went on the harmonic convergence in '87 to Sedona—"

I say, "South of Flagstaff, one of the energy vortexes, right?"

"We went camping out for a few days. That's what the New Age Movement means to me—doing earthy things like camping out. So after we got back after the convergence we got bombarded by people telling us we were witches. Now, for me I don't understand the controversy. Of course, there are these New Age people, a lot of them are really, really into it and I can sense that fine line.

"You know what I mean? But then a lot of them just want peace, they want love, they say they believe in the Christ, so it can be confusing. I think I've come up with my own ideas because I've done a lot of studying of different churches and the differences in philosophy."

Ellen goes on: "My girlfriend who was really getting into it started going to a psychic and started doing tarot cards, talking about her past life and all that. Well, the problem with that, what came to my heart, I think really from God, is that she's so focused on the past and the future that she's not living the moment—and all we have is the present."

Gino says, "Ellen, you know it is so true what you're saying about focus and about feeling. People tend to focus on their experiences and their feelings about the experiences. But somewhere along the line of experience when you have multiple experiences you have to ask yourself, 'What is true?'"

I add, "Not so much, what do I feel is real, but what is true?"

Gino says to Ellen, who glances around to see that her other tables aren't swearing at her under their breath for refills on Perrier water. "Now, for instance, I communed with spirits. I have conjured devils. Now another person might say, 'Excuse me. Spirits and devils aren't real.' And I say, 'Excuse me, but I have experienced that; so what the spirits have told me is true because it was a real experience.' And they say, 'Excuse me, it wasn't true because it wasn't real because I've never experienced it.' So which one of us is true?

I try to clarify what I'm hearing: "So what you're getting at is that what we base our lives on might be real but might not be true, right? Just because a spirit really did appear to you doesn't mean that what you learned from the experience is true, right?"

Ellen says, "This is so fascinating. I have a book that I want to tell you about. I'll let you all finish and then . . ." and she rushes off across the restaurant balcony.

I say to Gino, "You were talking about that first experience. It was real?"

"It was real. I remember the thrill of realizing that the spirits were real and that I could talk to them. Then the next thing I did was go to a seminar in San Bernardino, California, on past life regression. I altered my state of consciousness while I was there and this guy guided me to a past life regression in Tibet. Now, Jerry, when I closed my eyes, it was like a movie that came to life. And I was flying through the sky and there were white clouds and beautiful blue skies and I was like in an airplane and I came to a mountaintop and there on the mountaintop in a lotus position was a Buddhist monk.

"Here's what happened. For a moment, I looked at that monk, and he looked so familiar to me. And then I focused on his feet; and believe it or not, they were my feet. You know how you know different parts of your body? And I go, 'Hey, I'd know those feet anywhere. Those are my feet?'

"And then it clicked. That's me! That is me! And for that split second, Jerry, I was that Buddhist monk on the top of that hill and I was also in a hotel room in San Bernardino, California.

"I was both people, and it was real.

"That's how I got hooked. That's how I got sucked into the idea that I could know truth, and I could know spiritual truth based on altered states of consciousness. I began to divine things through tarot card readings. I would use, you know, what I thought was supernatural skill coupled with good old-fashioned horse sense to bring people to a point of vulnerability. And once I could bring people to a point of vulnerability I could manipulate them. But it was all positive; you see, at the time, my intentions, as Ellen was mentioning, were good, were love, were peace, were reconciliation and healthy, whole relationships."

"You were saying some of the negative side effects started hitting you in the tenth grade?" I ask. "Like what?"

"Like I became suicidal. I had an unhealthy preoccupation with death. I started getting visions in the evening of blood, of decapitation, mutilation."

"Can you think of a specific instance?"

Gino bites his lip. "I would be in my bed and I would see people who were mutilated and decapitated bleeding all over me. At one point I went to Mexico, and my brother was staying in my room, and he had a vision too. My brother was not even involved in the occult. But he had a vision of a bleeding hand coming right toward his throat and he ran out of my room. I had occult paraphernalia all over my room. I would also become severely depressed. With all the lights out, I would look into a mirror when it was absolutely black. And I would gaze into the mirror and I would see blood and death and gross, perverted forms of sex.

"And I became increasingly more depressed to the point where I took a whole bottle of antihistamines and aspirin. Who knows why, because all it did was make me sick. Gave me a horrible headache—made me hurt, but it didn't kill me. But I kept thinking about dying. I kept thinking about cutting my wrists, or wanting to inflict pain on myself."

I ask, "By then, when you went into your altered state of consciousness, were the spirits still beautiful and feminine and—?"

"No, no. They'd become increasingly more aggressive, increasingly more hostile, and increasingly antagonizing me to destroy myself, to destroy others."

"Could you conjure up the nice, loving ones? If you really worked at it?"

Gino says, "No, at that point I couldn't. I got pot luck at that point. Because I wanted the love and I got the hate, I got the aggressive, I got the hostility. I got the demons that were now self-destructive. But you see, there's something about the power that's intoxicating. So that even though you don't want to die you still want the power and you almost—" He fishes through his untouched chef's salad and tries to convey his thoughts: "It's like addictive, compulsive behavior. You become drawn to it. You have to do weirder and weirder and more bizarre things in order to get a deeper and deeper spiritual high, so to speak."

Ellen the waitress comes back to the table. "I'm on break for a few minutes," she explains. "I'm just going to eavesdrop. I'm not going to interfere anymore, but I would like to sit down and just eavesdrop, if you wouldn't mind."

"Of course not; have a seat," I say. I start to ask Gino a question but Ellen beats me to it.

"What did you believe?" she asks.

"I did have a whole set of basic beliefs and denials," says Gino. "I was taught well in the occult and in metaphysics. And it was a belief system."

I say, "What do you mean by basic denials?"

Gino lists, "There is no personal God, Jesus is not the only Christ, sin is not real, Hell is not real, there is no judgment—"

"Now wait," I say. "Were you really taught those things, or did you come up with them yourself? How were you taught?"

"No, as a metaphysician, as an occultist, as a witch, I was taught those things, not only by my spirit that I communed with or by the demons I conjured, but by every book I read. There was always something to reinforce this new belief system."

Ellen asks, "'Taught by the spirit you had conjured—'? Did you conjure up the spirit and it would sit down and give you lectures?"

"Yeah," Gino nods. "I would talk with the spirit, either through automatic writing, through divination, through a ouija board, or I would alter my state of consciousness and just receive from the spirit. What I was actually doing was inviting the spirit to possess me and then to commune with me. But at the time, I didn't know that. I didn't go, 'Yeah, now I'm going to become demon-possessed, and I'm going to talk with demons.' See, I thought they were spirit guides to instruct me, teachers, ascended masters."

"Do you think you were ever possessed?" I ask. Ellen fidgets a little at the question.

"You know, I've often wondered that myself. And I think so. I think there were times when I was actually possessed by a demon or demons in the natural course of the trances of divination, especially when I was divining different things about people's past or present or future.

"For example. You know how kids party when they're in high school. We're partying down; we're going to this place; we're all in a car. Everybody's laughing and I'm being a normal teenager. Then all of a sudden I said, 'Everyone, be quiet. A police officer's going to pull us over in about five minutes. We need to ditch the beer, he's just going to say that you have a taillight out.'

"Five minutes later a siren goes off and we get pulled over. See, by this time the kids are freaked out. Not freaked out because we got pulled over, but freaked out because I prognosticated the event. And the officer says, 'Don't worry, you have a taillight out. I'm going to give you like a fix-it ticket, and I'm going to ask you to come into the station later on to demonstrate that you have fixed it.' See, we had ditched the beer; there's nothing in sight; we've all eaten mints since then, and we're ready for it. But you see, you know what that did? That event only reinforced the credibility that I had among my peers, got them more hooked because there really was something happening."

"And you think the incident was demonic," I say.

Ellen gulps and Gino nods. "That was demonic. You see, and I've often wondered, and people have always asked me, 'If only God knows the future, then how can occultists successfully prognosticate the future?' And I say, 'You know what? Devils don't know, but they can guess better than anybody.' See, if you're not in the kingdom of light you're in the kingdom of darkness. If you're in the kingdom of darkness you can be influenced and altered by the forces of darkness to be in a certain place at a certain time in order to accomplish a certain reality. And so, if I am a demon and I'm in charge of this officer, and I'm a demon and I'm in charge of Gino, and I can coordinate so that they meet at just the right time for just the right reasons, then I can pull off something that looks to be weird. And real."

Ellen says, "Wild, that's wild."

I backtrack for a minute: "Gino, back to where you said this satanist guy Steve contacted you. Did the two of you get into larger group rituals?"

Gino says, "Most of the time I did it on my own. And the only other times were with people like Steve. We would make a pentagram; then we would chant and offer certain kinds of prayers to the spirits in order to accomplish our goal. I never was in a coven, but I read extensively about it. And I knew of one close to me that I was hoping to someday join.

"The thing about being able to join a whole coven with its rituals that really thrilled me about witchcraft was the sexuality. Because, you see, I'm an adolescent, dealing with all these sexual, hormonal kinds of things and I'm reading these things and looking at these pictures and I notice that in black witchcraft the altar is a nude woman. And part of the worship for a young teenager is you get to have sex with the altar."

Ellen glances at her watch. "Yes, well. Break-time's over," she says and scurries away.

I'm reminded of Gino's quip hours later when in the middle of the night I drive into the Burger King in Amarillo, Texas. With the rest of the crew Carla in brown braids and brown uniform is just closing up. But she graciously takes my order.

"Kids into satanic stuff around here?" I ask Carla.

"No," she says, looking a little concerned. It is, after all, midnight.

"Witchcraft, ouija board sort of stuff?" I explain to her the legitimacy of the book project. That I'm one of the guys in the white hats, not one of the black-hatted satanic villains.

"Well, there's a group of real weirdos. Metal music stuff. They talk real loud about blood. That kind of stuff. And—" She hesitates. "They do, like, orgies." She shrugs. "Some kids who aren't into anything still go to their parties. So they're perverts, too. Big deal."

And I drive off into the Texas night thinking that, yes, satanic sex is a big deal. One more enticement used to bait teenagers in the very areas of their deepest desires. They want power, experiences beyond their dull everyday lives, and sex. Satanic groups offer it all with a contract in which the small print about destroyed minds and lives is too fine to read—until it's too late.

▶ 8 ◀

The Derangement of Satanism

It's getting grisly.

I'm tired of digging up the same demented themes in crime after crime committed by teenagers in the name of Satan. There's always the drug theme, the inch-by-inch progression of involvement, the disembodied voices lusting for a kill, the murders "just to watch someone die":

Just to Watch Somebody Die

John-Michael Trimmer was then 17. Michael Cravey, 19. Harold Smith, 17. A 16-year-old unnamed participant and a 16-year-old girl. In 1985 they beat, stabbed with a knife and pipe, choked with a scarf, and set on fire with a cigarette lighter 19-year-old Keith Medler in Houston.

As Houston police sought motives in the slaying, the suspects said they did it "just to watch somebody die"—the phrases used in the Sean Sellers murders and in the Steve Newberry case.

Transcriptions of their confessions show one of them leaned over the body and said, "Hey, Keith, it was nothing personal." They had lured Keith, a friend, to the grassy field behind the Resthaven Memorial Gardens cemetery on the pretense of gathering mushrooms to get high.

A self-styled satanic group, several had been suspected of other violent crimes. Cravey was subsequently implicated in the stabbing death of 25-year-old Ronald Monahan. Trimmer was convicted of attempted capital murder in the attack on 25-year-old Donald Dill, who survived with a slashed throat and arm. "We're devil worshipers," Trimmer said.

We could dig through the tragic rubble of Tommy Sullivan's family. He slashed his mother to death, tried to burn his father and brother alive, and committed suicide by cutting his wrists and throat and bleeding to death on

54

the snow in New Jersey. Tommy had begun his gruesome descent into satanism only months before. His father says the change in his son was demonic. Urging his classmates to pursue satanism, Tommy had told several friends of a satanic vision to kill his parents.

Or we could grovel in the morbid details of the Gary Lauwers case. Ricky Kasso, who later hanged himself in his cell, led a group of Long Island buddies into self-styled satanism that resulted again in death. Before a crackling fire in a patch of woods in upper-middle-class Northport, Ricky repeatedly stabbed his former friend Gary Lauwers, yelling, "Say you love Satan! Say you love Satan!"

Ricky and two friends buried Gary in a shallow grave and showed the spot to classmates over the next two weeks.

But we're not after grisly details of death and dismemberment. *True Detective* magazine is more for those craving the macabre of crime. What we are interested in is acknowledging teenagers' experiences in this disturbing netherworld so we can start pulling them out of the pit. And I think we've gone far enough profiling Satan's new children. You've got the hint—a hint as subtle as a two-by-four to the back of the head: Satanism is dangerous to teenagers' mental health.

Frankly, from my non-mental-health-professional perspective, I think these kids who've dabbled in the demonic are in some ways seriously mentally ill—which may be the most impressive scare-tactic to keep teenagers away from the devil.

Here's another noncriminal profile of a teenage dabbler. Unfortunately I've had to edit most of the hour and a half of conversation I had with Mark Madden; I think you'd catch even more the struggle Mark's having, figuring out what's been real and what hasn't in his occult-drenched life. Mark, a darkly handsome young man, is dressed in black and speaks articulately:

It Began with Molestation

"How'd you get into all this demon business, Mark?" I ask.

"Well," he says. "When I was five years old something happened that really disoriented my life. I was molested. And I think because of that, I wanted to run away from reality. I started having my own little fantasy world that I would escape to that wasn't this real world full of sin.

"I'd add things to the real world and I'd take things from the fantasy world, like from movies. Like you know, when I was young I'd watch 'Bewitched' on TV; I didn't go, 'Gee, I'd like to be an occultist,' but I do remember thinking that if I had that kind of power I'd use it for good. I think that's the way a good percentage of kids getting into the occult feel—that they'll just use it for good."

I say, "The idea that you could walk into a room, wiggle your nose and do something fun, something good is pretty appealing, right?"

"Yeah, or that I could have control over a situation. Let's see, at 12 I started practicing self-hypnosis for the first time and that's when I had my first out-of-body experience. I just sat up out of my body and I looked around the room and then I realized that my body was still back on the bed and I went, "Whoa!" Laid back down and went to sleep. Eventually I really got into astral projection and energy projection, things like that. Through the spiritual side of martial arts I became a rainmaker, where I could control the weather through use of the spirits. But I didn't know they were spirits, of course. I thought it was just, as one of my instructors said, the universal mind, you know.

"This was like my first couple years of high school," Mark continues. "And from that time on there was a lot of demonic appearances, false apparitions, stuff like that that was trying to sway me in the direction of magic."

"How can you tell the false apparitions from the real ones?" I ask.

Mark shakes his head slowly. "I was lonely; I had no girlfriends. I was the outcast at school. So I had this imaginary girlfriend and I called her Rhiannon, which is the name of a real Welsh witch. Only in my mind she was a good witch and never did anything evil and stuff like that. At 17 I got into drugs a lot so along with the hypnosis, the martial arts development of my chi, the meditation—

"I've had some interesting things happen while meditating. One time I was lying on my back in the dark meditating while listening to the live version of Led Zeppelin's 'Dazed and Confused.' You know, and I thought backward masking was take it or leave it. And I was lying there and in the middle of it there's a line taken from a '60s song. It's supposed to say, 'If you're going to San Francisco, you're going to meet a lot of gentle people there.' Well, I was lying there and suddenly this neon green pentagram was floating in the air in front of me and I went feet first straight up in the air and I landed on my feet and I said, 'Okay, what's going on here?' So I listened to the song again and it was all buried and mild guitar and stuff, but the line actually says, 'You're going to meet a lot of devil people there.' I went, 'Okay, good place to check for backward masking.' And I played it backward and it went 'Worship . . . worship.'

"But I've had many, many things like that happen.

"One time when I was into the astral projection side of it there were these people who were giving me bomb threats and murder threats and stuff like that. And voices started telling me to astral project and kill them in their sleep. And I wouldn't do it because I was deceived into believing my power was from God and I couldn't use it for evil. One time the voices of the demons woke me up. I was in a half-astral-projection state; my body was on the bed but I was coming up from the downstairs and the voices got louder. When I opened my eyes the voices were in my room and there was a heavy presence—it just felt like thousands of pounds of pressure on me. I went to move and I was totally paralyzed. The only thing I could move was my eyes and my tongue just barely. It was like someone had their hand on my tongue and I just forced the words out, 'Jesus, help me.' When I finally could sit up I consciously got back into my body and the demons left the room."

"—For a good night's sleep," I say.

Fantasy or Reality?

Mark is engrossed in his own story: "I've had other kinds of occurrences, like I had a witch—like I said, I used to have this fantasy girlfriend. Well, when I went back to visit friends where I started growing up in New Jersey, I went walking through the woods. It was autumn so all the trees were bare, and even though it was near sunset, there was quite a bit of light coming through them. Well, I passed this one street and in the middle of the street, there she was in a long black robe. And it was like—It wasn't like a vision, like it was a real person in a long black robe, with curly blonde hair, and I thought, *My dream's come true, I've finally met her*. And I went to walk up to talk to her but when I got about 25, maybe 35 feet away, she turned, took two steps to the side and disappeared right in front of me. And I was totally bewildered. So I walked off into the woods. Like I said I could still see, there was enough light I could still see all the way around me and I heard footsteps walking up toward me crunching the leaves but there was no one there. And I took off out of the woods because I'd heard there's a place somewhere in the backwoods in New Jersey called the Gates of Hell and it's a satanic ritual place."

"You know, Mark," I say, "that a lot of kids would still love to dive into these weird experiences because they think there's power there. What do you think?"

"Of course there's power," he says. "You know, a person doesn't have to sacrifice children on a mountain or drink blood, or commit mass acts of immorality in an orgy to be a satanist or a satan worshiper. And the power looks inviting. I mean, I would say of all people, even though I wasn't part of a coven, I was probably a pretty powerful dude considering—Well, a good example: during one meditation, it was on Christmas Eve, and the Jersey newspapers would probably back this up. They were expecting it to be dry, no white Christmas or anything, all the way through New Years. And I was listening to Led Zeppelin's 'No Quarter' and it talks about Thor and the winter winds. And so I meditated on it as I was doing my projection and I woke up the next morning and there was a foot of snow on the ground and the weathermen were astounded."

"I'll bet they were," I say.

"When I came back out here, as I was coming through Arizona I meditated that it would rain. And by the time I got to Los Angeles my dad came and picked me up at Union Station and said, 'You know, this is the first rain we've had since you left.' And so, I'd say I had the power. But I got to know who it was who was giving me this power and I baled out on him. So anyone who's listening to me and wants to get into the occult or satanism anyway, you know, I'm telling them, they're after a murderer. Satan presents himself as cool, and the satanists who appear on 'Eye on L.A.' say, 'Oh, we just want peace,' but their god tells them to lie. And if their god tells them to lie, what makes them think their god isn't lying to them?"

"Mark, what's to keep them from thinking, *Well, he was really on drugs. That's why he couldn't handle it and I can handle satanic stuff because I won't do drugs*"?

"Well, I never did any drugs until I was 17, yet I had occult experiences dating back way before that. From the time I was young, like I said my first astral projection was when I was 12. No, the demons weren't drug visions. And during many of the occurrences I'd been straight for I think it was three years."

I say, "And the demons were real?"

"Definitely," Mark says. "And powerful. That's where all the power actually comes from—whether the magician recognizes it or not. Some people say, 'I had a confrontation with a spirit and he left just like that. But they've never had a confrontation with a principality, which is a much more powerful demon. Before I totally got out of it for good, I had a principality. I used to go places; I'd walk into a restaurant or walk down the street and I had like an entourage of spirits, you know, like a celebrity has an entourage of people. I had this one major spirit that was called the Overseer and he had all these other little spirits around him. Every time I'd walk past babies they'd start bawling, like, 'Get this ugly thing away from me; get this guy away from me and all of his ugly friends.' I'd walk down the street and dogs would bark for a quarter mile before they even knew I was coming.

"One night I was on LSD and it happened to be a satanic holiday. I was just freaking out because everywhere I'd go I'd see people, all the people who were given over to Satan acting totally bizarre. And every time I'd walk down the street, as far south, as far west, as far east, and as far north as I could hear, there'd be dogs barking. Everywhere I went from one side of La Mirada to the other.

"So I know dogs for one don't like demons, unless a person's actually into drugs or the occult because I have come across a couple of animals who were subject to their owners and they were demon-possessed. But the instances were very rare.

"But really the power in the occult is nothing because in the first place, Satan was going to make me powerful and give me plenty of women and plenty of money through music. He lied."

I met two other teenagers whose minds I began to worry about: Flancy and the Jester.

Flancy and the Jester

All right, all right. So you'll have to guess where I am on this interview.

Let's say we're in Portland, which we're not. The teenagers who agreed to talk with me at length on their occult involvement insisted that everything be changed—their names, how I contacted them, where we are. Both insisted that they wanted this anonymity to guard the secrets of their little self-styled satanist group.

But I keep getting the feeling that it's closer to the truth to say their insistence on anonymity is based on fear.

We're in a tiny Waffle House and it's about three in the afternoon. Rhonda the waitress is curious about my tape recorder setup and insists on yanking out the old juke box at the end of the counter to turn down the volume knob. The yellow-and-brown appointed restaurant thumps with a country version of the old Eagles song: "Somebody's gonna hurt someone before the night is through. Somebody's gonna come undone; there's nothin' we can do."

"Naw, leave it up," Jester yells to the waitress. He looks like an 18-year-old Ichabod Crane: lanky limbs, scraggly brown hair, an attempted mustache, eyes that can only be described as beady, and a wonderfully hooked nose. "So that'll be what you call me, right? Jester."

"Sounds good to me, Jester. You're in a coven now?" I wave my empty coffee cup to Rhonda for a refill. "So you meet when?"

"Whenever we want."

"Like once a month or on the holydays or what?" I ask. I like this kid.

"Whenever we want. Like maybe twice a week. Most every weekend. We play basketball Saturday mornings at the Y and then usually load up at somebody's house and then see what happens."

"Load up?"

"Do some drugs. Nothing spectacular. Mushrooms. Then Saturday nights or sometimes Friday nights we'll just be having like a party and when we feel like it do some magic."

"Magick with a 'k'?"

"Huh?"

"I hear magick with a 'k' is about building power in rituals and with a 'c' is conjuring."

"I don't know about that," Jester says affably.

"So describe what the group does."

"Well, we kind of clear out the stuff in the room—"

"Where?"

"In somebody's house. Somebody's place like—" He hesitates, then makes up a name. "Like Horatio's where nobody's ever home. So we clear out the room and draw the circle."

"Who does the drawing? And with a marker or something?"

"With tape sometimes. Masking tape or once I did it with sugar; just poured it like you're chalking a line for soccer. And I'm the one who does it 'cause I'm the magister. If I'm not around, _____ does it. What're you gonna call her?"

"Whatever she chooses. Or you choose."

"Flancy," he says. "She'll like that."

"So you or Flancy draw the circle. Then what?"

"Then I stand in the middle and everybody gets inside around the edge of the circle."

"How many are there?"

"Depends on who has to work or who's there. There are nine of us but it's only once in a while everybody's there."

"Then?"

"Well, the candles are lit and I lead chants from Necronomicon and they repeat whatever I say. Then we get blood from either one of us. Somebody volunteers to cut themself with the athame. That's a knife. Then we dribble it into a chalice and pour in some red wine and pass it around. Then we pray. We used to have a fire but it got too hot during the summer and only two places have a fireplace. You can't just do a fire on the floor."

"Why not do it outside so you can have a fire? What's the fire for?"

"It's one of the elements—earth, wind, fire, water. We first used to meet down by the creek by the cemetery but I guess somebody called the cops 'cause a cop car would cruise back and forth and it got to be a hassle."

"You weren't doing anything wrong, right?" I say.

"Naw. Just who wants to get hassled? And somebody'd have dope. We usually use mushrooms so it's not illegal but it seems like somebody's always showing up with coke or something. It just got to be a hassle to find a good place around here. If we were out in the hills . . . ."

Jester rambles on about how his little group plans to go backpacking in a few weeks in the hill country, about how they're all going to live further out so they can get serious about their satanism.

"You're not serious now?"

"Well, sure. But we're not doing the real stuff."

"Like—?"

"Like real sacrifices and whole weekends of ceremonies. And get in with other covens so the ceremonies are huge."

"Why would you want that?"

"Well—" Jester tries to hide a lockerroom grin. "Most of the rituals are—" (I'll translate: sexual orgies) "—and it gets old with the same girls."

I guess I sigh too obviously.

"That's not what it's about, you know. I mean, we're serious about dedication."

"You said something about 'real sacrifices.' What did you mean?"

"Like humans. All this other stuff is like preschool. I mean, it's good to know; like I know how to skin a cat now. I was taught by this little kid. We do a sacrifice on full moons."

Flancy has pushed through the glass door to hear Jester's last comment. "But we got to get real drunk to do it," she says.

"We don't get drunk," Jester says.

"You don't," she says. "I gotta take something or I throw up." Flancy plops a large black purse on the table and scoots into the booth next to Jester. She's overweight, with a very pretty face, brown shoulder-length hair and blue eyes made up with swept-wing blue eyeshadow. Hard blue eyes above a Levis denim jacket, red T-shirt and jeans. "We're not doing anything wrong," she begins.

"Who said you were?" I ask.

"You guys are always pickin' about something."

Jester and I look at each other. He bursts into a laugh: "Hostile, hostile."

Flancy shrugs. "I just get tired of it. Why can't we just do what we want to do? It's not hurting anybody else."

"You've been hassled about this?" I ask.

"Oh, they're doing TV shows on Satan taking over the world and making a big deal. We've got a right to practice religion however we want. It's not hurting anybody."

We sit silently for ten seconds. Then I say, "Are you happy, Flancy?"

She swears.

Jester says, "What's with you?"

"So this guy gets Mr. Chauncey to set this up and it's just so he can tell us how bad we are."

"That's not what's happening here," I tell her. "I just want to know what you're all about. How'd you get interested in satanism?"

"My dad and mom go to this church and have meetings at our house afterwards on Sunday nights. They do meditation and astral travel and mental telepathy and stuff."

"What church is that?" I ask. "What kind of a church?"

"Church of Religious Science."

"They're into New Age stuff?"

"That's what Mom says. My dad says that's a fad."

"So how'd you get to satanism?"

"I'd get hypnotized at the meetings with my parents and just got into spiritual things."

"Such as—?"

"Astral projection. I've got beautiful spirit guides."

"Such as—?"

"One's called Mother Clara. The other one I don't tell anybody about."

"Why?"

"That's the way he wants it."

"So that led you—"

"No," she seems to be warming up a bit. "I knew him."

Jester says, "We're calling me Jester."

"I knew he was into something and went to a party at this guy's house and they asked me if I wanted to stay to do a ceremony. This was after I'd told them about astral projection and the guy in my dad's church who can levitate objects. So I stayed, and I've been in it ever since."

We talk further. I need to leave, while it's obvious they're still wanting to talk. Both Jester and Flancy seem to be trying to top the other with stories about how bad they are, about the prevalence of sex in their brand of satanism. "So," I say, "you do mushrooms, some of you get drunk, you skin cats and have sex with as many as you can afterwards. How long have you been doing this?"

They look at each other as if to say, "Yeah, we're bad." Then they decide: "About a year."

"Why?" I click off the tape recorder and stand to leave.

Again they look at each other. Then they laugh—happy, mischievous, teenager laughs. "It's fun," Flancy finally gets out.

"What can I say?" says Jester.

I smile because I care about Jesters and Flancys, thank them for the interviews, and push through the greasy glass door of the cafe feeling stifled with a kind of despair—because I care about Jesters and Flancys.

Crimes in the Name of Satan

Young girls, from 11 to 14 years old, began telling police about rituals in which men gave them alcohol and drugs, read from a satanic bible and forced them to participate in dozens of bizarre sexual acts. At first, the detective was incredulous. Most of the girls wouldn't identify their assailants, and there was little evidence linking anyone to a crime. Then physical exams showed that 11 girls had been sexually assaulted, and a 19-year-old arrested for burglary of a church began substantiating the stories.

On March 1, four months after a 16-year-old Greenville boy disappeared from a local theater, police found his body in a shallow grave. A 20-year-old indicted for the slaying has been charged with luring the youth to an area, beating him with a club and stabbing him to death.

The 20-year-old has a 666, known as the mark of Satan, tattooed on his forehead. Police found a robe, black candles, a satanic bible and occult literature in the man's car.

In December, Kennedale police found an amphetamine lab at the eastern edge of the city and found occult paraphernalia suggesting that the woman charged with running the lab was conducting satanic animal-mutilation rituals.

Occultism: The Fad of the '80s?

Dallas/Fort Worth area police say that virtually every high school has at least one small group dabbling in the occult. Much of that is only for shock value, little deeper than an interest in heavy metal/rock bands whose satanic anthems and album cover pictures of weird symbols and gore are guaranteed to bother almost any adult.

But officials, including mental/health professionals at a number of area psychiatric hospitals, say they are seeing indications that a growing number of teenagers are more seriously involved.

"About one in every five kids we see have experimented with books or black mass or an animal sacrifice. One or two percent of the kids we see seem to be involved in something organized," said Dr. Richard Cancami, a staff psychiatrist at a private Arlington psychiatric hospital.

One high ranking official of the Fort Worth police department was shocked and defensive when I informed him of the name of the special covert agent on the force dispatched to uncap satanic crime. He reminded me that should I be careless with this privy information his life and family could be in jeopardy.

In the Dallas/Fort Worth area, police have found ties between deviant occultist groups and white supremacists such as the neo/Naxi "Skinheads."

In one case, a North Richland Hills detective said, an adult believed to be a leader of "Death Babies," a group of about 50 adults and teenagers involved in occult activities, was also a Skinhead. The detective said the man and others in the group were being sought for vandalism and other petty crimes.

An FBI behavioral sciences expert believes some of the rising interest stems from a simple itch to ride the edge of social convention. "People want to toy with forbidden things. They're kind of like moths flying around a damn flame just to see how close they can get without getting burned. And you must consider how little is forbidden today," said the agent, assigned to the FBI training academy at Quantico, Va. "We accept things now that would've been unheard of 20 years ago. That's one reason why what's attractive is so much more extraordinarily evil."

Satanic Crimes on the Rise

At a special conference on satanism and occultism held this past spring, 150 law enforcement officials from across the United States told of the rise in satanism-related crimes. They stressed the importance of recognizing the signs of devil worship, including mutilated animals, cemetery robberies, and church break-ins. Los Angeles author Joel Norris said that of the 300 serial killings he studied, 30 percent were involved in satanism in some form.

A letter stating requirements for joining a teenage satanic coven in the area was recently discovered at a local school.

The list was handwritten and had been drawn up by an eighth grader in the school. Among the 50 requirements listed to join the "Church of Ozzy and (the child's name) and the Devil" were worship of the rock group Black Sabbath and the KKK, participation in oral sex, taking drugs, burning crosses, killing 666 people, killing your grandmother and mother and biting "off your dog's head." Drawn on the list in a rough pen sketch was a figure clutching two blood-soaked knives standing over a person with his chest cut open.

Salt Lake City Deseret News   Utah   May 8, 1986

Local Police Say Satanism on the Rise

Crime linked to satanic worship is becoming so much a trend that Metro police officers now are being trained to recognize the signs of devil worship. Sergeant Mark Wynn began teaching a course in satanic crime at Metro's Police Training Academy in February. Wynn helped identify numerous Satanic worship items found at the home of Robert Brian Canter. Canter, 32, of Madison, was arrested Saturday on stolen property and sex charges. Wynn said police discovered elements of satanic worship during the investigation of Travis Sacchinelli, a Madison man who was sentenced to 25 years in the death of his grandmother, Geanne Saverio, in December. Sacchinelli's mother insisted to police her son was "demonically possessed" and showed them numerous "demonic" drawings she had found in his room.

Although both Canter and Sacchinelli are from Madison, Wynn said, there is no heavy concentration of devil worshipers in the community. Demonic worship paraphernalia is easily obtainable in Nashville, Wynn said, noting the number of mail/order catalogues available in most bookstores. The satanic bible published by Avon Books can also be found in a number of area bookstores.

Nashville, Tennessee, Banner   May 5, 1988

Satanism Reports Concern Local Officials

Increasing reports of local students dabbling or participating in cultic activities, particularly satanism, has officials concerned about how to respond to the situation. Representatives with Charleston Area Medical Center report that at least a third of the teenagers checking into their adolescent Care Unit are involved or dabbling in satanic activities.

John Adams Junior High School vice principal Carla Williamson said schools got involved after parents began expressing concern about their children dabbling in the topic. "I've had many parents ask for help in this," Williamson said. "But I didn't know how to help them . . . . We feel inadequate to deal with it."

A representative with the Care Unit of the Medical Center said the children admitted to the alcohol and drug dependency program do not come from any particular section of the county or social class. "There are just as many preppies as there are flashers," she said. Most (professionals) involved, however, agree that there is one thing that seems to tie the students together: heavy metal music. Some of the groups supposedly followed by the youngsters are Motley Crue, Black Sabbath, AC/DC and Iron Maiden.

Charleston Daily Mail   West Virginia   May 5, 1988

Cult Rumors Stir Up Maine Towns
School Officials, Police Debunk Stories of Devil Worship

Island Falls. Island Falls, like neighboring Smyrna Mills, is a town torn by rumors—rumors of a cult of high school students that worship the devil. School authorities and police totally debunk the cult rumors, citing it as a textbook example of how hysteria can sweep a small town.

In the kitchen of a farmhouse overlooking Smyrna Mills, a student at the Southern Aroostook Community School talked about the so-called cult. "It was easy to pick them out . . . . They have these eyes, really it's scary. They look at you as if to say if you do anything wrong, they know where to get you," said the student. She said the cult members were dressed in jackets inscribed "Teens against God."

John McElwee, the Aroostook County district attorney, said he could not recollect any specific criminal incidents being attributed to a cult, and he is mystified by the rumors.

Bangor Daily News   Maine   November 21, 1987

The Devil Cults

Ed and Lorraine Warren (the celebrated ghost-hunting team who battled demons in a house now famed as the "Amityville Horror") are now involved in the legal defense of 19-year-old Arne Johnson, charged with the bizarre murder of Alan Bono, 40. They are trying to prove that the softspoken teenager was possessed by the devil when he suddenly flew into an uncontrollable rage and slashed the life out of his best friend and neighbor in Brookfield, Connecticut.

In Sacramento, California, a 13-year-old girl shot her 11-year-old sister to death. The youngster later sobbed to police that she didn't want to harm her sister, that she was under the control of Satan.

Denver Post   Colorado   March 12, 1988

Satanic Altars Arouse Fears

West Haven, Conn.—Local police are on edge, and townspeople and clergy are nervous about possible violence in the wake of the discovery of a devil-worshiping cult in this working class town. Since last month, police have been probing the discovery of two satanic altars—one in an abandoned incinerator site, the other in an old warehouse—where the sacrificial remains of a slaughtered mink also were found nearby.

. . . What really has police on edge is the possibility that the cult group's sacrificing of animals could eventually turn to violence against townspeople. "Nothing has happened yet, but in case something does, we want to know more about it. If there is a crime committed that is related to all of this, we'll know what to do," said Assistant Police Chief Theodore Forbes.

Paul D. Valentine, an admitted "satanist" in nearby New Haven, who heads the Worldwide Church of Satanic Liberation, said the discovery of this cult shouldn't be taken too lightly . . . (and he) also said the group is capable of violence because its members have turned to sacrificing animals as part of their devil-worshiping ritual. "These people are taking what they do very seriously, way too seriously," added Valentine.

Boston, Massachusetts, Herald   *November 22, 1987*

Some Criminals Drawn to Satanism

It's only natural that many people suspected of heinous crimes would proclaim their allegiance to the Prince of Darkness, experts say.

Fort Wayne authorities confirmed last week that several of the men questioned in connection with the disappearance and slaying of 8-year-old April Marie Tinsley have admitted being involved in satanism. April disappeared from near her West Williams Street home on Good Friday, April 1, and was found dead three days later. An autopsy showed she had been sexually abused and suffocated.

Margaret Singer, a professor at the University of California at Berkeley, said it is not unusual for criminals to declare they are involved in satanic worship. "It gives them a way to convey to their colleagues in crime that they have mysterious power," she explained.

In recent years, satanic worship has been tied to a number of crimes in Indiana.

Terry L. Lowery, 26, is on death row in Michigan City, awaiting execution for the May 1985 murder of 13-year-old Tricia Woods. Lowery has told authorities he is a devil worshiper who hears and sees Satan.

Garrett Police Chief Jerry Custer has investigated a number of reports of satanic worship in N. Eastern Indiana. His investigations have taken him to abandoned farm houses where "magic circles" and inverted pentagrams were drawn on the floor— evidence that satanic worship had taken place.

(Custer) explains that the main concern is children who become involved in Satanism. "It's the ultimate rebellion, with rituals guaranteed to shock parents." For many children it's a fad, a set of rituals they temporarily dabble in because it's shocking to adults. But Custer says he has run into many examples of youngsters who have lost the ability to differentiate between reality and fantasy.

Journal–Gazette   *Fort Wayne, Indiana*   *May 8, 1988*

Anti-Social Behavior Cited in Experimental, Occult Cults

Last month, Bob Miller, Greene County chief deputy prosecutor, got a call that a dead wolf had been found in Greene County. A dead wolf is unusual, but the fact that it was found in the center of a pentagram in the stone house near Linton where 15-year-old Cindy Lou Mason was murdered in 1983 made it remarkable.

Miller said the finding represents another piece of evidence that satanic activities continue in Greene County and in other areas of southern Indiana. A few weeks after police verified the report of the dead wolf, another animal—probably a coyote—was found in the woods just behind the stone house. Its head had been cut off and there were bits of fur and dried blood on the pentagram.

"We get reports of animal mutilations frequently," Miller said. "And we get lots of reports of activity at the stone house—fires being lit, chanting and sightings of candles or torches being carried around. The dead animals there are something new."

Herald-Telephone   *Bloomington, Indiana*   *June 22, 1986*

Adolescents Susceptible to Satanism

Experts say the growing interest in satanism among Coloradans might come as a surprise to most people, but that's because they don't know what to look for.

Wayne Van Kampen, chief pastoral officer at Denver's Bethesda hospital, said the typical satanic worshiper is an underachiever, suffering from low self-esteem, experiencing conflict in peer relationships and alienation from his family and his family's religion.

Van Kampen, having seen a sharp increase in the number of patients at Bethesda who once were involved in satanic worship, said adolescents are the most likely to succumb.

Dr. John MacDonald, director of forensic psychiatry at the University of Colorado Health Sciences Center, said parents need to be more aware of the warning signs in their children.

"They'll have the robes, they'll have the ceremonial chalice—but they'll say they weren't really doing anything, that it was just something fun to talk about," MacDonald said. "Then you come to find out from other sources that they're very deeply involved in it. . . ."

Rocky Mountain News   *March 16, 1987*

Kern Drops Satanism Case

Kern County's largest criminal case ever—a child-molestation investigation that involved allegations of Satanism and later resulted in a $500,000 state review—ended Thursday with a burst of hugs and smiles by freed defendants who got a "deal too good to refuse."

The only two defendants in jail were released Thursday night after pleading no contest to felony charges. Charges were either dismissed or promised to be dismissed against four other defendants in the case.

Gerardo Gonzales, 33, pleaded no contest to one count of molesting a 5-year-old neighborhood girl in 1984.

The Rev. Willard Lee Thomas, 34, ended nine months in jail with a plea of no contest to a charge of child endangerment and to a charge in a separate case of unlawful sexual intercourse with a 17-year-old girl.

The no-contest pleas mean that the defendants are not admitting guilt but that they are offering no defense. They have the option of denying the charges in another legal proceeding.

In exchange for those pleas, Deputy District Attorney Stephen M. Tauzer agreed to dismiss 117 charges against Gonzales, 43 charges against Thomas and 43 charges against Gonzales' wife, Cheryl.

Tauzer told The Californian outside of court that he also would be dismissing 133 molestation charges against Brad and Mary Nokes, ages 29 and 32, and two charges against Kathy Scott, 28.

"I don't feel good about ending the case this way," Tauzer said. "But it is ended."

Tauzer said the plea bargain was arranged because the case "was difficult if not impossible to put on."

He said he believed the initial statements by children that Gonzales, Thomas and others molested them, but he didn't know how he could convince a jury in light of the same children making later accusations that couldn't be proved.

Those later accusations were that 80 adults molested 60 children and killed 29 babies at sex orgies inspired by devil worshipping. Among the accused were a social worker, a Kern County sheriff's deputy and a deputy district attorney.

Tauzer added that he wanted to spare the children the trauma of having to testify. He said a psychologist recently strongly recommended against the testimony of a key 8-year old witness in the case.

Bakersfield (California) Californian   *January 23, 1987*

Parents, Teacher Urge Action against Satanism

A teacher and several parents of junior high school students say they are upset and disappointed with the way threats linked to incidents of alleged devil worshiping have been handled by school administrators.

Audrey Marshall, a Lincoln Junior High School special education teacher, and four parents talked with *The Coloradoan* last week.

Marshall said some students are in great fear of the group that she said is well-organized and looks for the vulnerable student.

"I've estimated that 30 to 40 percent of my class alone has been either victimized, threatened, beaten or in some way bothered or terrorized by this group," Marshall said.

She said she has observed students meditating on satanism.

"It is really, really scary and really serious. The gang goes out actively recruiting kids at school. It's been going on a long time."

Parent Kathy Allred said she removed her daughter from Lincoln Junior High last fall after her daughter was beaten up downtown on Halloween night by three girls who attended Lincoln.

Allred said the teens involved in the incident give out satanic literature and wear cult symbols such as upside-down crosses. Allred said her daughter was instructed by the girls not to tell anyone about the assault or they would kill her.

Allred gave *The Coloradoan* a copy of a handwritten, two-page piece circulating among students called "Servants of the Devil." It describes forsaking Christ and denying baptism for the devil, along with definitions of satanic terms, a list of holidays and details of ceremonies instructing readers to eat stolen communion, to tear up Bibles and to sacrifice roosters.

Fort Collins (Colorado) Coloradoan   March 20, 1988

▶9◀

The First Victims
Are Not Human

Animal Mutilation

The hayfields have just been cut around northwest Arkansas; they look like golf courses between rows of shelter-belt trees and brush. A grizzled farmer swears about the summer's lack of rain. "It's only my second cutting this season. Pretty dry fescue," he says from his perch on a tractor with hay baler behind. I've stopped to get directions from Bugscuffle near Highway 158 in Hogeye to Clinton in Van Buren county. "Got a good ways to go. You be careful over there, son." The old man wipes his forehead in the 90 percent humidity of the 95 degree morning. "They don't take to foreigners over there."

Van Buren and the surrounding counties of northern Arkansas are renowned for their eccentric citizens. The area is thickly forested and riddled with an obstacle course of small mountain ranges that further north are called the Ozarks. Paved and dirt roads snake around seemingly every other hill, interlacing and emerging out of the thick trees only at wide spots with gas stations, country markets and occasional tourist attractions: "Wild Donkeys Here!" or "Mystery Cavern" or the regionally famous "Dogpatch USA." These "towns" are really only supply posts for the county's inhabitants: families that make the Beverly Hillbillies seem sophisticated, survivalist cults, aging back-to-the-land hippies who bought into these nearly inaccessible acreages in the seventies when the price was only a few hundred dollars an acre. "Primo place for marijuana growers," a kid tells me at a gas stop where the pay phone is still only ten cents, and you have to drop the dime in after the party on the other end has answered. And, reputedly, the area obscures several hardcore, generational satanic covens.

Driving south out of Harrison on Arkansas 65 I mull over yesterday's phone conversations with Gary Wilson of the National Cattlemen's Association headquarters in Denver, Gail Eisnitz and Dr. Randy Lockwood of the Humane Society of the U.S. Whether in teenage dabbling, self-styled groups or the primary satanic cults, invariably, Satan's initial victims aren't human.

Oddly enough, this strange phenomenon of ritual mutilation of animals has all sorts of serious implications. Animal mutilations would indicate the presence of satanic groups in an area, groups which had stepped from religious worship into crime—since the torture or ritual killing of an animal is a crime. Animal torture by an individual also indicates a dangerous psychological state, a serious signal that the perpetrator is well beyond intellectual involvement in the occult. And yet many parents or neighbors who know of teenagers' torture of animals avoid reporting these incidents.

The U.S. National Cattlemen's Association doesn't keep nationwide statistics on livestock mutilations, although most local NCA chapters have data on local incidents. Local law enforcement officers generally don't record reports of "companion" animal or pet mutilation or disappearance because these are humane society matters. Local humane societies sometimes keep loose records of mutilations, but till now haven't forwarded these statistics to any national agency. As far as I could go into the red-tape catacombs of the U.S. Department of Agriculture, the government is apparently not tracking these obvious signals of conspiratorial crime—it takes more than a single perpetrator to bleed a horse to death—and destruction of farmers' property. The FBI doesn't tally or track animal mutilations because they don't fall into a category of felony crime.

So it was with frustration that Gary Wilson of the NCA tried to steer me toward an overall answer on how serious livestock mutilations are. "Just last week I was in on a couple incidents of wildlife—one was a mountain goat—and household pets being mutilated. But I'm afraid we're not the ones keeping track. All we have are news clippings of occurrences, so unless a newspaper reports something, we don't hear about it."

Animal Mutilation a Crime

Gail Eisnitz' specialty is the growing problem of animal tortures and killings in the Santeria religion. "It's nearly impossible to track," she said. "Most of the carcasses are bagged or buried. Though we know animals are being killed in rituals, it's real difficult to get a handle on just how often."

Gail referred me to Dr. Randy Lockwood. "We're fighting an uphill battle," he said. "These incidents are usually dismissed with a 'boys will be boys' attitude. Or they're labeled as relatively minor misdemeanors, so there are no national statistics. The U.S. Criminal Reports Center catalogs only felonies and convictions. Animal mutilation is usually either plea-bargained or not prosecuted at all."

"Yet," I said, "it could be such a key to stopping a lot of these groups that go on to more drastic crime. What do you think, Randy: Are the mutilations slacking off from the heyday of reports in the late '70s? Or is the media just tired of reporting the same never-solved incidents?"

"Well," he said, "it's my own perception that we just don't know whether the problem is abating or increasing because of the reporting problems we were talking about. What I hope is increasing is the public's awareness of the possibility that crimes against animals are preludes to violent crimes against people. Geraldo Rivera is bringing this idea out in some of his shows. There seems to be a new segment of society that is taking this problem seriously. For instance, I think people were shocked in the Carl's Junction, Missouri, murder of that boy by his classmates—"

"Steve Newberry. By Jim Hardy and Pete Roland and—"

"Right. Those kids killed hundreds of animals for apparently years before they progressed to human sacrifice. It's incredible that no one in the community caught on to the state of those boys' minds from the number of kittens and animals they boasted about having killed. My degree in psychology—and I'm no clinical psychologist—allows me to suggest that cruelty to animals suggests a serious psychological disturbance.

"And yet," he continued, "it's usually discounted. For instance, as far as I can study in the DSM III—the basic bible of psychological disorders— there's no mention of animal cruelty as a distinct symptom of psychological disturbance. We're finding most homes in which animal abuse has occurred are also the homes in which child abuse occurs. Several of the more diabolical serial killers we've seen lately—Berkowitz and others—were known to be violent to animals. Yet these symptoms are ignored."

"What do we do?" I asked.

"Well, a new program we're developing called 'Project Empathy' is providing a model for communities that don't know what to do with youthful offenders caught abusing animals—whether in rituals or for kicks. A Greensboro, North Carolina, judge came to us with two juveniles arrested for animal mutilation. Community service, painting the animal shelter fence, probably wouldn't change a thing in these kids' feelings about violence to living things. So we set up a program involving these kids in sensitivity building by working with the police canine corps and so on.

"Another thing we're doing," he continues, "is trying to follow up on our premise that animal cruelty is directly related to later crimes of violence against people. I'm sending out a briefing to that effect to the 100,000 members of the U.S. Association of Chiefs of Police. And we're encouraging local humane society organizations to start forwarding their statistics to us. We've got to start monitoring this problem on a broad base."

UFOs or Satanists?

Yesterday when I called Steve Watts, he described his experiences in documenting the victimization of animals by satanic groups in Idaho and Montana. Steve was an Idaho state investigator during the '70s when the phenomenon of animal mutilations popped up regularly in the news throughout the U.S. and Canada.

I remember an old neighbor telling me the latest accounts of the dozens of blood-drained cattle carcasses found in Indiana, the dogs skinned alive left on a California beach, the sheep surgically dissected on a hillside in Kansas, the 140 dogs found ritually tortured around Phoenix. "UFOs," old Mr. Clay had explained as he offered me a handful of mulberries one afternoon. "Yep, little saucers come zipping in and beam them poor animals up. Then they do experiments on 'em to see what earth is like. See, they don't know a human from a Jersey. So after their research they drop the critter back down the hatch and zip away."

Old Mr. Clay had some of his evidence right, at least. Often the animals were found in a completely different pasture than the one they'd been left in for the night. Most often there were no footprints anywhere near the carcasses. The absence of blood and surgical precision of wounds ruled out rabid coyote attacks.

But Steve Watts was gutsy enough to present another explanation. "Satanic ritual. Nobody wants to acknowledge that that much satanism is going on in so many locations. Because if it's true, we need to be alarmed, and we're already alarmed at the threat of nuclear bombardment, abortion, overspending on our credit cards and on and on. When I'd have to report on these mutilations I found even we had to practically fight against simpler, less threatening explanations in order to give the facts of the incidents. I think the veneer of civilization is very thin. Often we'd find the stress of ritually mutilated animals brought locals to hysterical, vigilante-type action."

Steve went on, "Extensive investigation both in Idaho and Wyoming established the methodology used by occultists who allegedly collected animal body parts and blood for ritual purposes. Tranquilizer-type dart guns—many stolen from local dog pounds—were used to inject fast-acting animal tranquilizers such as Ketosin and Detoset, I believe, which rapidly block the nervous system."

I had always wondered how these mutilations had occurred in places such as a farmer's barn near the house without the animal raising a ruckus. "No noise, then, right?" I asked.

"Right," said Steve. "The perpetrators would then surgically remove tongues, eyes, sexual organs, large pieces of hide, and even entire rear legs from full-grown cattle. Sometimes catheters were inserted directly into the animals' hearts to pump out the lifeblood.

"Some incisions were made with pinking shears, probably in an effort to disguise the cuts, making them appear to be made by predators' teeth. Microscopic inspection of these cuts clearly negated the 'critter' theories.

"After the deeds were done and the suspects had left, the quickly dissipating tranquilizer would wear off, the animal would regain some consciousness and sometimes walk off for quite a distance before it died. That explained why no human footprints or blood signs were found near the carcasses. Also, in open pastures, other animals milling around the scene would quickly obliterate evidentiary traces."

High-tech Mutilation

Pulling up to the county courthouse in Clinton, I'm given access to the records I need by a friendly graying clerk who explains, "Of course, that transcript is a matter of public record since the Kahaner book came out." She smiles.

"*Cults That Kill,*" I say.

"Yes," she smiles.

The transcript gives interesting insight into satanic animal victimization.

To: Sheriff Carl Stobaugh
Subject: Animal mutilations
On 8-14-79 Sheriff Gus Anglin (Van Buren County) Arkansas, chief investigator, Jerry Bradley (Faulkner County), Sgt. King (ASP), and this officer interview a 23-year-old white female whose identity must be kept confidential in reference to the recent cattle mutilations in this area. The young lady related the following story to us.

That for five years she was a higher echelon member of a satanic worshipping cult which was headquartered in Tulsa, Oklahoma. During her five years there she was involved numerous times in trips to outlying remote areas where cattle were killed and the blood drawn out by use of an old embalming machine, which they had converted to battery power. They also removed the cows' eyes, tongue, sex organs and sometimes the udder.

She related the cult she belonged to was quite wealthy and had a helicopter and several van-type trucks which were used in obtaining the organs and blood needed from the cows to be used in their rituals. She also stated that doctors, lawyers, veterinarians and other prominent persons belonged to this cult and were all taught by doctors and vets how to precisely cut the parts needed and exactly where to stick the needle to draw out the blood.

She stated the blood was put into gallon jugs and kept cool for baptizing new cult members. They were baptized in the same manner as most churches do except the baptismal vat would be filled with blood which had been extracted from the animals. The eyes taken were boiled and eaten by the cult members at rituals. The sex organs were used in the rituals, also, because the cult believes in free sex to everyone.

When using the helicopter they sometimes picked up the cow by using a home-made belt-type sling and one man would go down and fasten it around the cow, and they would move it and drop it further down from where the mutilations occurred. This would account for there not being any footprints or tire tracks.

When using the van trucks they would also have a telescoping lift which she stated was 200 feet long, mounted outside the truck. They would use that to extend a man out to the cow, and he would mutilate it from a board platform on the end of the boom and would never touch the ground.

She stated that they love the publicity that surrounds the mutilations, and as long as the publicity is in one area they will keep returning because they like to baffle law enforcement.

She stated that they would repeatedly go back to one farm if there were a number of roads coming into the area which would be accessible for a quick getaway route. If not, they usually hit one time and then moved on to another location. They sometimes do three or four cows a night.

The cult usually prefers the dairy cattle but will mutilate any type of cow when no dairy herds are easily found. They will also mutilate cattle which have died if they are still fresh and haven't started to deteriorate. They have mutilated bulls, horses and dogs to get blood for their rituals.

She left the cult about a year ago because one couple sacrificed their 15-month-old baby. They placed the little girl on a table at one of the rituals and placed oil on her body and cut her up with a large knife to prove their love for Satan. She said that after seeing this she realized that the cult was not for love and left. A few months later she was beaten by some cult members who located her and was apparently left for dead.

She has agreed to cooperate in any way she can as long as her identity is kept a secret, because she fears for her life.

Ray Coffin
Chief Investigator

Immediately I ask myself the ever-present question in this infernal issue: Is it true? I've heard too often in the past several weeks that satanists and even ex-satanists lie. And do it well. It's always interesting to me that so many of the ex-satanists claim to have been in the upper echelons of a cult; I've yet to hear a reformed satanist confess about how "I was a nobody in satanism." But again, the story needs to be considered, to be taken with a grain of salt as it's matched against corroborating stories. I decide to match it against an account described in *Jay's Journal,* a book edited by Beatrice Sparks. I pull it out of my bookbag in the trunk of the car and sit on a concrete bench outside the Arkansas courthouse in the strong sunshine. The book is actually an edited version of a journal or book of shadows found in the closet of "Jay," a sixteen-year-old whose addiction to the occult ended in suicide. On pages 166 through 170, where Jay refers to Satan as "O," I read Jay's account of his initiation into animal mutilation:

December 7
The whole weekend seems unreal. Driving along pasture roads until Mel found exactly the right bull. Mel's bow with the electric arrow made from a many times increased

battery powered cattle prod, but with a charge strong enough to stun said bull. Our rushing to the beast as he tried to struggle then fell to the ground.

I remember the blood sloshing up into my ears as we raced into the pasture. Dell held the flashlight while Mel made precise little surgical cuts in exactly the right places. He had practiced in the van on a big chart we'd ripped off from the market showing a side of beef. Oh, first we siphoned off the blood from a careful tiny slash in a vein, put it into gobs of gallon jars we'd ripped off from the A and W and the caterers, trying not to spill a drop. It would be used as part of a ritual when we returned home. Mel, like a surgeon, cut out the eyes, tongue and balls. Then we had to go for another animal. Taking all the parts from one would lessen the power they retained. Each organ was immediately sealed in a fruit jar, and whisked off to the van. That kept me and Brad jumping. Besides, the bull smelled like nothing I'd ever smelled before and made strange gurgling sounds in his throat and belly even though he was dead. It was bad enough to see the eyes and testicles in jars. I don't know how Dell managed to watch Mel do it. Actually none of it really seemed real!

We were half way through before I was even aware that all the cattle that had drifted away from us were mooing and making other strange noises that I didn't know cows made. It was spooky and I wanted to get the _____ out of there. When Mel finished and we sprinted across the field with the last of our stuff, I wondered if anyone would ever suspect we had been there. Mel had had his knives so sharp they had gone through the cow's hide so clean and almost bloodless that I had been amazed. A few flies on the cuts and no one would ever know what had happened except that parts were missing and that jars and jars of blood had disappeared.

In the van, Mel and I sat in the back while Dell bounced back towards the highway with his lights off, all of us grateful for the big clear moon. Even with its light, however, we hit chuck holes and rocks, without it we might have highcentered at any point and found ourselves in a mess I don't know how the hell we would have gotten out of. After we'd been on the highway for about half an hour Mel and Dell pull over and we added anticoagulant something to the blood and parts. It was important, Mel said, to keep them as exact as possible. I couldn't wait! Kept wondering if Bootan really would work! The excitement was intoxicating!

After about another hour of driving we took off on a second side road and started looking for a cow that came up to all Mel's requirements. It didn't take long to find one and soon we had downed it and slit its vein also, the tiniest little incision. This time each of us took turns drinking the warm blood directly from the female animal. It was hard to get down because it came out in such great spurts, and was so hot, so much hotter than I had expected, or maybe it was me. Again we drained the blood, this time not so carefully, and took a few parts, Mel having informed us that all living things are composed of both female and male whatevers.

It was a relief when we got back to the highway and started heading towards home. Mel wouldn't even let us stop, though, and the excitement had about exploded our bladders.

All four of us squeezed up in the front area and Mel told us how ranchers from at least 22 states had reported cattle mutilations. Man, "O" must be even bigger than I thought! Brad, who was driving, slowed down when Mel added that various rural groups had gone together and put rewards up, some as high as $25,000.

The blood we had drunk was supposed to have given us the strength of the animal and at that time I'm sure if we had stopped we could have lifted the van. We felt like T.V. or comic strip supermen. Dell wanted to try but I guess we were all more afraid of getting caught than we were anxious to test our powers.

So we started reading each other's thoughts. It was amazing how accurate we were. I wonder if the foreign substance in our bodies had anything to do with that. After a while we all had to stop and throw up. Then it was gone, all of the excitement as well as the strength. We were just a bunch of bitching young turkey tails, mad about everything and wanting the _____ to get home to nice soft warm beds and some decent food.

We drove right past the ski resort turn-off and into a motel just three hours from home. I was bushed and it seemed like such a _____ stupid thing to have done, wasted all that meat, drunk gobs of blood, which just made us throw up, and . . . oh _____ . . . the whole thing was a bummer. How did I ever get sucked into this weirdo sick kind of thinking? It doesn't have anything to do with mind control and expansion, it was just the old fashioned, superstitious, stupid, childish kind of stupid thing the world hates and suspects about cults, and rightly so. We were just four _____ kids looking for excitement—any kookie, hair-brained thing to explode the boring, boring, boring every-dayness of average life.

Flesh Is Cheap!

God, what's got into me?

Both accounts somehow have a ring of truth about them. But regardless of technique, the hardiest suggestion that animal mutilations can be traced to satanic ritual comes from the demands of the rituals themselves. Anton LaVey's Satanic Bible disclaims any necessity that there has to be sacrifice.

Why? We'll need to do some saturated study on satanic belief systems as to exactly why—but for now let's just say the purpose is power.

Power is the answer to any number of questions about satanism. The satanist believes he amplifies the life force of an animal by terrifying it, torturing it. Then he absorbs that power of the sacrificed animal by eating and offering in ritual the most "potent" body parts—the reproductive organs, the heart, and so on—and by drinking the blood.

Widespread Animal Victimization

From the bottom of my bookpack I pull out a mashed manila folder of newspaper clippings. I sit back on the bench in the hot Clinton, Arkansas, sunshine and leaf through:

"Mutilations Raise Spectre of Satanism," an Erin Emery article in the May 25, 1988 Colorado Springs *Gazette Telegraph*. It says:

Discoveries of mutilated animals in an isolated area on the city's west side have fueled concerns by police that satanism . . . is growing in popularity among local teenagers, police said.

Six dogs, six rabbits and seven cats, many that were decapitated, skinned or gutted, have been found in the past year at the "old mill" near 21st Street south of US 24, said Colorado Springs police sergeant Richard Realing.

"We think it's juveniles," he said. "But again, what kind of kid sits there and takes apart dogs and cats and rabbits at that age? [Police had identified 24 satanists age 13 to 19 in the neighborhood.] "You just can't write it off when they are taking animals apart for kicks. What are they going to do when they turn 20?"

A 16-year old girl . . . said, "I know the people who took the skull and the one who took the paws [of a black Labrador retriever] for a necklace. . . ."

A Lee Hancock feature in the April 20, 1988 *Dallas Morning News*— "Crimes in the Name of Satan"—reports that "in December, Kennedale police raided an amphetamine lab at the eastern edge of the city and found occult paraphernalia suggesting that the woman charged with running the lab was conducting satanic animal mutilation rituals. Police Chief Dave Geeslin said the lab was adjacent to fields where Arlington police repeatedly had found mutilated animals in the months before the raid."

Apparently some areas of the country are more concerned than others about the victimization of animals by occult groups. Magnolia, Mississippi, police chief Smithie Buie said in the April 1988 *Clarion-Ledger* that "A cult ritual scheduled Thursday night in Lincoln County met the same fate as area baseball games—called due to rain."

Terrified parents kept hundreds of students out of McComb schools on Thursday as a precaution against a rumored list of potential student victims. But Buie said Friday that cult members are equally frightened by the paranoia that has swept the county.

"They're keeping kind of low," said Buie. He said the cult has existed since at least the 1960s, its members occasionally sacrificing animals but never known to harm people.

He said the group traditionally meets at midnight and new members are required to sacrifice an animal. The meetings are frequently in gravel pits or wooded areas, are attended by between five and twenty couples and are followed by group sex.

"They sacrifice any animal they can get—dogs, cats. I was told they prefer goats, but that goats are hard to come by," Buie said.

The account seems to suggest that Chief Buie isn't too concerned about the animal sacrifices—not nearly so much as San Antonio's Deputy Constable Cynthia North, an animal cruelty inspector with the Bexar County Humane Society. In a San Antonio *Express News* story on January 17, 1986, staff writer Tom Edwards asserts that teenage satanists are responsible for the mutilations and deaths of about 50 animals on or near the campus of the Leal Middle

School on Southcross Boulevard in San Antonio. A teacher at the school said some students are "very serious about their . . . satanism. It's all that power stuff," she said.

North says that in most cases involving devil worshipers, a trail of blood usually leads to a mutilated animal. "It's more widespread than the public realizes. I think most of it can be attributed to satanic cults.

"I've seen a resurgence of this. I think there's a lot more going on out there than anybody knows about," North said. "Some people just don't recognize this as being part of the work of a cult."

Worship in any religion is legal; mutilation of an animal is not—any more than is the mental/emotional/physical mutilation of a human.

▶ *10* ◀

Human Sacrifices

Obviously one of the hot topics of sensationalized satanism is human sacrifice. But frankly I'm not going to dredge through the mire of possibilities on the topic. There's just flatly no evidence to corroborate the stories about the thousands of children and women and men who are allegedly sacrificed to Satan. Every survivor of childhood ritual abuse as a member of a traditional satanic cult testifies that human sacrifices have occurred and do occur. Nearly every ex-satanist says the same. But there's no hard proof, and I don't feel like launching into a segment of sensational speculation as if I'm writing for the pulp tabloids.

Satanic literature alternately calls for or denies the necessity of human sacrifice:

Aleister Crowley, father of much of modern satanic practices, writes on page 95 of his meandering book *Magick*, "For the highest spiritual working one must accordingly choose that victim which contains the greatest and purest force. A male child perfect in innocence and of high intelligence is the most satisfactory and suitable victim. It is a mistake to suppose that the victim is injured. On the contrary, this is the most blessed and merciful of all deaths, for the elemental spirit is directly built up into the Godhead." Crowley's "magick"—actual demonic technique, distinguished from simple sleight-of-hand "magic" in Crowley's vocabulary—was responsible for the alleged sacrifice of 150 human victims yearly from 1912 through 1928.

Richard Cavendish in *The Black Arts*, page XX, says that blood sacrifices provide energy and a psychological boost to ritual. Since blood is the source of life energy, as blood is drawn and eventually consumed, that victim's life energy flows into the magician.

But Anton LaVey of the well publicized Church of Satan in San Francisco writes in his Satanic Bible, page 89: "Under no circumstances would a satanist sacrifice any animal or baby!" LaVey contends that the true magician can develop his own energy and does not need the blood energy of a sacrificial victim.

"The only time a satanist would perform a human sacrifice," LaVey writes on page 88 of his bible, "would be if it were to serve a two-fold purpose, that being to release the magician's wrath in the throwing of a curse and more important, to dispose of a totally obnoxious and deserving individual." So LaVey allows curses to be thrown on enemies, but ritual sacrifices are unnecessary. Weaker witches, he suggests, believe they must perform sacrifices because "as a creature is dying, bioelectrical energy is given off into the ritual to help empower it. 'White' magicians or occultists wary of the consequences involved in the killing of a human being naturally utilize birds or other 'lower' creatures in their ceremonies. It seems these sanctimonious wretches feel no guilt in the taking of a nonhuman life as opposed to a human's."

Another public, religious satanist, leader of the Temple of Set, is Michael Acquino. He likewise disclaims any blood sacrifices in his sect's rituals.

But then, in order to be a public, religious organization which can enjoy tax-free status as it accepts membership fees, the Temple of Set as well as the Church of Satan have to disclaim criminal activity, right?

Satanic Human Sacrifice

Most of the circulating reports on occult crime in the U.S. and Canada give accounts of human sacrifice. The first substantiated case of satanic murder was the San Francisco Clifford St. Joseph case.

The March 15, 1988 *San Francisco Chronicle* reported the conviction of St. Joseph for the occultic mutilation murder of a drifter in June, 1985. The victim was apparently killed during a gay satanic rite in which a pentagram was carved on his chest, the body's blood was mostly drained; he had been sexually mutilated and had wax drippings in the right eye.

At the moment I'm freezing in the computer room of the University of Arkansas in Fayetteville; the temperature is kept around 65 for the welfare of the electronic systems. Certainly not for the welfare of students or T-shirted visitors. I'm keying in some of the information I've dredged through in the school library including two items from two decades ago—items which make me think that once law enforcement and historical researchers coordinate their expertise in investigating the satanic underground, we might end up with surprising insights.

For instance, the *Los Angeles Times* on July 10, 1970 reports "Satan Worship Tale Unfolds in Slaying Case." Apparently a Steven Hurd and two other "brothers of the shadows" were apprehended for the ritual murder of a 31-year-old schoolteacher. The woman's heart and lungs had been cut out and her left arm—emphasizing satanism as "the left hand path"—had been amputated. With the characteristic sloppiness of a dabbler group, the men had performed the sacrifice, according to Hurd, "because the devil's cult believes it's all right to snuff people out providing a portion of the body is used in a sacrificial offering."

The other old article I skimmed on microfiche was from the August 2, 1969 *San Jose Mercury* of central California. The article recounts Chief of Detectives Barton Collins' shot-in-the-dark homicide investigation of two girls who were stabbed 300 times and yet "there was no trace of blood."

And perhaps there have been more satanic-related homicides which simply weren't tagged as such. Apparently police occasionally find bodies which bear the markings of ritual abuse—I'm reading one such report now that's so gross I'll bear you the graphics. But tying such physical evidence to a specific place-and-time ritual is practically beyond the methodology of conventional law enforcement. So the homicides have been simply reported as homicides. Without stirring up public panic, it's probably tough for law enforcement to do anything else when strange murders have occult overtones.

Cops are having a tough time with these rumors of satanic human sacrifice. There are almost too many similar stories to completely discount the possibility. But then it's nearly impossible to come up with any hard evidence on a specific incident. Cops' efforts to try to infiltrate satanic groups has met with disaster, although I was told the FBI has successfully planted informants in at least one traditional satanic cult. Corroborating testimony about sacrifices is hard to come by; participants are conditioned with a loyalty to the group and a terror if they informed. And true satanists are extremely intelligent in planning their activities; they know well how to precisely plan, execute and dispose of evidence.

So the prevalence of satanic human sacrifice is still anybody's guess.

A Utah Corrections officer guessed from the reports of ex-cultists how many covens were operating in the U.S. and Canada. He multiplied this number by the ritual dates during the satanic calendar which call for human sacrifice. The dates, which vary according to which satanic group you're researching, can include February 25 (St. Walpurgis Day), March 1 (St. Eichatadt), April 26-May 1 (a Grand Climax), July 1 (Demon Revels), September 20 (Midnight Host), October 29 (All Hallow Eve), and December 24 (High Grand Climax). The corrections officer therefore announced that 40,000 to 50,000 human sacrifices are performed every year by satanists in North America.

The problem with picking a number, of course, is, as Cult Crime Impact newsletter editor Larry Jones told me, "Nobody's counting the beans." Satanism is such a slippery, secretive phenomenon that we don't have even a vague idea of how many groups there are out there. A few organizations offer lists of satanic groups, but they seem to include any organization that has anything to do with any form of the occult. There are no statistics on how many true satanic covens there are.

Jones says that we further haven't a hard-evidence clue as to what they're doing in human sacrifices. He attributes the chicken-or-the-egg syndrome for much of the mystery of satanic victimization: There are no statistics on occult crime; and because it's not therefore recognized as occult crime, it's not reported as occult crime. So there are no statistics. But that's what his organization based in Boise is attempting: to count the beans.

Rationality and Human Sacrifice

In Los Angeles, detective Pat Metoyer had told me several of the reasons he discounted the 40-50,000 human sacrifice numbers:

"Let's say we're all good satanists and I'm initiating you. I take this little baby. Picture an actual, squirming, sweet-faced baby. And I laid it down on a block of wood or an altar and I said, 'Here, I want you to kill this baby or I'll kill you.'

"You wouldn't do it. And secondly, if I put my hand on yours to hold the knife, you would end up fighting against me. This is human nature."

Pat's been working homicide for twenty years—in L.A.—and knows murder. "But how, then," I asked him, "do we come up with so many firsthand, eyewitness testimonies of satanic human sacrifices?"

"Look at it this way," Pat said. "It's just like an auto accident where a guy says, 'Yeah man, I saw the whole thing.' And actually what happened was he heard a squeal of tires and he heard the big crash and he saw smoke coming up out of one of the cars, and he looked across the street, back and forth, to run across to help. And he ran over there and saw a guy fall out of the door of one of the cars. He says, 'Yeah, I saw the whole thing' when, in effect, he saw maybe two or three seconds of the actual action that took place over a twenty- or thirty-second period.

"I often mention in lectures on this subject, that in the same way, here I am the high priest. We have those women standing around scared out of their wits—even if they're satanists, there's a surge of fear in the rituals. That's part of the kick. And I say, 'Now I'm going to kill the baby' and raise the knife. There's not a one of you in the crowd that wouldn't close his eyes. I don't care how tough you are or even if you're not remotely squeamish. Whoever you are, you would grimace at that. You would even for a second close your eyes, and not have actually seen the whole thing. And when you opened your eyes there would be blood all over, and the baby would be being carried off. Or chunks of meat would be being whacked into pieces on the messy altar."

"You think a lot of this is staged?" I asked.

"It's pretty good magic," he said. "Staged is the word. Ever see a really good magician? It's incredible what they can do with sleight of hand. You put somebody that good in a dark, spooky setting with drugged adults or imaginative little kids and he could have them swearing they'd actually seen almost anything.

"Then," Pat continued, "you add in the fatigue of the worshipers, their predisposed belief in what's going to supposedly take place, the hypnotic chanting and rituals to dull the senses. That magician—and I don't mean 'magick' with a 'k' but plain old magic. That magician has the ideal circumstances to make anything look real. And you've got 'solid' human sacrifice testimonies."

The phone rang and as Pat answered, I sat wondering why a coven leader would go to such lengths to make a staged production of a sacrificial ritual. Then I remembered the constant input I'd heard on the lucrative porno and drug operations invariably tied to many of these groups. I guess a loyal-to-the-death, deluded cult of followers who believe demons are tracking their every move would be a master criminal's dream gang.

Pat finished the phone conversation and without missing a beat continued: "And then there's the drugs, of course. You'll hear that everybody but the high priest and his chief sidekicks drink the potions, take the drugs—which is another way these stories keep popping up.

"Drugs are appropriately called hallucinogens. For instance there's a guy, a heroin addict, played with LSD and all kinds of stuff. He gave this great big confession about how they killed babies. Yeah, he really had regularly killed babies in satanic rituals. And yet he described a lot of details that were absolutely impossible or don't jive with satanic ritual: 'We didn't have an altar, we just did it on the ground. We did it with a knife and cut it up and ate parts of it, burned the rest and then scattered the ashes around and we had a portable crematorium.' But nothing he told us panned out."

Pat said, "These things were completely real to the participant as he was not only involved in a hypnotic ritual but was on drugs as well. These kids on drugs really believe that this is what they were involved in. In fact, if the kid took a polygraph test he's probably pass with flying colors because he believed it to be his true experience."

The peer pressure of the group is another factor in perpetuating the stories of human sacrifice. Pat characteristically used another analogy: "It's a kid that steps outside," he said. "And he looks up into the sky and squints. His buddy comes along and looks up and squints, and then a crowd forms and the first guy says, 'Yeah, I saw such and such.' Of course the second kid isn't gonna be a dummy and say, 'Well, I've been standing here for 15 minutes for nothing,' so he's gonna say, 'That's right; it was like this.' And pretty soon most of the group is going to be 'testifying' about the actuality of something that never was actual at all."

He rolled his eyes and said, "I myself participated in going down to the L.A. River and trying to dig up bodies. A whole raft of participants in some of these rituals said and swore that that's exactly where they buried the bodies. So with all that corroboration, we thought we finally had something.

"So we go ahead and dig and try to find something—anything. And while we're there it's evident to any expert that the ground itself has not been disturbed for decades and yet the participants were saying, 'Yeah, it was exactly right here. I know it; it was only a matter of weeks ago.'"

Pat said that consequently he's not only sifted all the occult crime questions as the resident cult cop, but he's also the resident skeptic: Too much hooplah and sensationalism is being pushed about how wild and tight these eyewitness accounts of human sacrifice are.

"It's like the child porno kidnapping stories," Pat said. "Now, just as in the satanic homicides, some of this is going on. But not nearly to the extent that either paranoid or sensationalist people would have us believe.

"Like the stories of these high-tech smut networks. It may be happening in a few isolated cases. But the nation isn't being run by pedophiles who call each other up and say, 'Yeah, I need a kid. Bring him out here and I'll sodomize him for a while and I'll ship him back to you on the train.' Or 'I'm doing a snuff film; why don't you send me out a couple of kids?' 'Sure, no problem.' That sort of stuff is not happening every day. These things are really, really difficult to pull off. There are national law enforcement personnel and vice squads across the country who track activity, there are paper trails, there are bystanders who report suspicious activity and neighbors who get concerned. This is not TV; horrendous crimes such as nationally linked pornography or satanic human sacrifices are really tough to pull off. Nearly impossible to pull off consistently without detection."

Pat concluded, "Yes, occultic human sacrifices have been committed, and probably are committed. But not to the extent of some of the statistics I've seen such as thousands or even tens of thousands per year."

So some satanist experts say human sacrifice is widespread, others insist it's not. What's interesting is that both camps do acknowledge it has happened and is happening. The only question is how often. And a verdict on how often satanists have tortured and murdered children, men and women will just have to wait until the evidence is in.

But another area of satanic victimization has already accrued plenty of evidence. Satanist groups from cliques of dabblers to self-styled covens to generational cults are adept at terrorizing those who speak out against them and those members who decide to get out.

Satanic Terrorism

Richmond, Virginia. I'm racing down one street past the Mr. Bojangles statue and up another in the city where Patrick Henry shouted for liberty or death. Richmond, Virginia, is an old town with friendly people who'll yell directions to anywhere—even if they have no idea where you're heading. I'm looking for the State Library, but finally give up for a lunchbreak.

The Shockoe Slip Cafe is on cobblestoned Carey Street. The place is filled with old photos—of Ronald Reagan drawing his pistola, of Humphrey Bogart looking with a long face up from his hand of cards—of old advertisements and of young yuppies.

I tell the waiter about the book and he says, "A book on the occult, huh? I never knew stuff was going on around here till there was this story in one of the—Let's see, it was *Style* magazine last spring. Told about this woman who'd been chosen as a child to be in one of those satan cults and now they were trying to harass her to get back into it. There's supposed to be a lot of that going on."

"*Style* magazine?" I jot another note. I dig back through other pages of my yellow pad and note the name Lisa Antonelli as a writer speaking at an occult crime seminar for law enforcement and mental health personnel. She writes for *Style*.

The next day I arrange to meet her at the Manchester Courthouse. She'll be hanging around all afternoon with the other Richmond media as they await a jury decision on the rape-murder case of Timothy Spencer. Spencer was already convicted of a similar murder in Arlington, is being tried here in Richmond, and regardless of the outcome will be tried again for yet another murder in Chesterfield, Virginia. One of Spencer's victims once worked for *Style*.

Lisa is sitting on a sidewalk curb with other media reporters, and in classic Virginia friendliness she quickly introduces me to the group.

She hands me a *Rolling Stone* magazine; I look a bit puzzled; then she explains that her *Style* piece on satanism is tucked inside. Apparently she doesn't want to advertise her authorship of the story. She starts telling me about how her dog went stir-crazy after her story on satanism was published because she and her husband wouldn't let it out of the house for two months.

Stirrings of excitement among the milling cameramen and reporters signal that the jury is about to re-enter the courtroom with a verdict on Spencer. Part of the particular interest in this trial is that, as in the Arlington conviction, the prosecution used the results of a radical new method of identification—the DNA patterns of a hair found at the crime scene match the DNA of the suspect.

We all file quickly into the colonial brick and white-trimmed courthouse to watch the drama of the jury's announcement. The fifty-ish jury foreman stands, hands a sheet of paper to the sheriff who hands it to the bailiff. She reads the findings: Spencer is determined guilty of robbery, of rape and of murder. The judge announces a recess before sentencing, and Lisa excuses herself to phone her magazine.

A few of the bystanders in the hallway tell me how Spencer would strangle his victims with everything from vacuum hoses to socks until they passed out.

Then he'd revive them; then strangle them again. He'll probably get a death sentence again as he did in Arlington because, I'm reminded by a reporter, people won't stand for such brutality.

During the recess I read about another crime in which a woman was tortured, raped, brainwashed, burned in an attempted murder, kidnapped, beaten and terrorized. Only this crime is still ongoing. And in this crime, there's more than one perpetrator; in fact, a whole group of people have conspired to torture the victim. And because the crime doesn't quite fit the psycho-sex motivations of Spencer's homicides, these people haven't been apprehended; nobody's checking for DNA fragments of the maniacs this woman has struggled with. These criminals probably won't be caught—they're incredibly intelligent. And their terrorism has rendered the victim's mental state to such a helter-skelter level that she's often not taken seriously at all.

I'm sitting at a sheriff's deputy's desk in the Manchester Courthouse hallway reading Lisa's story on the satanic victimization of Cassandra "Sam" Hoyer from the January 19, 1988 *Style* magazine. And I'm getting angry:

Lisa begins her story with "It was one of those hot July days, the kind where a splash in the pool or a cold-water bath provides only momentary relief. Cassandra 'Sam' Hoyer had spent the morning quietly indoors at a friend's apartment at the corner of Floyd and Davis in the Fan.

"Shortly after her host left that afternoon, Sam answered a knock at the door. Two men, one carrying a gun, pushed their way in. Without a word, one shoved her onto the bed, rammed a gun against her head and told her to strip. As she removed her clothing, her assailant repeatedly pulled the trigger on one empty chamber after the other.

"Forced to lie on her stomach, Sam shivered as narrow swaths of icy liquid were sprayed down her back. Then one of the men rolled her over and the other finished spraying her down. When they were done, the men simply stood back and watched. Sam lept off the bed, grabbed her keys and a shirt from the floor and fled through the back door.

"Sam jumped in her car and keyed the ignition. As she adjusted the rearview mirror, she saw the reflection of a woman in the back seat. The woman leaned forward and, pressing a gun against Sam's neck, told her to drive. 'Where?' asked Sam. 'To that woman's office,' replied the woman, naming Sam's therapist.

"Ten minutes later, Sam pulled into the parking lot beside a private West End psychiatric practice. The woman ordered Sam to park, then told her to get into her therapist's car and to stay on the floor. Sam waited for what seemed like hours until her therapist arrived to coax her out from under the dashboard. It was then that Sam realized that she had been painted black down one side, white down the other—the satanic designation for defectors."

I look for Lisa in the courthouse hallway, but apparently she's still reporting to her magazine; I'm wondering if Sam is still in Richmond. I read on that Sam Hoyer has been abducted six times in the six months prior to the story; she's changed her residence that many times as well.

Sam's victimization began at birth, when her mother gave her up and she lived her first sixteen years in a Roman Catholic orphanage in New England. "There," writes Antonelli, "several of the orphanage's administrators—priests and nuns—practice satanism, according to Sam." Her mother visited occasionally, sometimes wearing ritual robes for ceremonies held at the children's home.

At age nine, Sam was chosen along with several other children to be tested for the role of high priestess. Sam and five other candidates were strapped to crosses and burned. Sam alone survived, and consequently was selected to be indoctrinated into cult leadership. Lisa notes that Sam bears the scars from the burning as well as telltale signs of other childhood abuse.

The child was forced to have sex with cult members, as were most of the orphanage children, according to Sam. Also, "as part of her grooming," the article states, "Sam was required to watch other children being sacrificed; then she was forced to witness and participate in cannibalism. If she told anyone, she was warned, she would be killed."

Some of Sam's training included travel to various cities for satanic holiday rituals. Lisa writes, "Richmond was a routine stop. On these occasions, the children were introduced to major figures in cult hierarchy.

". . . For the 24 years after she left the orphanage, Sam's life was, on a conscious level, cult-free. Mercifully, she had been brainwashed by the cult to forget the horrors of her childhood, a practice considered routine by medical professionals working with victims of ritual abuse. The cult invests years of 'programming unconscious responses which can later be reactivated by simple gestures, phrases and visual images,' says Kathy Snowden, L.C.S.W., a psychiatric therapist in an established West End practice."

Snowden says she has ". . . 'on many occasions witnessed Sam vividly reliving in detail brutally traumatic childhood experiences of the satanic cult. . . . Sam has experienced body memories involving intense pain, physiological sensations associated with terror, specific tastes and smells, visual images and unusual auditory memories that we have come to realize are associated with decapitation, dismemberment and torture. Other ritual abuse survivors that I have treated have also relived similar and often identical trauma.'

"Last June," Lisa's story goes on, "the cultists began their campaign" to reclaim Cassandra Hoyer. The cult had kept track of her all these years.

Sam was abducted as she walked behind her Grove Avenue home and driven to a barn outside Richmond. Draped in a white robe, she was placed in a procession of 20 or 25 satanists who walked to a nearby field where a large ritual circle had been cut out of the grass. Lisa notes that police later confirmed that a circle had indeed been cut into the grass of the field. A terrified young boy was also draped in white and forced to watch the rituals as a high priest chanted to summon the demons Sabboth and Aglon.

"Over the next few hours, Sam and the young boy were harnessed and lowered into vats filled with blood. Then they were taken to a stream and cleansed. Later, Sam and the other hostage were forced to watch as cult members tied a woman to a cross which was then hoisted into the middle of a fire. After the woman was determined dead, Sam claims that cult members then participated in acts of cannibalism. After the ordeal, Sam was shoved into a car, driven back to Richmond and dumped in the alley where she had been captured.

"Over the following months, Sam would be forced to endure other atrocities every two weeks to a month. In the course of her abductions, Sam was raped, urinated on, and forced to witness another human sacrifice. On other occasions, attackers forced foreign objects into her body." Such incidents resulted in Dr. Sally Sange recording that she removed from Sam's body objects such as a red Maybelline mascara case with a paper reading 666 and a chapstick cap with items stuffed in it.

I find myself thinking, sure, but perhaps Sam Hoyer is just a little off and came up with all this to get some kind of psychotic attention. Lisa writes that "the most devastating part of the experience was trying to convince people that what she was living was real."

Apparently her therapist Kathy Snowden believed her even without corroboration; but when Snowden herself began to get threatening phone calls, warning letters and death threats, the experiences were more believable. One caller laughed and said, "Your little puppet strings are about to be broken." Then Snowden began to network with other medical professionals across the U.S. and Canada who were dealing with similar cases. Victims in other parts of the country were reporting similar abuses; for instance, the chapstick cap is reported by experts to be a common ritual of reclamation.

Other victims have corroborated Sam's story. "Several victims like Sam are identifying satanists, including many local professionals, prominent Richmond citizens and at least one highly respected religious leader. A half-dozen victims —former practitioners who either joined a cult or who were raised in the "religion"—have come forward to tell their stories to Richmond police. Separately and independently, these victims who have never met have corroborated Sam's story, including names, places and specific ritual practices involving rape, child abuse and murder . . . . Health care professionals are hearing the same accounts from children . . . . 'Their descriptions are very specific, and they corroborate each others' stories,'" according to a psychologist at the Virginia Treatment Center for Children. The Center is joined by Charter Westbrook Hospital and the Chesterfield Department of Mental Health as a Richmond-area facility seeing a distinct rise in satanic abuse cases.

Lieutenant Larry Haike of the Richmond Police Intelligence Division stated, "With everything we've heard from a variety of sources, victims and other law enforcement agencies, I believe that Sam is a victim of ritual abuse. People hear of people out there worshiping Satan, and they think it's not a problem. It is a problem. There is serious criminal activity associated with it. It took a lot of time to develop information to meet our criteria for confirmation. I'm satisfied we have it."

A state investigator added, "We are investigating several things that have happened to Sam. We have physical evidence corroborating her story."

After racing through the Richmond International Airport like O.J. Simpson in his old TV commercials—all right, at perhaps a bit slower pace—I'm letting my heart settle down from the run and from the adrenalin cranked up by Sam Hoyer's story. While the Delta cabin attendants smile through their preflight instructions on how in an emergency we should be prepared to panic in an orderly fashion, I pull out my laptop to write and listen again to an impromptu interview I had with Detective Bill Lightfoot of the Richmond police. "We've got six of those people in the same situation of being terrorized by satanic cults," he had said. "Six that we know of, who've reported to us. We provided some protection for a while after the story came out, but after a while it's just a question of manpower. We just couldn't keep a man on her 24 hours a day month after month."

I asked, "Did disclosing her story help? Did the threat of telling all stop the harassment?"

"No," said Lightfoot.

The middle-aged man next to me finally leans over from his seat by the window: "What is it you're working on?"

I click off the microrecorder I've been holding to my ear. "A book. On satanism."

He huffs.

I hand him the photocopy of Lisa Antonelli's story on Cassandra Hoyer. "Just to keep you out of mischief, how about reading through this and give me your response?"

"Sure," he says. He clicks on the reading light as we take off and reads.

I've clacked a few notes and put away my computer by the time my seatmate is through with the article. "What do you think?" I ask. "Believe her story?"

He tosses the article on the seat between us, swears loudly enough that the lady across the aisle from me glares at both of us, and turns to look out the window at Virginia disappearing in clouds.

Part Two

◆▶

Signing in Blood:
The Devil as Recruiter

"To a teenager, satanic worship is sex,
drugs and the antithesis of a Christian
upbringing all rolled into one."
                    —Juvenile Intake Officer
                    John Thompson

A Medieval engraving depicting Hell and Satan. The Bettman Archive.

▶ 11 ◀

Getting In

I'd been driving north from Washington DC, the stereo in my rented Taurus cranked up to WAVE "Power 105" to find out what music and events Washington teenagers were tuned into. The ads were the best: Movin' Tommy was plugging a car dealership in Fairfax. "These are fair facts, see? Like Fairfax? They got four by fours, one by sixes, two by twelves—" A sound engineer asked, "One by six? Two by twelve? This is car stuff, Tommy. Trucks."

"Yeah," says Tommy. "These are all-deranged vehicles."

"That's all-terrain," said the engineer. "No, like off-road, off-highway, over-the-ditch deranged vehicles." Then he sang, "Home, home on derange. . . ."

I turned the radio off. Interstate 95 north under a gray-flannel sky, with towering oak and maple trees lining both sides of the freeway, is like driving through a tunnel. A bit boring. So there's plenty of time just to think. I was trying to construct a list of exact reasons why teenagers want to get into the occult. Or, a more dangerous way of putting it, why the occult so perfectly fits what teenagers want.

When I pulled off 95 just after the Fort McHenry tunnel into the overcast parking lot of the Baltimore Travel Plaza—Roy Rogers Restaurant! 24-hour Exxon! Days Inn!—I got at least one item for the list: Teenagers are told that by giving in to evil they can have one of their most desperate wishes fulfilled: They can be magically attractive.

I made some calls in the lobby of the Travel Plaza, then ordered a large coffee in the empty Roy Rogers restaurant. A man in his late twenties in a restaurant uniform of black pants, white shirt and red jacket nodded and rang up my purchase. For the second time in two weeks, I was amused that the total popping onto the cash register display was overpriced. "Pretty expensive coffee," I grinned.

"Oh, my gracious," he said. "I don't know why that came up. Must have been a previous order. The coffee is 90 cents."

I picked a table near the wall made of windows full of the gray Maryland afternoon, flopped open a notebook and map and wasn't surprised when he sauntered over and sat down. He noticed my material.

"The reason I know the occult is a roommate I had was really into it. Black magic. Now, I'm Puerto Rican and I know about black magic. But he was into Satan. He said he'd made a pact with the devil when he was a teenager."

"What was the deal?" I asked.

"To become gorgeous," he said. "I saw pictures of him as a teenager, and I don't mean as a 13-year-old. As an 18 or 19-year-old; and he was homely. He was grossly fat and his face was just a lump. So he told me he had sold his soul to Satan to become attractive. And he was. When I met him he was gorgeous." He talked about how in his late twenties David, the roommate, could have anybody he wanted in the gay community around Baltimore.

"Did he have powers?" I asked.

"Everybody said he did. He said he did. But I never saw him do anything magic, actually. But he would do things. You're not going to believe this—I didn't—but he said he was a vampire. Had the spirit of a vampire. He told me that when he said he was hungry, he didn't mean for food. He'd actually bite people, draw blood and lick it off." He explained that David did this as a kind of kinky come-on to other homosexuals. "But he was serious. He'd go pacing around the apartment—mostly when he'd had something to drink, some alcohol—saying he was hungry for blood. He was very disturbed. Very disturbed." The cashier jumped up to check out another customer and called back over his shoulder, "But it was all in his head. Mind over matter stuff."

I remembered Sean Sellers in the McAlester state pen saying he'd drive frantically around Oklahoma City hungry for blood. I also thought about how many teenagers are hungry for success in attracting admirers. And even mentioning David's success in becoming attractive might itself be an enticement for a kid to say, "What have I got to lose besides my soul?" and dig into the occult. This is definitely going to be a slippery topic to hit in my high school assemblies. After reading Michelle Smith and Lawrence Padzer's book, *Michelle Remembers*, for instance, I read a File 18 report that British Columbia teenagers were fascinated with the book, which is set in Victoria. Satanic cult expert Gloria Corliss of Vancouver Island reported most of the locals chose to view the book as fiction. But she said several youth into satanism are furthering their practices with information from the book's graphic descriptions of rituals.

The cashier came back to the table to finish his cigarette. "Remember in high school, those 'lit' books with the story called *The Date Catcher*? It was in every tenth grade lit book in the universe. It's about a teenage girl who thinks of herself as plain and she buys a hairclip in a fancy store and it's called a 'datecatcher.' That's what the saleslady tells her and she's a little skeptical but then decides to believe it. So she goes out of the store but there's this man who looks like he's trying to follow her so she rushes down the sidewalk and dives into this little maltshop. I guess it's set in the fifties or something—a maltshop. And who's there but the guy of her dreams who never ever notices her at all and he's surrounded by all the cheerleaders and homecoming-queen types? Then she remembers the power of the date-catcher and goes ahead and talks with the guy in wonderful, witty lines and he suddenly is interested. In fact, he's so interested he asks her out for a date that weekend. She's just amazed that her datecatcher worked so fast. Then as she's leaving the maltshop that man who'd followed her in the fancy store comes rushing up and says, 'Here, young lady. I was trying to get this back to you; you dropped it in the store a while ago. And it was—"

"The datecatcher," we both finished.

"Yeah." He tamps out his cigarette. "That's all it was. It was just auto-suggestion. David just told himself that what he wanted he was getting from Satan and it basically worked. We had lots of fights about how easily he could have as many guys as he wanted. But it was only in his head, I'm sure planted there by a grandmother he said he had in South Carolina who knew all this satanic power stuff. And for him it worked—like the date-catcher story. He got what he wanted."

"Which," I said, "is why a fad of the occult hitting teenagers falls right into their laps."

"You better believe it." He swore. "What teenager in the world would refuse what they think is an offer to become attractive?"

"Any chance I can talk to David about his satanism?"

"No," he said. He stood to go back to work. "Last May—May 23. We had a spat and I left. And then when I got back he was dead. He hanged himself in the corner. May 23."

I didn't know what to say.

"He got what he wanted," he said, and disappeared behind the kitchen doors.

I gathered my notes and pushed out through the gray afternoon to the car.

—Which is where I started thinking about this list idea of reasons why teenagers—why anybody—get into this evil business. If a person believes there is an entity called Satan and that he offers powers and opportunities, that person must also believe that he's actually selling his soul. And anyone who would willingly sign up for self-destruction is, like David, disturbed.

Maybe if I were talking with a 14-year-old freckled kid named Greg right now I'd say something like: "So I think it's one thing to want to be amazed, to be curious about something that doesn't usually happen in your typical routines. But it's another thing to think about committing yourself to any-thing occult. That's the sign of a problem, a disturbance. It means you need something. And maybe it'll take some help to find out what that something is." I wonder if we can say that anyone who seeks occult involvement is seeking help?

My folder labeled "Signing in Blood: Why They Get into Satanism" has five categories scrawled on the outside: Recruitment/Curiosity, Books & Movies, Fantasy Roleplaying Games, Metal Connection(?), Psychological Needs.

Satanic by Birthright

Of course, one of the reasons why teenagers are into satanism is that they're born into it. It's something most mainstreamers in Canada and the U.S. probably would deny simply through ignorance. A group of people can't keep a secret forever, most of us think. So if there are whole families who practice wild satanic orgies at least eight times a year and sacrifice animals and babies, somebody would spill the beans.

But what I'm finding is that people have spilled the beans—and they end up in mental institutions. Jerry Simandl is investigating 30 cases of patients whose psychoses have involved "delusions" of satanic ritual—patients incarcerated in psych facilities. They apparently have confessed to law enforcement agencies which, since much of the disclosure has come years or decades after the alleged incidents, can do little other than record these bizarre tales. But of course the general public doesn't hear of these unsubstantiated stories because they're perceived as drug-dreams of crackpots. And satanists who were born into the "religion" have divulged their stories to therapists across North America. And the therapists, intent on the healing of these beleaguered minds, have simply had to listen to the accounts, accept them as believed-to-be-true by the patient, and avoid publicizing these confidential disclosures. But some therapists are hearing too many similar stores and are willing to speak out. A rare few, such as Jacquie Balodis whom we talked with in California, are themselves from a generational satanist background. And they know that being born into the cult is one sure way to become a dedicated satanist:

"Generational cult membership," Jacquie writes in her unpublished paper on brainwashing, "is an inherited way of life, passed from one generation to another. It is the elitist group of members in the cult, consisting of intermarriages to form a high level of blood purity. The cult carefully selects a child's parents, who will produce an offspring with a high IQ and spiritual and racial superiority. A child's parents may be married to each other, or both may be unmarried, or both parents may be married to separate spouses. Multigenerational intermarrying produces a clan-like network, which assures safety and continuance of the cult."

The special issue of *Passport* magazine I've stuffed into my bookbag, Lyle Rapacki's INTEL occult and deviant crime reports and the Cult Crime Impact Network File 18, all recount a horror story by a girl who is warped by satanism simply because she is born into it:

I think my father was trying to gain satanic power. I remember going with my father to a man's apartment. It seemed as if it was as a seedy neighborhood. He wanted to buy a woman. I thought my father was good because he didn't sell me. The man wanted to exchange the woman for me. He wanted a clean blonde, no makeup, in her early 20's. I was a seven-year-old kid at the time.

Later when she came into the room, they made her take her clothes off and lie on the table. There were men and women in the room. They tied her up. She screamed a lot. She looked at me and I couldn't save her. They raped her before and after she was dead. I felt like it was my fault. I felt I should have saved her. But I thought that if I had asked my father to save her I would have been next. They had a stainless steel trough under the table to catch the blood. My mother held my arms and made me cut her wrists with a razor blade. They made me lie on top of her when she was dead.

They would toast the devil with the blood. Usually they would take the heart out and offer it to the devil to be blessed. Sometimes they would use a scalpel, sometimes a dagger. They would always push a piece of the heart in my mouth.

One Easter I was tied to a cross alongside a dead man. I remember feeling ill because I was upside down. They took his intestines out and cut him down. They wedged me partially inside the cavity. I was supposed to be born to this man. They put the man in a coffin and put me on top of him. They had a box of live kittens, and they crushed their heads and threw their bodies into the coffin. Then they closed the lid. I can remember screaming. But I worked really hard to calm myself down. I could hear someone walking across the wooden floor. I had to go to the bathroom. Later, when my father let me out, he told me I was a stinking pig and I smelled so bad. I had to lie on the floor in the back of the car and he threw a rug over me.

Losing my virginity in the Bride of Satan ceremony was, in a way, not as bizarre as some of the other things they did to me. It was after going to the opera in a prestigious hotel. Six people, three men and three women, including my father. Usually there were 13 people at ceremonies. They have no choice but to go.

It was the usual coven. It was nighttime. Father was standing by the altar. I walked to the altar alone. The people there said—they were chanting—"Hail, Bride of Satan. Welcome, Bride of Satan to our midst." I was crying. They were greeting me with clenched fists. They told me to kneel on the altar in front of my father. They all walked around the table twice and touched the top of my head. They told me to lie down on my back on the table. Then they took turns having sex with me. They were burning incense. It was inside a building. The robes were black and purple. Father's had a lot of embroidery . . . .

Lisa Antonelli's story on Cassandra "Sam" Hoyer's battles to renounce satanic involvement includes a section on another woman born into a Richmond, Virginia, area cult. Lisa's January 18, 1988 *Style* magazine story states that "generational satanism . . . is hardest to break . . . . Separately and independently, these young victims [being treated in local psychiatric facilities] are relating nearly identical accounts of torture, mutilation, even murder committed under their parents' tutelage."

Lisa quotes Virginia Treatment Center for Children therapist Mary Margaret Kelly: "It's nearly impossible to terminate parents' rights. But if you can't get the children away from their parents, I don't think they have another chance [to] become aware that there is another reality out there."

The *Style* feature then profiles "Sandee," a generational product of satanism who grew up in an upper middle class family that baptized her into the cult at age four. Sandee's parents are a medical professional and an elementary school teacher. As a preschooler, Sandee attended a local religious daycare center where she recognized some of the teachers as participants in satanic ceremonies at other locations. These teachers, according to Sandee, "gave drugs and explained the upcoming ritual to the children."

As she grew up, Sandee "attended public school during the week and went to Presbyterian services with her parents on Sundays. Like all practicing satanists, she says, Sandee's parents did nothing to give themselves away." By the time she was a junior higher, Sandee had allegedly participated in the stabbing sacrifice of two infants; she witnessed several ritual homicides, and then fled the area to flee the cult.

"'I had to fully accept what I had been involved in,' she says. 'I had . . . to continue the involvement or to take the chance of talking and being killed. I knew I had a clear choice to make.'" Speaking out has its terrors, too, for the generational satanist. First, there's the threat of reprisal by the cult: Sandee once was given a lesson on what would happen to her if she tried to escape the group:

"While Sandee watched," Lisa writes, "a woman was raped, stabbed, tortured and eventually dismembered, Sandee claims. There were no other women in attendance, she says, nor was anyone dressed in robes, only dark clothes. 'It wasn't a ritual, per se,' she says. 'It was a lesson to show what would happen to me if I talked.'"

The other terror survivors of generational satanism must face if they decide to tell their stories is flat disbelief. "People aren't going to want to hear," said Sandee, "what they have to say."

Recruitment

Now the sun is dropping out of the clouds over the Joppa, Maryland trees, and the rain stops. I leaf through the paper on brainwashing given me by Jacquie Balodis; as an ex-cultist she knows that kids get into demonic occultism because they're actively recruited:

"Youth and self-styled satanists are recruited into the cult by lures promising companionship, excitement or thrills, free sex, free drugs, money, power and recognition. These lures are intensively persuasive to a person from a dysfunctional family whose values conflict with the family or society. Recruitment locations include schools, parks, satanic and non-satanic churches, occult bookstores, bus and train stations, counseling centers, daycare/preschool centers, parties, psychic fairs, science fiction and fantasy conventions, heavy metal concerts, fantasy roleplaying sessions, satanic computer bulletin boards and cult hotlines."

I decide I need to talk over more specifics with Bette Naysmith, the winsome lady I met in Chicago. She's an administrator for the American Heart Association and a part-time researcher for the Cult Awareness Network (C.A.N.). She'll be at an occult-crime conference in Richmond, Virginia, this week; maybe I'll get a chance to ask her some more specifics on why teenagers get into satanism. Why is this satanic fad hitting at the high school and college level with such force?

Back in stuffy Room 19, I leave the door ajar and open as many windows as possible, and switch on the laptop to pull up the file of my first interview with Bette. I read over the Naysmith transcript. Ms. Naysmith is wonderfully astute. I had first asked what Bette thought was the most dangerous part of teenagers getting into little groups dabbling in the occult. Mind control, she asserts, is the killer issue.

Bette says, "I think teachers, students and parents all need to be warned about teenage involvement in any group. Some cult groups are adept at mind control techniques that most people would think are impossible in our society. But it isn't. There are people out there who know how to identify individuals when they are vulnerable and how to take them a step at a time until they have control over them. I think it's key to get across to teachers, parents, and the students themselves the fact that teenagers must develop a habit of critical thinking during those difficult phases of life, the teens and early twenties. I think most adults, reflecting back, would say that those are some of the most difficult times of life."

"And formative years too," I say.

"Right. You walk a fine line at certain times in your life. There are times when your parents don't seem to know anything. You may respect them, but all of a sudden you run into ideas that are almost opposite if not the opposite of your adult guiders' belief system. And you want to try something new."

And trying something new is what dabbling in satanism is all about. I switch off the computer and dig out some of the materials Bette had given me from the Cult Awareness Network. One pamphlet asks, "Who Is Vulnerable?" and answers, "Everyone. Even the brightest get hoodwinked!" The pamphlet is about when, where and by whom people, especially teenagers, get recruited into destructive cults—satanic or otherwise. Some of the categories cover:

When? Youth get involved during normal transitions including a change in lifestyle, during a sudden illness, accident or death, during a time away from home. Where? On campus, at a self-improvement seminar or activity, in religious organizations, at a dance, party or concert. By whom? The friendliest person you ever met, by a person too interested in what you like to do, by someone who has all the answers. The C.A.N. pamphlet closes with, "Remember: There is no such thing as instant friendship or a free lunch!"

A December 28, 1987, Gilroy, California, *Dispatch* newspaper account I pull from my folder mentions that therapist Lilia Sandoval in Morgan Hill reported that ten of her patients, aged 14 to 16, "have complained of being approached by Satan worshippers. She said the groups lure local children with promises of power, protection and a Satan-induced 'high' that is more powerful than drugs."

Devil Parties

Bette and Chicago detective Jerry Simandl in their unpublished article, "Dabbling Their Way to Ritual Crime," affirm that "adult leaders lure [teenagers] in through involvement in free sex and drug parties. Reliable information reveals two types of adult leaders, one involved for self-gratification, the other recruiting for upper levels of cult involvement."

I remember Jerry Simandl's description of these parties: "If the lure is a party, the prospective member learns there is a special room a select few may enter. During the party this person could be put into a compromising position and photographed or video taped. Then, if invited into the special room, candidates are introduced to the new belief system and possibly urged to sign a contract to Satan stating they will sacrifice themselves at a certain age. If they are hesitant to sign, the rape or photo can be used to induce participation."

I pull out of the folder a clipping from the *Dallas Morning News*, April 20, 1988. Lee Hancock has written a feature, "Crimes in the Name of Satan," which asserts that "police have evidence that some youth groups are being orchestrated by adults."

The article reports that Fort Worth police "identified a teen club opened by adults who attracted teenagers with free alcohol and drugs. Police found that the teenagers were told to learn about Aleister Crowley, an occultist considered the father of modern black magic and satanism.

"Police in a southeast Dallas suburb found an identical operation; and last December, police found another in Fort Worth. Each of the clubs was closed after operators were charged with misdemeanors. 'We have information that similar operations have been set up in other Texas cities,' said a Fort Worth investigator. 'While we have not tied any directly to organized groups, we have interviewed juveniles who claimed that their interest originated with visits to these operations and that after going to the clubs, they became involved in organized groups.'"

Occult recruiters. Missionaries for Satan. Frankly, it's hard to believe. I pull up on the computer the Naysmith interview and note what Bette said on how even teenage dabblers can be sucked into adult-organized satanic cults. I had asked, "Do they get involved in these secondary and primary groups? And if so, how?"

"Some of them do," Bette had said. "Certainly not all of them. In the article that Jerry and I wrote about the dabbler, we note that some of them will get out when the recruiter tries to introduce them to the upper levels. And the ways they get out are escaping through hospitalization, entering a substance abuse program or committing suicide. But those who go on are pretty much seeking bigger thrills, more excitement in different ways. They get bored with the routine they have gotten into at the dabbler level. In some cases, if they are involved in drug dealing, that may be an incentive to go on and get involved in more dangerous stuff all across the board. Some of them do go on to primary level satanic groups. I hope we discover that it's a minority."

I had then asked Bette about whether she'd read the book, *Jay's Journal*, by Beatrice Sparks.

"I did. A long time ago. That's out in the Utah area?"

"Yeah," I'd said. "Do you think it's accurate in the way it represents a typical method of recruitment?"

"Yes," Bette had said. "It's conceivable that that is the way it would occur."

Personal Recruitment

At the Lakeside Motel in Joppa, Maryland, I dig out *Jay's Journal*. Outside the sky has cleared and a brilliant three-quarters moon reflects on the little lake; by Saturday it'll be a full moon. And Saturday is the 24th, which—remember—is supposedly a critical date to practitioners of ritual satanism because of that protocol established at the 1981 W.I.C.C.A. convention in Mexico.

I don't expect human sacrifices to be wantonly carried out by these groups on the 24th of every month, however; I still suspect the authenticity of that document. I mean, why would any covert group need to put down as an international agenda the item that they should—or could—get people to increase their personal debt or to "destroy government agencies by over-spending and public opinion"? It strikes me the way a story would of an old geezer deciding to cause international mayhem and carnage by announcing he'll force all old geezers to spit their tobacco juice on the floor instead of in spitoons. Regardless, the moon is beautiful tonight.

I again leaf through *Jay's Journal*, the diary of a 16-and-a-half-year-old. An intelligent, creative teenager, he fits one of the profiles of an occult dabbler —he's an overachiever, is frustrated in his relationships with the opposite sex and he's incredibly curious. Let me read some of his entries to you as, busted for messing around with drugs, he's recruited into the occult by an instructor at the juvenile detention facility:

September 16

Today Pete took me into the city to have the school station wagon repaired. I can't recall ever having had a more fantastic day! Maybe it was just because I've been in stir for so long, but then again maybe there is something to all the strange alien stuff he believes so completely. Just because it seems unnatural to my little sheltered provincial mind shouldn't mean anything. Man, it really is heavy thinking. This is the first time I've been emotionally stimulated since I don't know when. To expand my intellect . . . to comprehend things incomprehensible . . . to actually experience other planes of existence that have not even been complete fantasies before. Man, could it be possible, conceivable, feasible? Did Atlantis genuinely once exist? Does it still? I've never been so upped in my life before, even on drugs and booze. I wonder when we will be able to get together again.

September 17

Last night I met Pete after lights out. We talked for hours about my aura, which shows fear and grief and pain. I can't see auras on other people like he does, yet, but Pete says I can learn, actually I really think I saw a soft whitish glow around him, denoting spirituality, security, dependability and honor. I've got to change mine. As my self-conditioning changes, my aura will change. I want to learn everything all at once, but I know I can't. It's so frustrating! Pete is going to help me find myself! My true self! My inner aura.

September 18

Pete gave me a herb to chew before I go to sleep. He says it will relax me and give me wonderful dreams. It will show me my inner aura, my own aura and the aura I can yet obtain. I know I saw Pete's aura tonight and also I am beginning to see the dark sinister ones around Cal and Jim and some of the others. It's a new plateau of existence that I didn't even know existed before. Man, it's so strange and exciting.

September 19

Last night I really did experience cosmic consciousness . . . something supernatural. Pete was right! My psychic self is a slumbering cosmic power. It is my link with infinity to be drawn upon at will. It was not like being stoned. I saw bright colors and stuff but it was like I controlled them instead of them controlling me, and I understood the harmony that governs the world in space and the tiny atom. Pete had said that the consciousness that directs the physical universe also pulsated in the cells of my being. He was right! Right and wonderful! He will teach me the mastery of life. Oh, I can't wait. Orthodoxy has ruled my thinking far too long. I and the universe are one. There is no division of supernatural and natural. I must . . . I will, control my karma, thereby controlling all things around me and within me.

September 20

Pete is teaching Tom and Dave and me about ESP. He said he would awaken me at 1:47 a.m. and he did! Oh, these wonderful powers that mankind wastes!

It's the middle of the night again and I can't sleep. How can a person really know what's real and what's unreal, what's right and what's not right?

I suspect that the herbs Pete has given me a couple of times, once to chew and once to drink, were some kind of natural hallucinogens, but I couldn't have been hallucinating when I saw him levitate coins and when he woke me to the minute with ESP or the aura bit.

October 12

When I got home from school there was a phone message that I should call Pete. It really zinged me. We talked for about an hour. Dad will go straight up the wall when he gets the bill, but he can just hang it in his ear because . . . Oh Judas, Pete's got me even more confused than ever. Something inside me could buy the Astro stuff and the Cosmic Concept . . . but witchcraft, that seems too childish and scary storylike . . . but he did . . . he really did . . . right over the phone levitate the pen. He says white witchcraft is of God. I wish I could talk to Pete in person.

October 16

I cut out and hitchhiked up to see Pete for a couple of days. I had to! It was like a magnetic force. Exciting as hell. Now that I'm home and grounded again nothing seems real or exciting. It's like some dumb midnight movie, or I was half stoned or something. Pete wants me to get Brad and Dell in. He said he could feel good vibes from their pictures.

October 17

Brad and Dell and me cut our last two classes and went down to the lake. Mom's at a convention so I "borrowed" her car. At first they both laughed when I started to tell them about Cosmic Consciousness but I understood because I remembered how uncomfortable I'd been when I first introduced it. Pete told me to be sure and not bring in the witchcraft part until after they'd been in a couple of weeks at least. Judas, I know if Pete had thrown witchcraft at me the first time, I'd have told him in no uncertain terms to blow it out his rear end. It's funny how hypnotic the concepts are though once you get into them. Brad and Dell both seem as curious and fascinated as I was. I'm glad! It's not fun to be into things alone.

October 19

There is something hypnotic and right about Pete's people and his teachings. I'm thinking more and more about them. It's like they and I can communicate in ways besides letters and phone calls. I wish I knew more . . . In some ways I'm repelled in even the little I know . . . it's dumb . . . I'm scared and repelled, yet at the same time, drawn and, almost out of my head, curious. I think I'll forget it, all of my background and teaching tells me Pete and his concepts are wrong . . . But what is wrong? Pete says "wrong" is only programming . . . conditioning . . . tradition . . . Man, I wish I had a sleeping pill.

As I finish reading, I'm again curious about the authenticity of the journal. Back in the room, I track down the phone number of the author/editor Beatrice Sparks and ask her just how accurate the published version of the journal is.

"Well, when the boy's mother first contacted me," says Beatrice, "she had said she had several letters and this diary leading up to her son's suicide. I initially thought the suicide was drug-related since my book *Go Ask Alice* was about the drug culture. So I knew nothing about the occult, and other than a bit of research, the occult information in the book comes directly from the boy's diary."

I mention, "Most of the people who are knowledgeable in the occult feel it's a genuine representation of what goes on as teenagers dabble in satanism."

"That's good to hear," she says. "That's been the response coming to me from various sources, too. So I feel the diary is genuine. In fact, it seems to have such an impact that it's being reprinted by Simon and Shuster this year."

"Well, thanks for your time," I tell her. "But frankly I was hoping it was just a fictionalized account. There's too much sadness, too many demons in it for a bright 16-year-old."

"I know what you mean," she says. "But maybe it'll keep another bright 16-year-old dabbler from going over the edge. Incidentally, what is the name of your book?"

"*The Edge of Evil,*" I say.

▶ *12* ◀

The Onslaught of the Occult

I've driven back to Richmond to try to catch as many of what Larry Kahaner called "Cult cops" at an advanced seminar on occult crime partially sponsored by BADD—Bothered About Dungeons and Dragons. The organization was founded by private investigator Pat Pulling after the death of her son in 1982 in a suicide prompted, she feels, by his involvement in the game of Dungeons and Dragons.

Fantasy Roleplaying

I find most of the conference-goers worried about security from satanic cult threats, and consequently—as a nonlaw-enforcement entity—treated pretty much as a persona non grata. So my anticipated goldmine of experts to interview is virtually a bust, but I do wander off from the Bell Road Holiday Inn with some specifics on how teenagers can get overinvolved in fantasy roleplaying and thus hooked into an unhealthy preoccupation with the occult themes of these games.

Back in my room, I leaf through the materials I've accumulated on games like Dungeons and Dragons. From the *Battle Cry* magazine, I read: "A psychiatrist in a Canadian court said that the violent fantasies in the game Dungeons and Dragons played a significant role in the conditioning of murder suspect Michael Leduc. Leduc was accused last month of bludgeoning to death Norma Kowhel and severely injuring her husband and daughter.

"Through his massive involvement in Dungeons and Dragons, the boundary between fantasy and reality was weakened, Dr. Stanley Semrau told a British Columbia Supreme Court jury." The article goes on to report that Leduc spent up to 60 hours weekly playing the game. Dr. Semrau said he was "horrified at the incredibly sadistic nature of the [D&D] materials.

Evil is the more desirable aspect of the game" as it stresses "violence, aggressive behavior and murder."

The article editorializes: "Those who have come out of the occult tell us that D&D is one of the most comprehensive and effective training materials used to prepare young people for entrance into witchcraft."

The same magazine carried another article profiling the frustration of Lafayette, Colorado, detective Gregory Corrie's discovery of 12- and 16-year-old brothers Steven and Daniel dead, their legs entwined in a macabre deathlock. Steven had shot his brother and then himself. Their 13-year-old brother seemed to have been expecting it, according to Corrie, because of their longtime involvement in D&D. The detective found they had left D&D about a year ago since it was no longer challenging. "Friends said they had discussed astral projection where they could ward off demons and devils in the spirit world if they traveled in pairs." Daniel left a farewell note in the stilted D&D style: "I am sorry, but a man without freedom is not a man at all and, therefore, this man is targeted for termination. So shall it be."

Some of BADD's materials list other fantasy games. The list first emphasizes that the version of D&D that encourages players to lose touch with reality is played without the gameboard, played entirely in the minds of the participants. Other roleplaying games deemed questionable by organizations such as BADD include Tunnels and Trolls, The Arduin Grimoire, Runequest, Empire of the Petal Throne, Nuclear Escalation and Demons.

Electronic versions of similar games are available to anyone with a computer and modem who can link up to a users' network. For example, a computerized fantasy roleplaying game called "DND" is currently available to north Texas computer users through a bulletin board linkup. The instructions begin, "This game is not for everyone. As Gary Gygax [originator of Dungeons and Dragons] explained in the foreword of the original edition of Dungeons and Dragons, ". . . we invite you to read on and enjoy a 'world' where the fantastic is fact and magic really works. If you dare, I will take you to such a world, but beware! You will find that this is somewhat more than just a clever computer game, that the characters you create may contain a tiny bit of yourself, and that the urge to return and explore just one more level down, if not carefully controlled, can begin to take precedence over work, family, eating, sleeping."

The game, of course, is meant for simple entertainment, but even its creator recognizes the lure of fantasy roleplaying. And escape—whether through too much television, drugs or overinvolved gameplaying—coupled with constant emphasis on the occult is a volatile combination for susceptible teenagers. That these games emphasize the occult is obvious in a comment Pat Pulling offered in a 1986 Occult Crime Seminar: "Where is the fantasy in this fantasy role playing game if all the characters, deities, gods, spells, incantations, skills, and traditions are firmly embedded in actual occultism, demonology, sorcery, necromancy and magic? What D&D actually comprises is a crash course in sorcery which equips the avid player with the skills necessary to . . . perform satanic rituals."

Rosemary Loyacano of the Denver branch of BADD also lost a son to D&D involvement. Steven Loyacano committed suicide in 1982 at the age of 16. He had over $150 worth of D&D materials in his room along with occult paraphernalia including ritual candles, swords, knives, homemade weapons, animal bones and occult books. With other players from his Catholic school, Steven learned occult rituals and with them began dealing drugs before his death. A final note to one of his D&D buddies said Steven was departing on his long journey in the underworld to meet his master.

Just as fantasy roleplaying games can lure the susceptible teenager into occult involvement, another moneymaking enterprise piques the interest of too many teenagers: Horror movies.

Movies

I'm back in Southern California, heading up 101 to the fading glitz capitol of the world. Hollywood is replete this morning with hostile traffic, smog and characters straggling down Hollywood Boulevard: a clown-suited legless man on a rolling cart, a punk with what looks like a skinny black stovepipe hat but turns out to be his hair, hundreds of everyday-looking people who know Hollywood is just like every place else.

I went last night to see "Spellbinder," a gripping movie about a satanic cult. I'm trying to track down the occult consultants who interjected into the film such realistic trappings of satanism. From what I'm learning about the nature of the beast, these consultants know their stuff.

Occult Movies

Sam Webster operates the Studio City consulting firm Occult Influences. Sam describes himself on the phone as a "sorcerer."

I tell him, "I'm not so much interested in the blood-and-gore horror films, but more the occult movies that are particularly accurate. There's *Rosemary's Baby*, right? Sort of the '60s introduction to the idea of modern satanic cults. Then *The Exorcist*'s popularization of demon possession. *Excalibur* with its Arthurian-era chants and spells. Any other movies that carry an authentic stamp of satanism?"

"Well, of course," he says, "there are plenty of accurate occult scenes in many films. For instance, one of the incantations in the movie version of the musical *Camelot* is authentic. But get back to me for a broader list."

I later meet Sam at a posh office near L.A. International. He's slight, pale with a well-trimmed black beard. His eyes are dark, opaque, almost black. Cultured and articulate, Sam offers me this list of magickally accurate movies: *The*

Golem (1920) by UFA in Germany, silent, directed by Paul Wenger. Based on a Hebrew Caballah myth, the film involves conjuration of the spirit/demon/god Ashtoreth to imbue a clay manfigure with life. The Mages use the Star of David on the forehead of the creature along with a "name of God" to bring it to life. When one letter is removed, making the word for death, the creature dies.

The Black Cat (1934) by Universal Films, directed by Edgar Ulmer, with Boris Karloff and Bela Lugosi. Karloff is head of a satanic coven and some of the incantations were apparently taken out of an old classical grimore.

Curse of the Daemon (1958) by Columbia Pictures, directed by Basil Keys. Based loosely on the life of Aleister Crowley, the film portrays a magician who conjures up demons to get rid of his enemies. The central demonic character, the Daemon, is somehow attached to a parchment which has magickal runes. Whoever has the parchment becomes the Daemon's victim. In the end, the magickian is killed by the demons he summoned.

The Devil Rides Out (1960) in England, based on a Dennis Wheatly novel, with Peter Cushing. This film gives an excellent example of a sorcerer's "circle of protection" which the good guys construct to save themselves.

Sam mentions in the list that this film "is flawed in that it equates satanism with witchcraft."

Burn, Witch, Burn (1962) by American International Pictures, directed by Sid Hayers, based on the Fritz Leiber novel *Conjure Wife*. This is an accurate depiction of "sympathetic magic" in which spells force characters into otherwise unaccountable actions. Here the wife of the professor is able to fight with the evil witch by using magick herself.

The Raven (1963) by American International Pictures, directed by Roger Corman, with Peter Lorre, Boris Karloff, and Vincent Price. Karloff and Price play magickians who battle in what's sometimes called a "Duel Arcane." The movie begins with some especially interesting psuedotraditional incantations by Price as the "good" sorcerer to cure Lorre, the Raven of the title.

The Dunwich Horror (1968) by American International Pictures, directed by Roger Corman, with Dean Stockwell and Sandra Dee; based on the story by H. P. Lovecraft. The film portrays accurate ritual and incantations of malevolent intent such as "Yog Sothot," a call to summon back the Great Old Ones, beings from "outside." While somewhat fantastic, the film is believed by some to be a seriously authentic depiction of satanism, such as in its treatment of the "mythic black brothers."

The Wicker Man (1972) offers many excellent examples of authentic magick including the "Hand of Glory" (a candelabrum made of a human hand to keep someone asleep until the flames are extinguished). Most of the ritual scenes— the women dancing in the Henge, the sympathetic magick in the graveyard— are all accurate depictions of the ancient rituals.

"However," Sam adds his comment to the list, "the film mixes up all the old holidays into one, May Day, making its philosophy and customs some-what confusing."

Ghoulies (early 1980s) has excellent scenes in which a college student uses material from the historical Greater Key of Solomon to call up elementals, minor nature spirits. He is possessed by his dead father in order to raise his body back to life. The son battles the father until aided by the old caretaker who is an ex-cult member. Together they war magickally until the mansion falls down upon them and only the student escapes.

The Serpent and the Rainbow (1988) by Universal Films, directed by Wes Craven. The movie is about the Voudon cults of Haiti and provides beautiful scenes of religious Caribbean occultism. Both evil bocor and good hougan priests are represented accurately with allowances for drama. Zombies are explained in light of modern anthropological research.

Back downtown in LA for another afternoon of "The Nightstalker" case of Richard Ramirez, I got bored as another potential juror is dismissed. At least I'm getting lots of "homework" done as I sit in on these monotonous proceedings. For instance, I'm leafing through reports from an outfit called INTEL out of Flagstaff, Arizona. The briefings list Lyle J. Rapacki as consult-ant and chief analyst. Below an eagle insignia the INTEL sheet states: "Occult-Related Crimes and Deviant Movements." Under something labeled "CRM 100 File" the report suggests that one avenue whereby kids get hooked into the occult is through movies shown at school.

The report says that Diane Daskalakis founded her organization, Citizens for Better Education, after finding too much occult-related materials in her local schools in Plymouth, Michigan. Diane found that for the last 11 years all kindergartners were shown the cute, six-part animated film, "Tales of Winnie the Witch." In it Winnie and her cat Lucifer save the town by cast-ing spells and calling up the dead for advice. Each year the sixth graders in the system are shown the movie "The Sword and the Sorcerer" which opens with a witch calling up the devil in a room whose walls come alive with screaming, bleeding human faces. The witch proceeds to "worship the devil, licking and kissing him throughout several scenes"—according to the report. Junior highers' film fare in Daskalakis's district, according to the report, includes "What Are Friends For," a movie in which an 11-year-old prays to Satan and casts a voodoo spell from The Witches Bible to make her mother disappear. High schoolers are then shown—as in the other cases, without parental consent—the R-rated "Excalibur," the photographically beautiful and magically oriented Arthurian film.

Immediately I wonder whether the entire Plymouth, Michigan, school system is satanically oriented or if Diane Daskalakis is overreacting. I jot a note on my yellow pad to call her and to call somebody from the Plymouth school board.

The INTEL report concludes with a Citizens for Better Education run-down of some of the occult books in the Plymouth school libraries. One that particularly seems odd is *Witches and Their Craft* which, according to the report, contains information about spells, charms, the devil and the Black Mass. "In this book," the report asserts, "goats have sex with girls, people swear allegiance to Satan, animals are sacrificed and recipes are given calling for 'the brains of an unbaptized infant' and 'the flesh of an unbap-tized baby.' Many . . . rituals are described, like the drinking of women's menstrual blood."

I should mention a couple other titles found in elementary school libraries: *Meet the Witches*, a nonfiction book published by Mohargue in 1984, lists 30 steps to sacrifice a baby by boiling it alive. A fiction entry found on an elemen-tary school library shelf is *The Story of Witches*, published by Aylesworth in 1984. The story gives instructions for becoming a witch including renouncing Christ, renouncing one's godparents, spitting on the Holy Bible, proclaiming Satan as lord and saying the Lord's Prayer backwards.

Face it, I think: *If a kid wants to get into occult dabbling, he has to look no further than his school library holdings. Or even his school homework assign-ments.*

Occult Reading

The padded, carpeted courtroom in which the "Nightstalker" is being tried is getting stuffy. I decide to drive over to Westwood. On the way I pop in a cassette of Tom Elliff, a preacher I'd met in Oklahoma City a few weeks ago. I'd been standing in his nicely appointed, windowless study back in the catacombs of a huge new church building near Del City, Oklahoma, study-ing the National Geographic world map covering an entire wall.

"Given to me by my kids," Tom had said. Then he tapped the map at the southern end of Africa. "We spent some time in Zimbabwe. It's the world's best seminary on demonology. *Newsweek* said it has the highest number of witchdoctors per capita of any country in the world. A real hotspot."

"And that's how you were more sensitive to it when you got back?" I said.

"Not really," he said. "Since at first as we got back the demon activity here in the States was so much more subtle than the animist variety in Africa." Tom's voice was harsh with a touch of laryngitis, but he smiled—blond and tan, mid-forty-ish, wearing gold wire-rims—as he studied the map.

Now Tom's voice blares in on the cassette: "I had just taken a new church in Tulsa and had a bunch of kids that would hang around my office. One day one of the teenagers said, 'You know, I found out I could get good grades by praying to Satan.' I said, 'Now, where'd you get an idea like that?' 'Oh,' the student said, 'don't you know about the course we have at school?' He went to the largest school in Tulsa; and he began to tell me about this course called 'The Devil in Literature.'"

Tom continues: "I began to research that course and found out it was taught by a man who openly avowed to be a demon in reincarnated form. The classroom was draped in black. As I read the syllabus for this course—which had been taught for several years—I found that as a part of the course, the students had to study 'Rosemary's Baby' and books on the occult. They were challenged to go to every movie they could find on demonism and satanism. They were also to write a sample contract between some prominent figure in contemporary society and Satan.

"I campaigned against having that course in the curriculum; and one time after coming back from a conference we found the body of a goat sacrificed on our church communion table. On the deacon board chairman's front porch we found the goat's head.

"Out of this course—just to my knowledge and just from that current year—came no less than five students who told me, 'My life is so messed up and twisted because I've started praying to Satan.' And two of them told me they had made a contract with the devil, had sold their souls to the devil."

Listening and dodging traffic, I think about how anyone not of Tom's evangelical Christian persuasion could dismiss such confessions as meaningless teenage superstition. But that, according to Tom, is exactly the point. Even if the teacher weren't anything more than an imaginative instructor getting his students into the subject, even if there were nothing to a kid writing a pact with the devil, at least some of these kids believed it. Imagine yourself as a 15-year-old. Try to remember the normal mental and emotional upheavals of your fifteenth year. Now imagine the added mental and emotional upheaval you'd experience if you actually believed you had sold your soul to Satan.

I wonder how many other kids besides the five Tom talked with were hurting that year from getting in over their heads in this one course. I wonder how many kids felt twisted in all the years the course was taught in that Tulsa school. And how many schools have such a course?

On the University of California campus it takes me nearly 45 minutes to find the glass and steel library. I check out the UCLA trove of occult holdings. There's everything listed from western Apache witchcraft to the Kurdish Yezidi who for centuries in the Armenia-Iraq-Iran area have worshiped a fallen angel of evil. The hot occult books favored by the typical dabbler are listed, of course; but when I track them down through the labyrinth of shelves they're all checked out. Every one: *The Satanic Bible* and *Satanic Rituals* by Anton LaVey, Aleister Crowley's *Magick*, *Black Arts* by Richard Cavendish, Herter's *Symbol Dictionary*, *Necronomicon* and *The Witches' Bible*. And more. Judging by the listings on the occult, devil worship, demonism, witchcraft, etc., there's no end to the black arts literature anybody can read who has access to a large library. That is, if the books aren't already all checked out.

I then browse through the phone books for Montreal, Canada, hoping to find some listing of a group calling themselves CASH—the Continental Association of Satan's Hopes. It's a mail order outfit. A brochure I'd run across on the CASH book catalog intrigued me—mostly because somebody had torn off the coupon with the address, which meant at least somebody was falling for the ad copy. The CASH spiel goes like this:

> The mighty power of our lord Satan can now become part of you! Whatever you need or want, our lord Satan can get it for you quickly and easily! You can now discover for yourself a new world through the infernal power of the mighty Satan, lord and rightful ruler of this earth. Find out how you too can realize your lifelong ambitions once you pledge allegiance to the true king of this world. It does not matter what your goals are, whether you want infinite wealth or just a comfortable new home, fine possessions, love, companionship, new health and vigour, power over others, our lord Satan can bring it to you! You will be absolutely amazed how lifelong obstacles will disappear, and life will become such a pleasure to live, once our lord Lucifer becomes a part of your life.

The brochure might just be a quick buck for some diabolical entrepreneur; *The Magic Power of Satan* sells for $23. But fast-buck art or not, the brochure's authors know how to appeal to their target audience. They have the basic sale-of-satanism pitch down pat:

> Do you know that you can get someone to do your bidding, to accept your commands, to do as you order? Through the power of our lord Satan you can implant thoughts in other people's minds! You can use satanic power to dominate others! Control your boss where you work. Make someone love you. Attract women! Attract men! Leave your enemies wishing they were your friends! People will act toward you how you want! Best of all, no one will ever suspect they are under your power!

This is why I'm trying to track down CASH. They've been able to put into one mail-order paragraph what every God-fearing Sunday school kid has felt at one time or another: Why worship God when the alternatives are so much more fun? Think how your favorite teenager might react to the brochure's enticement.

No luck on the CASH listing in any of the Montreal references. Maybe I'll find somebody who knows somebody who's into the association when my quest inevitably draws me north. But it bothers me that any teenager who can read English can simply order such materials; I wonder how many underground satanic and black magic mail order firms like CASH are titillating young thrill-seekers to dabble in hell.

Mail order isn't the only odd source of satanic info. Kids can get into the occult through their computers. Phil Hansford in Tujunga has compiled a list of occult-related computer bulletin boards through which anyone with a modem can access files such as "Why Magick?" or "Astral Projection."

I jot down a list of the inroads kids can take to the occult—being born into it, being actively recruited, becoming overinvolved in fantasy roleplaying games, getting into horror films, reading books, seeking mailorder or computer bulletin board materials. I step out of the ice-cold air conditioning of the library to a warm evening and a huge hazy full moon rising over the UCLA campus. Somewhere among the buildings and lamplit walkways a rock band is belting out some industrial-strength music. I follow the noise as it ricochets among the class buildings and find a cast-of-hundreds crowd dancing on a huge square below three-tiered banks of amplifiers, below a few guys in glistening pants and no shirts, below the huge, odd moon.

They're good; a local band, a kid with a mohawk tells me. He says the concert is part of the fall semester orientation. I watch the momentum of the music, of the crowd. Two other students join the mohawk kid; they whoosh back and forth on huge skateboards along a sloping walkway, grate in a twirl against a curb, then whoosh back.

I pull out my minirecorder, mention some of the in-over-their-heads teenagers like Ricky Kasso with his "Say you love Satan" and ask them about students involved in the black side of the occult. They're not UCLA students but high schoolers who followed the sound of the band and who revel in the maze of skateboard-wonderful concrete walkways on the campus.

I ask them quick questions to encourage specificity. They're into heavy metal. They don't know any kids dabbling with satanism but as usual they mention a few really weird kids who do seances with ouija boards and claim to cast spells. Good stuff for the book, I think, as I try to find my way back to wherever it was I parked. It only takes a half hour to find the car and about 45 seconds to find that my recorder batteries had suddenly and inexplicably died while trying to record those pithy questions and interesting answers. I put new batteries in the little machine and hear a phrase I had first asked: In a slow, deep voice as if full of marbles, a voice grinds out, "love Satan." I'm spooked.

Pulling out of the parking lot, I hear echos of the band and I can't keep from mulling over one of the factors that continually pop up in this question of how kids get involved in such a wacko enterprise as satanism. The factor, I've often felt, is overrated, sensationalized and beat like a dead horse. But it seems to always be there. The factor is trash rock. Black metal music.

Metal Music

I'm in Santa Ana, California, standing in an Alpha Beta checkout line with my lunch. I watch the trio saunter in: the short, overweight man first, the girl, then the scraggly young man. The men are both dressed in black.

The cashier is arguing with a hard-of-hearing lady about cashing her check, so I'm still in line when the trio gets into the next checkout line. I'm trying not to appear too interested, but the in-his-thirties leader guy glances up just as I'm studying his outfit: he has black jeans and a black Black Sabbath t-shirt pulled over his belly, bare feet and long, greasy black hair. His eyes seem to glare back. He frowns at me. The girl is in her early twenties and could be pretty but looks worn out. In contrast to the men's colors, she wears faded pink out-of-fashion stretch pants and a pink striped sweater.

The younger guy is most intriguing: he too has a Black Sabbath t-shirt, his black jeans are cut off at the knees and his two left middle fingers are missing. He has so many tattoos on his arms I can't distinguish where one begins and the other ends. He's wearing about four silver rings on his right hand. He's holding a 25-pound bag of dry dog food. Just as I glance back at the first guy, he glares back at me so the whites of his eyes reflect light from the store window. I nod. He doesn't.

I decide the best entre I can have to talk with them will be about metal music because of their t-shirts and I'll go from there to find out if they know of any occult cults in the area. They check through, my line is still jammed, they leave—again walking in a line without talking—for the parking lot.

I finally get through and hustle out to the parking lot to catch them as they begin to pull away in an old Dodge van. Black. "Hey, I wanted to ask you a question," I say, suddenly feeling too clean in my white pants and gray Newport Beach t-shirt.

The younger guy is driving. He hunches across the steering wheel and says, "Yeah?" out the window.

"I'm trying to track down regular people instead of the ivory tower experts on metal music." The guy just looks, his face sort of loosely hanging. So I press on: "I noticed your Black Sabbath shirts so I figured you'd be able to tell me something about them these days."

I'm standing basically in the middle of the Alpha Beta driveway, the guy is revving up the van as if he can't wait to be on his way. He looks over at the older greasy haired guy who suddenly stiffens as he looks behind me. I turn and see a white-shirted kid running like Carl Lewis across busy Bristol Avenue toward us.

Fifteen feet behind him with nightstick churning as he pumps his arms charges a policeman. The kid flies across the parking lot and tries to jump a fence into the yard of a house but smashes into the fence instead, plowing through a couple boards headfirst. The cop leaps on him, whacks him a couple times with the nightstick and begins cuffing him.

The driver of the black van yells, "Outta the way," to me and squeals down the driveway and out into Bristol Avenue traffic. I'm left in the middle of the driveway holding my yogurt.

I watch the cop's handling of his prisoner as a little crowd gathers, then wander to my car mumbling, "So much for man-on-the-street metal opinions."

"Hey, I heard you asking about Sabbath." A teenager walks up behind me. He doesn't look like a metalhead. I'm disappointed but say, "Know anything about 'em?"

"Yeah, a lot of the groups are into it."

"What do you think? Heavy metal music gets kids into satanism?"

"No way. It's the black metal bands that play with the satanic stuff. And there's no way somebody's going to get hooked into demons by listening to a Venom cut," he says. "No matter how much preachers yell about how terrible it all is. I think their big gripe is they just don't like the music. Don't get it, know what I mean? But once a kid is into occult stuff, gets into drugs or meditation or whatever, then the music speaks. Loud."

"So it's not really a draw into the occult?"

"That's what I think," he says.

"Who are the metal groups into the satanic stuff?"

He rubs his head and scratches his hair from one ear to the other. "Let's see. Venom, Slayer, Possessed, Satan's Host. Maybe Megadeth, Fedev, Sodom for sure, Exodus, Bulldozer. None of them get airplay so it's just concerts and albums. Most of them are like in just one city since they don't go national much except for tours. Dark Angel, Fallen Angel, Metal Church, Demon. Then there's Satan, Metallica, Celtic Frost, Exciter, Abbatoir, Candlemass, Christian Death. Witch Finder, 45 Grave, Skulls, Nuclear Assault, King Diamond, Sentinel Beast, Flotsam and Jetsam, Kirax, Krank."

I think back over the stomach-gripping cases I'd researched. In Georgia two guys and a girl strangle a girlfriend in their car listening to Ozzy Osbourne. They pass her body out the window of the car, perform some rituals over her and bury her in a shallow grave.

"Son of Sam" David Berkowitz was a dedicated fan of Black Sabbath.

Midlothian, Texas, was the setting of the satanic-related slaying of undercover cop George Raffield with heavy metal playing.

Ricky Kasso's murder of Gary Lauwers in Northport, Long Island—as he shouts "Say you love Satan!"—was orchestrated to heavy metal. Kasso's favorite groups were Black Sabbath and Judas Priest.

The L.A. "nightstalker" Richard Ramirez was obsessed with AC/DC's "Nightstalker."

"Hey, thanks," I tell the kid. "What's your name?"

"Tommy," he says.

It's getting to be a warm afternoon. I pull out of Alpha Beta and cruise Bristol Avenue until I find a store. Inside I buy the November 1988 issue of *Power Metal* magazine. The clerk looks like Truman Capote. He leers up at me and asks in a whiny voice, "So you're into this stuff, eh?"

I'm clean, straight-looking, and beyond the age of most metalheads. So just to make Capote's day, I say, "Yes"; and have to pay two dollars for this piece of pulp that any kid in America can buy by saving lunch money. I sit in the parking lot and leaf through the issue.

My "Metal" folder is in the back seat, so I climb out and sit in the back of the car, pulling out a couple of clippings. One is from the April 1988 *Power Metal* article on King Diamond.

"It's my belief," this musician who wears upside-down cross earrings, bones around his neck, etc., says, "that there is a dark side within us all. I feel comfortable with that dark side, and I want to explore it in my life and in my music. I don't believe there is anything inherently right about the Christian God, as there is nothing inherently evil about Satan. I have spent a great deal of time studying satanic beliefs—I'm not the type to dabble with something as powerful as satanism without a proper understanding of the form. The music I am making is still heavily steeped in my beliefs."

A scrap ripped out of my folks' June 1988 *Reader's Digest* begins an article on "Shock Rock": "Recently several sixth-graders at Marion Elementary School in Belle Vernon, Pennsylvania, asked their music teacher about the meaning of some rock music lyrics. One record was by the group Venom, whose message was spelled out on the album cover: 'We're possessed by all that's evil; the death of you God we demand. We spit at the virgin you worship, and sit at lord Satan's left hand.' In the other album, Hell Awaits by the band Slayer, the lyrics glorified 'the relentless lust of rotting flesh.'"

I leaf through the issue of *Power Metal*, glancing up to see Truman Capote, the little clerk, watching me through the store window. I have no pride, so I read on:

A review of the group Sabbat's album "History of a Time to Come" suggests the group "mixes thrash influences with convention power metal fare like black magic, the occult and religion. '. . . we are interested in any subject we find fascinating,' Sneap [a Sabbat member] explained. 'People have called us satanists—but we aren't of course. But we do have an interest in magic. Who wouldn't? It's an incredibly mystifying field and a subject like that ties in so well with our music. It's a very natural marriage of sound and substance.'" The review then comments, "Can it be? A thrash band with brains?"

Messiah Marcolin, who wears a monk outfit in the band Candlemass, is quoted: "We tend to tackle subjects like death more than we do Satan. But we might take a few songs and deal with the satanic issue in our own way. We certainly won't be pro-Satan, so we'll be writing songs of warning."

Greg Hyses of Newport News, Virginia, writes in a letter to the *Power Metal* editors: "I'm a serious heavy metal fan . . . . I'd like to say that I'm not a devil worshipper and I don't do drugs. Lots of my friends think all heavy metal is based on that stuff, but I tell them it's not. I don't like Slayer and Possessed and other groups like that. With a name like Megadeth, people would think that they are devil 'fans,' but the lyrics prove they aren't. On 'Peace Sells,' one of the songs even says, 'Don't summon the devil.'"

But for all the protesting that of course the groups aren't preaching satanism, there are too many satanic dabblers addicted to metal music, too many other letters to editors of metal magazines like the following excerpt from an old clipping:

"There's a new breed of kids out here. The real metal—from Iron Maiden, Black Sabbath, Motley Crue and Ozzy have our spirit and love. We believe that Satan rules and would rather blow up this wicked world than let it fall to the communists. We live to be high and want nothing to do with reality. We don't care about ourselves, just each other. Violence to those we hate, love to our friends and the breed. May everyone be a slut. If you can understand, love to you. —Just One, Middleburgh NY."

Just how accurate the old clipping is in conveying more than one kid's opinion is anybody's guess. Most experts tend to minimize the effectiveness of even strong satanic messages in metal music to entice innocents into the black arts. But most further agree that, once into satanism and black witchcraft, a person's response to satanic metal music can be remarkable.

On page 19 of her excellent unpublished paper on brainwashing Jacquie Balodis states: "A person in a mind-altered state of consciousness is highly susceptible to the words of a song or incantation. In a trance state, the person identifies with the words and internalizes them. Many of the heavy metal songs glorify sex, Satan and committing criminal acts. [Ritual abuse] survivors report . . . being instructed by older cult members to listen to heavy metal music."

So in all probability thrash-mosh-black metal music doesn't drag unsuspecting kids into satanism. The teenager who wouldn't worship Satan anyway just listens to the stuff because it's one type of his '90s generation music. He knows how to shock adults, just as the '60s generation shocked the old folks with "I Can't Get No Satisfaction." And the '30s generation shocked the old folks by blaring one of the many tawdry renditions of "Pistol Packin' Mama" or "That Old Black Magic"—which was banned in many areas.

It's the kid already sliding into the pit who is susceptible to power metal messages about the dark side—even if the groups themselves only intend the messages to be theatrical. So metal music doesn't seem to be an enticement into but a reinforcement of satanic ideals.

It's getting hot in the car on the Seven-Eleven asphalt parking lot, and the little old clerk keeps looking out the window at me. But before I take off, I remember Mark Madden, an ex-satanist I interviewed, had related an experience he'd had listening to an old Led Zeppelin cut. I find the cassette and click it into my recorder:

"Yeah, there was one session when I was meditating," Mark said. "I was on my bed and intending to work on astral projection and I had this old Led

Zeppelin reel-to-reel on. And I'm concentrating and just when 'there's still time to change the road you're on' comes on—"

"Stairway to Heaven," I said.

"Right. Zing—something catches me right there. So I listened to it again and felt something right again at that phrase. So I reset the reels and right at that point but back-masked—that's where they recorded in messages backwards so you really can't hear them when it's playing forwards. Back-masked in it was the word 'worship!' Just 'worship.' But I guess because I was getting into altered consciousness it struck me even though I wasn't really listening consciously."

I'm concentrating on Mark's anecdote and typing it into the computer on my sweaty knees—it's a warm afternoon, remember—and I don't see the Truman Capote-looking store clerk till he bangs on the car door.

"If you don't mind my asking," he says in a whiny voice, "just what are you doing? We do have policies against loitering around the store."

"Well," I stutter, "I'm doing some research on teenagers dabbling in satanism and metal music seems to be associated with the problem."

His entire demeanor changes. He's suddenly courteous. "Well, why didn't you say so?" And he proceeds to rattle nonstop in a more cultured whiny voice on his son's involvement in metal music, on his own interest in the occult since he was in Korea in the army. He asks who was on the tape and I explain Mark's experience with the Zeppelin back-masking.

"Of course," says Capote as he notices a customer heading into the store. "You know who lives in the most famous satanist's house in the world—in Aleister Crowley's mansion in England."

"No, who?"

"Jimmy Page."

My mind bumbles through cobwebbed files trying to place the name. "Jimmy Page?"

"Used to be a guitarist," says Truman as he walks off and winks. "In Led Zeppelin."

▶ 13 ◀

Shocking the Old Folks

Why do teenagers get into this evil business? Not just because a devotee entices them. Not because they've played a fantasy roleplaying game or read a book on magic or gone to see the grossest spook film or listened to power metal. Bette Naysmith and Jerry Simandl write in their manuscript on dabblers: "Fantasy roleplaying games, heavy metal music, books and movies can influence and possibly enhance the dabbler's involvement in ritual satanism. However, if properly monitored and not taken to extremes, these activities are not considered dangerous." Teenagers get into satanism because they want to. Because they think they need to.

Psychological Needs

Satanism especially seems to fit the needs and wants of "middle and upper class teens of high intelligence who are creative, curious and possibly underachievers with low self-esteem," according to the Naysmith and Simandl article.

I'm sitting in the Memphis airport people-watching and thinking through the horrendous, secretive, contradictory and controversial input I've read and listened to these past weeks.

Then I start noticing faces: A haggard young woman pulling a monstrous suitcase and a four-year-old boy on a little plastic leash attached to his arm. An overweight teenage boy with all the wrong style clothing hauling his belongings in two cardboard boxes reinforced with twine. Two probably twelve-year-old girls with droopy, frankly homely faces plastered with makeup, both wearing oversized baggy white sweatshirts—one says "Shuck & Jive!" on the front—and tight, tight stonewashed jeans. A family: a fat, bald, pale dad and his immense blue-Hawaiian-tent-dress festooned wife; a grinning gap-toothed

119

seven- or eight-year-old daughter in a playsuit that looks too young for her; and a greasy-haired 14-year-old boy in jeans and red t-shirt who's obviously embarrassed to be seen with his family. "Keep up with us, Jeffie," his mother squawks at least three times as the troupe hustles past me, Jeff the son intently lagging behind. And a woman in her twenties who's trying too hard to be perfect: She's got expensive matching luggage, so much jewelry dangling from every corner of her body that the security alarms must have buzzed for an hour as she went through, a satin-looking crimson dress fit for the governor's ball, bleached blonde hair moussed to perfection, and an exquisitely made-up, homely face.

Write it down somewhere: Kids, teenagers, adults get into something as bizarre as worshiping evil not because they're maniacs but because they're needy. These faces we've been cataloging seem to say, "I'm trying like everything to be special, to be noticed, to have some control over what happens to me. But all that seems to happen is I get hurt or disappointed or passed by and I'm lonely and bored and feel stuck in my plain, plain life."

In our instant, quick-fix culture, the possibility of getting what you want through a shortcut is attractive. Even if the shortcut is risky since a teenager thinks he can handle it, he can get out at any point he chooses. Teenagers are always optimistic about how they'll quit something if they get in over their heads; I think of Beatrice Sparks' comment: "The voice of every pregnant girl, every kid hooked on drugs, alcohol or the occult [says], 'Not me! I didn't think it could ever happen to me. I was sure I could handle it.'"

Further, if the shortcut—to belonging, to being special, to having abilities to make people love you and get money—is something that will outrage a teenager's stodgy parents, all the better! Any kid who's going to mature in the next century knows that a key way to outrage stodgy parents is to shock them with satanism.

So I think certain teenagers are walking powder kegs of desires, disappointments and rebellion. And brash, alluring satanic dabbling can be just the match that blows them into a world of sex and drugs and stomach-twisting thrills. Then their growing addiction to the occult can pull them into derangement, pain and murder.

I've met too many teenagers whose entire lives focus on their desire to be free from overwhelming feelings of insecurity, loneliness and boredom.

"I was looking for something to hang onto, something to belong to, something to make me feel more secure." I'm reading the comments of a senior named Wendy at Cedar Falls High in Cedar Falls, Iowa.

Wendy said she'd been involved in satanism for about four years. "You get what you want," she said. "But you pay."

The article from the April 27, 1986 issue of the *Waterloo Iowa Courier* gives a solid glimpse into why teenagers find satanism attractive:

A friend of hers who was involved in satanic worship seemed to have everything. Wendy's curiosity about satanic worship grew.

She said her friend took her to what she described as "worship parties" in the Waterloo area where plenty of alcohol and other drugs were made available.

"Kids who are feeling low will reach for anything," she added.

Wendy already had a drug problem, and if she needed drugs, she got them. If she needed money, it was provided.

"It's not like, boom, there's a car in your living room," she explained.

But in exchange for what she termed "recruiting" people and other errands, she had all the drugs and money—and "friends"—she wanted.

"They give you nifty presents, but when you try to get out, you owe them. You can't turn down their requests," she said.

Kids who get involved in satanic worship only end up hurting themselves, Wendy warned.

"You think you've got friends—till you get busted," she said. "They don't care about you, and you don't care who you hurt."

Wendy recalled that after four years of devoting just about all her time to satanic activities, some of which she says included criminal mischief as well as drugs, she became paranoid and began having nightmares.

"I said, 'I've had enough. I'm done. What you've given me, I've given back. I'm getting out.'"

I underline the phrases Wendy used on why she got involved in the first place: "You get what you want. Something to belong to. Something to make me feel more secure. Kids who are feeling low will reach for anything. They give you nifty presents."

Some of the rest of the article chronicles Wendy's struggle to break out of the self-styled satanic cult. Apparently it wasn't easy. Another section of the *Courier* piece explores the mindset of "Adrian," a practicing satanist.

He seems like a typical sophomore from a local high school—his bedroom is adorned with AC/DC, KISS and Ozzy Osbourne posters. But then the writer notices the upside down crosses, a couple of skulls and an altar against one wall. He tells the interviewer he's been into satanism for about four years and believes in the rituals and their effects. Ann Heise Kult writes:

"Christianity, Adrian and [his friend] Manitou say, limits life and glorifies death. Christianity tells you everything you can't do in anticipation of an afterlife that might never be. But satanism, they have gleaned from reading the Satanic Bible, says life is the ultimate indulgence; death, the ultimate abstinence.

"According to the two teenagers, other kids are a little bit leery of them and their alleged demonic doings. 'With fear comes respect,' says Manitou."

Several school officials commented on the satanic involvement of Cedar Falls area students: "It appears to be directed to a group of kids who might not otherwise feel accepted by their peers," said Holmes Junior High principal Lee Mickey.

"Kids are going to extremes today to get attention," said Cedar Falls High principal Les Huth.

Curt Nedoba, a local social worker, said satanic worship is appealing to adolescents because it's mystical and magical, and offers them an avenue to express the aggression and discontent that is normally associated with that age group.

Paul Smith and John Thompson, Black Hawk Country juvenile probation officials, commented that satanism is an excuse for kids to do the things they're not supposed to do. They agreed that, to teenagers, satanic worship is sex, drugs, and the antithesis of a Christian upbringing all rolled into one. "Kids like to shock people. And satanic worship is a good one for that," said Thompson. "It usually comes out when kids are angry. They use satanism in an attempt to scare off adults . . . . Kids want their freedom."

Jammed into my mounting mishmash of carefully organized notes is a quote I picked up somewhere from the Sunday *World-Herald*, February 14, 1988: "It's a shortcut to power, and the only thing you have to do is stick your neck out. There's the element of danger," says Linda Blood, a former member of the Temple of Set, a group of religious satanists.

"It's like the occult version of the Marines—'Are you man enough for this? Do you have what it takes?'"

Gino Gerachi's descent into heavier forms of the occult was probably a model of a lot of teenagers' progress in seeking resolution of their felt needs in the black arts. Gino had said: "It's esoteric. It's hidden, and the appeal for the general student is power and experience. If you can have an experience, this is your experience, and you see, this is the appeal of the occult.

"It's 'I saw the ghost, I saw the spirit writing, I had the reincarnational experience, I was able to cast a spell, I was able to do this or that.' So that firsthand experience is what I worship in the occult—it's the thing that I think about in the morning, the thing that I live for during the day, the thing that I go to bed at night thinking about, that's my god. The thing that occupies me emotionally, physically, spiritually, that is my god. And as a person, as a young person involved in the occult, my god became knowledge, and power and using spirit beings to acquire knowledge and power."

I had asked Gino, "Did you use any of your powers up to then to try to get things, to rise in the big bad world?"

"Yes, yes. I would use my powers, or my so-called powers, to try to get knowledge and information about people. You see, Jerry, when you have knowledge and information about people, you have power. Because, you see, if I can talk to you and I can say, 'Your mother and your father were like this, so you had this kind of a background, and when you were four years old your uncle did this to you.' And you see, demons can give you power, they can talk about hidden things, awful things, that you never told anybody about. And you see, if you are a girl, and I happen to know that you have an uncle named Frank and he molested you when you were

11 years old and you certainly know you didn't tell anybody, what are you supposed to think about that?"

"Were you able to do that, Gino?"

"I was able to do that." He said it a bit smugly even now, years later. "I was able to talk about people's hidden feelings. Now some of it was supernatural, but some of it was just intuitive. For instance, intuitively I knew, as a high-schooler, that everybody felt like me—lonely, hurt, afraid. Intuitively, I knew that they went home at night and looked up at the ceiling and cried because they hated their life. And so, when I was able to confront my peers with their feelings they would say, 'You're right. How could you be so honest, how could you be so real? How could you know?' You know what happens when you have intimate knowledge about another person? You have power."

"Interesting idea," I said.

"With that power, I was able to form relationships and friendships. I started thinking about girls more and more in relationships. And for some reason I wasn't able to have a really good relationship with girls. I contacted a person who was a satanist, because he told me that if I really wanted real power that I should see him. And that if I really wanted a girl I could cast certain spells and offer certain ritual sacrifices and be assured of a girlfriend. He came up to me at school and said, 'I'm Steve and I also heard you are interested in the occult. Why don't you come over and visit with me?' Steve, by the way, was also the California chess champion. A brilliant young man, he was a genius. He used to take 14 chess players, line them up in the library, and play each one of them and beat each one of them. And I thought, *Ah-hah. Here's a person who's psychically in tune, who understands the occult, but who also isn't an idiot. I can talk to him.* He told me about ritual magic, how to make pentagrams, how I could mix blood and urine, say certain things, and drink it and have certain kinds of powers."

"Did it work?" I asked.

"It worked one time. I had wanted to have this girl like me and I performed this particular ritual and she couldn't keep her hands off me. But you know what, the part that they don't tell you is there's a price to pay.

"It is bad news. But you know, you would be surprised what kids are willing to do if they think, not only it will work, but it can get them an intimate relationship. See, you've met hundreds, perhaps thousands of kids and so you know, you can tell kids they can have a genuine, loving relationship with another person completely. They're drooling for it. Then satanism asks, 'Well, what would you be willing to do?'"

"So you drank it."

"I drank it."

My flight in Memphis is boarding, so I tuck the *Courier* clipping back into a file and notice as I do a quote from Dave Balsiger's unpublished article on heavy metal: "Deputy Harry Hatch, San Bernardino County, California, Sheriff's Department, says, the kids out there worshiping Satan, holding ceremonies and writing graffiti on the walls probably aren't really worshiping Satan. I think, for the most part, they're probably feeling unloved by their parents, or just feeling lonely and bored."

But whatever the reason teenagers or anyone gets involved in the occult, the enticement to go deeper is part of the program. What is the progression like? Their descent into hell is, from the reports I've gathered, typically like the story of a 19-year-old from Louisiana. A police chaplain recorded the youth's story in a city jail. With my computer, recorders, mashed shirts and sundries stuffed into the 737 luggage racks, I click on an overhead light after takeoff and read through a segment of the transcription provided in Lyle Rapacki's INTEL "CRM 200 File":

When I was fifteen years old, I seemed to be drawn to something other than Christianity . . . . I thought I would start my own cult, so I started reading things. I read the Bible at first; I couldn't find anything else that I thought was spiritual. Reading the Bible, I decided that Satan was probably the good guy and had not been thrown out of heaven, but had come to earth to let people have a good time and do what they wanted to do . . . . I started calling on Satan to help me. Then I saw an ad in a magazine about learning to be a witch. The Church of WICCA somewhere in California or Texas. I started doing the things that it said in the pamphlets and books they sent me.

I did an altar and started saying some of the chants and things that they told me to say. We (I had some friends do it with me) had some dope along with it. Then some people told me there were some other things going on that I might be interested in. I think they got my name and address from those WICCA people. WICCA also sent me some information on where I could go and buy some potions to make charms with. I think the satanists here . . . got my name from them. They took me to different places and I met people and there was a lot of drugs and a lot of sex. I was very interested in that. I was also interested in worshiping Satan and I believed that he was really real.

We went to different houses, some very nice . . . and some not so nice. Sometimes it was out in the woods; sometimes it was just me when I did it by myself and the largest group that I was with was out in a cemetery way out in the woods . . . and there was, maybe 90 or 100 people. The leaders were in their middle to late 20s, no more than early 30s, and they told us what to do and how to do it. There were other groups of people that didn't come every time. They came to special rituals and they were older people . . . "the watchers," they called them, "the overseers." I think that some of our leaders had services with them at another time. We were the younger group.

Finally they asked me if I wanted to become part of their group. I said, "Yes." So they took me to a cemetery way out in the woods. We got there about dark and they had quite a to-do. At the beginning of the ceremony they rolled out a sheet of paper that was probably 12' wide and 30' long. They rolled it out on the ground and had me start at the top and read it. It was pledges . . . to Satan and what I would do. I didn't like all that I read, but I wanted to be with them so I had to agree to all of this. I wanted to sign but they said, "You can't sign yet. You have to be buried and resurrected first." They opened one end of a grave and made me crawl in it. They didn't let me have any drugs or anything. They put me in there at midnight and then they sealed it up. There was a body in there, but it was nothing more than a skeleton. So I had to lay there with this skeleton.

There were a few cracks in the top of the grave. They did other things outside; they chanted and danced around, and did a lot of things. I don't know what because I was scared and I got kind of cold down there. They poured some kind of liquid on the grave; they may have urinated. It ran down through the cracks and got all over me, and that made it worse. I went all through the next day, and they took me out at midnight. I was there 24 hours. I guess probably an hour and a half before they came to get me out, my body began shaking and it was uncontrollable. They let me out about midnight and all those people were there. I cut my wrist and bled in this cup. Then they took that from me and they had three bowls: a black bowl, a white bowl, and a red bowl. And they took stuff out of those bowls . . . . had some kind of liquid in it and poured it also with my blood and stirred it up and passed it around. A lot of people took a drink out of it. Then they brought it back to me and told me to drink the rest of it. I drank it and then they had me sign this big piece of paper in my blood.

They had a banquet; they were celebrating, but they didn't let me eat. There was a couple of motor homes . . . and the women came with a lot of food. There was people there in motor homes, cars and motorcycles. Some of them had robes on and some did not. They began to eat; it was all bird meat. I did like the mushroom tea. After they ate, a lot of them started having sex with each other . . . in celebration of me . . . for a long time.

I kept going to the meetings and there were things that they required us to do. I had to agree to go to a Christian church at least three times a month. And they like us to go to a spirit-filled church to show that the power of Satan is stronger than the power of God. You could go there and mock them by being there and make them think that you were one of them, make a mockery of God there.

They would take children and make them get naked and . . . stand in different places [during ceremonies] to represent things. [At a house] they had children standing in the hallways. Out in the woods one time they had children lining a path going to where we were going to have the ritual. They were naked and holding candles. The children always watched and just stood there.

. . . The group here is strict; they don't allow you to paint symbols or graffiti. They keep you under control, so that's why you don't see paintings or symbols here.

I see my elderly seatmate on the Delta flight eyeing my reading; she's all white—white suit dress, white shoes, white hair, white skin. "What is it you're working on, young man?" she asks. She looks frail.

I give her my spiel.

"Do you mind if I read that report?" She seems genuinely interested.

I hand her the report, suddenly remembering the parts that were either too gross or semiobscene to be put into the book. "It's a bit raunchy," I say. "But it seems to be a typical account of how teenagers get into the adult satanic cults. I hope you won't be offended."

She winks behind bifocals. "I was reading *Lady Chatterly's Lover* before you were thought about," she says.

She finishes reading and I ask, "What do you think?"

"Well, as an English teacher for nearly 41 years, I'd say someone has either made this up or has doctored it considerably."

"My thoughts exactly," I say. "For instance, a kid who uses grammar like 'people was' would hardly also say 'they may have urinated' or 'my body began shaking.'"

"Or 'required us to do,'" she adds. "But there's something there. I've done some occult investigation myself; and there's something to this. Perhaps." She hands the paper back and smiles as a stewardess leans over to ask what she'd like to drink. "Jack Daniels," she says.

"What I'm being told by cops and therapists," I say after I've ordered my paltry V-8 juice, "is you can figure about 80 percent of what anybody coming from deep occult involvement says is—"

She finishes my sentence with a flourishing expletive that says it exactly. "But then there's the possibility of 20 percent," she says. "So tell me, if you can perhaps acknowledge 20 percent of all you've heard in your research, what's going on?"

I begin to ramble about what I've found, what I really think. It helps sort out this amazing stash of jotted notes and taped interviews and phonecalls and briefings, newsletters, seminar details and books I've been amassing. "You won't be bored?"

"I'll be delighted."

"Well, something's going on. I don't actually think it's a cosmic surge of world-changing proportions as do some occultists and Christian eschatologists. Not yet anyway. But basically teenagers are cycling through a satanism fad while unfortunately the rest of the culture is cycling through an occultism fad while unfortunately the real satanic cults are—for perhaps the first time in centuries—in the mood for new recruits."

I briefly sympathize for the little lady having to be a sounding board for what I've been mulling over lately. But the sympathy seems to evaporate as I fall into a different mode: I admit it, I love an audience. "Teenagers whose parents were radicals need to break away from the old folks somehow. And they can hardly make a big statement of independence to shock Ma and Pa by smoking dope since Ma and Pa have been doing that or were into it 20 years ago. And they can't state their youthful independence by brashly jumping into sexual relationships when they shouldn't because that's what the establishment does—everybody from presidential front-running candidates to famous preachers to their teachers to everybody in the movies is sexually active in illicit affairs. Now, they'll get into drugs and sex, but it's just another growing-up experience like learning to ride a bike. Doesn't carry much of a statement to the world that 'Here I am and I am a unique individual apart from my parent!'"

"So they've got to do something unusual, something their parents will peg as 'This is something I myself would never do!'" says the little old lady. "So they turn to the occult?"

"Not really the occult," I say. "The occult is anything hidden, mysterious; and most occult practices require a lot of careful study, mental discipline, time. So the teenager who's been conditioned in our quick-kicks culture, the kid who wants to make a statement of personal autonomy jumps feet first—usually through a drug experience—into the pit of satanism. Just yesterday I was talking with the wife of an occult bookstore proprietor who said that no one under the age of 30 should ever tamper with serious paranormal practices, and then that adult should proceed only after years of careful mental and psychic—I'm not sure what she meant by that exactly—but careful psychic preparation."

"I know what she meant by that," the old lady smiled.

"So whether you believe in the mystical end of the occult, whether you even believe in an entity called Satan—they do. Especially since on the teenage level satanism always seems to involve drugs and sex, they're destroying themselves—body, soul and spirit."

I'm getting depressed even summarizing what I'm feeling. "Most of this satanic stuff is just a fad and most kids won't get involved. But about 5 percent will get involved, and from figures I've been shown, about a fourth of those—with addictive personalities, with pathological tendencies—will get in way over their heads."

She laboriously pulls up her handbag from under the seat, scribbles on a business card and hands it to me. "Call Don Blythe when you get to Los Angeles again," she smiles.

"Don Blythe," I say.

"Yes," the immaculate little lady smiles. "High priest of the Brotherhood of the Ram."

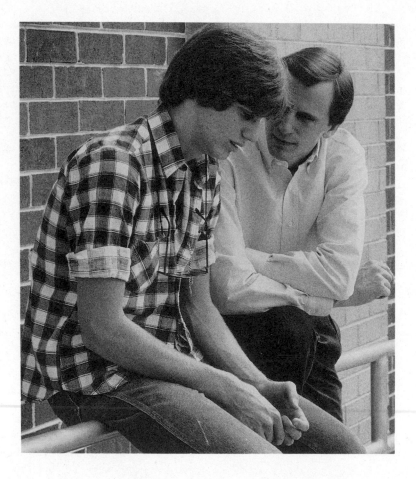

Jerry listening to one young man's cry for help.

Part Three

◀▶

Descent into Hell:
The Occult Groups

"I live in the managerial age, in a world
of 'Admin.' The greatest evil is not now
done in those sordid dens of crime that
Dickens loved to paint. It is not done
even in concentration camps. In those
we see its final result. But it is conceived
and ordered (moved, seconded, carried
and minuted) in clean, carpeted, warmed
and well-lighted offices, by quiet men
with white collars and cut fingernails and
smooth-shaved cheeks who do not need
to raise their voice. Hence, my symbol for
Hell is something normal. Very normal."
—C.S. Lewis
From the Preface to The Screwtape Letters

Accused serial killer Richard Ramirez, the "Night Stalker," display-
ing a pentagram at his arrest. The Bettman Archive.

▶ 14 ◀

Branches of the Occult

"Bhodi Tree. Best occult bookstore in Southern California," advises Dave Balsiger, one of the country's foremost occult investigators. "Occult bookstore of the stars."

Sure enough, it's in Hollywood. It's a warm September night and at ten o'clock Melrose Avenue in West Hollywood is popping with revelers from the J. Sloan Saloon ambling out into the street and couples wandering around the plaza of the Pacific Design Center. I stop to help an incredibly short Laotian jump-start his car. "Sibayadi," I say, my pronunciation probably worse than my spelling of the only Laotian phrase I know. "Bhodi Tree?" I ask him. "Bookstore?"

"Magic," he says and points down the block to a group of professorial types in heated discussion on the sidewalk. I park a block away on Melrose and walk past the huge glass-and-lights Design Center. Squarely in front of the block-size building is a funky fenced-off green shack almost buried in brush and trees; a sign on the shack reads: "Hugo's Plating. Silver—Gold—Bronze—Brass—Est. 1927." Apparently Hugo didn't sell out when the rest of the block did to the Design Center. Hollywood's got some interesting contrasts—such as the four men who looked like high school history teachers on the sidewalk outside the beige storefront arguing loudly: "Tell me I'm not suffering," one shouted. "Here I'm out of the body and Irma walks out on me!"

—Contrasts like the slickly commercial Bhodi Tree and the near-death pallor and squalid dress of the two citizens who adopted me in the section on occult black magic. Apparently I looked like a Kansas tourist who'd wandered somehow from the gardening section. "Are you looking for anything in particular?" a young man of about 20 asked. His black hair was slicked straight back; he looked emaciated, dressed in black Levis and black turtleneck t-shirt. His companion was a teenage girl from Hong

Kong also dressed in black with about two inches of black hair moussed straight up.

By now I'm good at playing the bumbling novice in these cosmic alchemies. What do I mean "playing" the bumbling novice, I think. A wild but subtle instrumental number is playing over the store stereo system and from the ceiling speakers that seem to make the insistent percussion come from everywhere at once. I find out from the clerk later it's Michael Harder's "Way of the Shaman." I ask the couple, "Look, what kinds of things can somebody get into if they want to find out about the occult? Like assume I know nothing and want to go all the way some day to tap into as much as I possibly can."

The girl is amused. The guy rolls his eyes: "All the way some day, huh? Sounds like a Republican slogan."

I've played dumb enough; they feel sorry for me and start throwing all sorts of interesting tidbits to this poor schnoock from somewhere in mid-America. "What're your names?" I ask.

"Mickey," she says.

"And yours?" I ask the guy.

"Mickey," he says.

Soon they warm up, browse through the shelves and pull out several must-reads. "Here you go," says Mickey—the girl—as she begins pulling out several must-reads.

A mustached bookworm-type young man saunters through our isolated section. "The Bhodi Tree closes in ten minutes," he says softly.

"Does Stevie Nicks really come in here?" I ask Mickey—the guy. My fresh-off-the-turnip-truck naïveté further charms them into spending the remaining ten minutes explaining and listing some of the typical occult practices anyone, they feel, can master.

"Actually—" Mickey, the guy, leans back against a shelf in a Percy Blythe Shelley pose and waves his white hands around as he talks. "Actually you can get good at divination with a well-worn-in Ouija board. Divination—that's sensing things you wouldn't normally know about a person as compared to clairvoyance which falls into the premonition or ESP category. Divination using tarot cards or the old tea leaves method or bones or animal remains. Palmistry, astrology, necromancy—contacting the dead through seances." He rattles off several other categories I missed since I wasn't running my recorder. "Using the crystal ball, all sorts of kitchen-table-variety paranormal experience such as extrasensory perception—which isn't extra at all."

The girl adds several occult practices: "If you want to include such disciplines as yoga, meditation. Anything hidden is occult, so you can include anything hidden—witchcraft, satanism, animism, psychic healing, voodoo . . . ."

The list was and is nearly endless. Entire libraries dedicated to occultic titles still don't exhaust the possibilities of the unexplained, the supernatural, the mystical. And about the time Mickey and Mickey are wearying of trying to educate me, I'm weary of keeping up with the list. Thankfully, I'm not writing a book on "The Occult."

"Well thanks for the overview," I finally say.

My occult guides ask, "So how come you're interested?" and I tell them about my work. "This is significant," says the girl.

"Yeah," says Mickey the guy. "And put it down: We're witches and we're proud. And if you want some advice for your teenagers in Saskatchewan or Coral Gables, our message is to go for it. Go for power. Give your soul to the oneness of the universe."

"You're happy, then?" I ask.

Mickey—the girl—scoffs. "Happiness has nothing to do with it. Power," she says, "is everything."

I pass a college-age guy with a shaved head who's explaining something intriguing to a long-haired young lady sitting cross-legged on the floor. I nod as if to ask if I can listen in; he nods without missing a phrase:

"Then he began speaking throughout Europe and he was an instant celebrity. They really believed he was the one. This was from about the turn of the century to 1910 or so. Whole organizations formed and raised money for his tours. Then," Kojak pauses for effect. "Then he comes to America."

"Who is this?" I interrupt.

"Jiddu Krishnamurti, the one they thought was Master Lord Maitreya."

I hate to not only be but look ignorant, so I nod as if I know all about Jiddu and Master Lord Maitreya.

"And to make the long story short since the place is closing," he says, "he bombed. Totally. America was just too Christian to open its mind to anything but hellfire and brimstone Billy Sunday preaching. Spent two years over here in Ojai just contemplating this turn of fate."

The earnest front desk clerk returns: "The Bhodi Tree is now closed. Closed."

The bald kid finishes his story which seems to strike the girl as incredibly sad; she keeps shaking her head. "Went back to Europe," he says, "and announces that he's quitting the job and disbanding his followers."

"Quitting as Lord Maitreya?" The girl stands, and I head for the door.

Outside I see Mick and Mick climb into a silver Mercedes 500 SL with an Iron Maiden sticker on one side of the back bumper, a "KNAC rock" FM sticker on the other, and an "I'd rather be marlin fishing" in the middle.

New Age History

Washington, DC. It's a bright blue fall day and the Pentagon gleams in the west as I drive off the 395 onto the Crystal City exit. Joe Carr works for the Navy, and in his JP2 building white-clad officers and frowning bureaucrats in pin-striped suits mumble with heads together as they hustle down hallways and jam the elevator. Joe is a big man, apparently big enough to take on anti-semitism and Neo-Nazis as he promotes his 1985 book *The Twisted Cross*, an exposé of the occultic, satanic background of Hitler's Third Reich.

His wife, who's a nurse with an avocation of songwriting, "won't let any more of this occult business into the house these days," Joe says as he climbs into the car and begins giving directions toward Arlington. "If it's still there, the best pizza place in the western hemisphere. It's Greek, right in the middle of a Vietnamese area."

Getting into Arlington, we stop for a second to see a patch of asphalt in front of a corner shopping center laundry. "You're sure we're in the right place?" I say. "Just, ah, what are we looking for?"

"There," Joe says.

On the parking lot asphalt is a two-foot square of new black paint.

"I think I'm impressed," I say.

"What do you see beneath the black paint? Look closely."

I squint at the patch and see, nearly obscured, a two-foot-square swastika.

"It's where George Lincoln Rockwell, the head of the American Nazi party, was gunned down by one of his own men, John Patton, with a .38 broomhandle Mauser pistol. The shopping mall tries to keep covering over the swastika Rockwell's loyalists painted on the spot; but every time they cover it up, it's repainted in a day or two."

We drive up the hill and Joe mentions that Shirley MacLaine grew up in this his old neighborhood.

"—Which reminds me," I say. "I've got two areas to ask you about. One is a 25-words-or-less sketch on Hitler and the occult—is there anything in that for us today? And the second is, I keep running into people who in passing mention the New Age movement as a sideline to what's going on in the occult today. What do you know?"

And I'm astounded over the next two hours about what this man does know. He's an electrical engineer in his top-secret career, has taught on university levels, written 50-some books, appears on talk shows and is excited about his wife Bonnie's music.

I ask Joe why he took on such a book as *The Twisted Cross*.

"I worked," he says as he waves directions to me, "for a Jewish family down in Norfolk, Virginia, when I was in college. And they were one of those families, you know one of those small businesses where you're not hired, you're adopted. The only gentile kid in the city that had his own Jewish mother. And it was such a positive experience that I came to really like those people, Frank and Dottie Weisel. A lot of their friends were holocaust survivors. So I decided when I got finished reading everything there was to know about the Civil War I would pick up the holocaust as the next study.

"It's been my habit all my life to pick a period of history and try to read all the literature on that subject. Because I do so much technical stuff, that's how I let the wind out of my head. So I read the entire Schlocken holocaust library, read every other book I could get ahold of on the holocaust. If you read the holocaust you've gotta read about Hitler, so I read every major biography of Hitler. And one theme that kept going through them is occultism.

"Every major biographer of Adolph Hitler mentioned the fact that he was an occultist. Even if it was only a passing mention of his interest in astrology. And then I started finding some of the occultic literature that dealt with Hitler such as Gerald Suster's book, *The Occult Messiah*. Another author I grew to admire is James Webb. He wrote *The Occult Underground* and *The Occult Establishment*. And both of them, if you want to understand modern occultism in the West, are the books to have. In fact, I would like to see a graduate student pick up the topic of occultism in politics, because I think occultism has had more to say about politics in the twentieth century than has hitherto been recognized.

"For example, the Adolph Hitler connection is obvious. However, an awful lot of nineteenth century western and central and eastern European politics were involving people who were ardent occultists. The Rasputin thing in Russia is an example. Most of the French hierarchy in the late nineteenth century were occultists. In fact, occultism, known as theosophy, was the primary world view in the late nineteenth century.

"There were two main world views. Christianity represented only 5 percent of the people. Only 4.7 percent of central Europeans attended church regularly at the turn of the century. And by the way, the percentage is roughly the same today. But the two main world views. First of all, you could be a rationalist, or a scientist, or a materialist. It had a lot of different names. And that's the world view that most Christians are aware of. Everybody was a Darwinian, Newtonian, the whole business. Well, it turns out that that was actually a minority viewpoint. A far greater viewpoint was the so-called theosophical viewpoint. It wasn't called that early on but the element that it congealed to turned out to be theosophy. Madame Blavatsky's theories. And they are the same theories that are at the bottom of the New Age movement today. The very same doctrine. And when I started realizing those I realized I was on to something that was worth writing about."

"Interesting," I say. "I was in an occult bookstore in Hollywood and the kid started telling me how Madame Blavatsky and her sidekick Ledbetter found Lord Maitreya and he spoke in Europe and went over like gangbusters."

"Well," Joe says, "that was later on. That was the Krishnamurti affair. It was Blavatsky's successor, Annie Basaud, who discovered Jiddu Krishnamurti in 1909. He's still alive, by the way. He's living in Ojai, California. In fact I just saw him, I met him."

"Lord Maitreya is alive and well . . ." I say.

"And living in Ojai," says Joe. "At any rate, Annie Basaud thought that she had found, she and C.W. Ledbetter, thought that they had found the Lord Maitreya in Krishnamurti. Interestingly enough, C.W. Ledbetter was a pedophile homosexual and something in the back of my head suggests that maybe the reason he saw stars over Krishnamurti's head had something to do with his sex drive rather than his spiritual insights.

"Regardless, they trained him. Now they came to Europe in 1925 or 1924, I forget exactly which, and he wowed everybody. One physicist who you'd think would be a very hard-nosed kind of fellow reportedly saw a crown of blue stars showering down from his head. He supposedly performed miracles all over Europe and encountered a tremendous following. Then he came to the United States. They docked on the S.S. *Majestic* in New York Harbor in 1925 or 1926 and he was just wiped out by what he called the spiritual atmosphere of New York Harbor.

"He was blasted his entire time in the United States. He was a great big embarrassment. So they went to Chicago to meet with a group of Theosophists. He couldn't perform any miracles there. So he went out to their Crotonas school at Ojai to recuperate and there he's pretty much remained the rest of his life. In 1929 he was supposed to go to the altar and allow Lord Maitreya to take possession of him.

"And he said, 'Nuts to this, I don't want to do it.' He threw off his robes, threw down his crown, and he told Annie Basaud to take a hike. And he has sort of given up messiahship ever since then."

"And how does that tie in with today's New Age business?" I ask.

"Well, true New-Agers are looking for the true Lord Maitreya."

"What about any New Age connections with Satan?" I ask.

"Well," Joe says, "they think Satan is an invention of the church of Christianity, and that it doesn't really exist. Their idea of Lucifer is summed up best in David Spangler's book, *Reflections on the Christ*, when he has a chapter called 'God, Christ and Lucifer.' In it he claims that Lucifer is merely the opposite pole of the same force as Christ. And that the evil imputed to Lucifer was actually man's own evil and that Lucifer is a neutral being whose forces are used for evil by evil people. They claim that Lucifer is the angel of man's evolution. And his task is to help man ascend to Godhood."

"Is there any way they think of him as an entity then?"

"Yes. They claim he came here from the planet Venus 18-1/2 million years ago."

"And he's still here?"

"Yes. To help man become a god."

"Do they only call him Lucifer?"

"Yes. You can find, well that's not quite true. There are some who call him Sanat Kamura, which is another name that they use. Of course, Sanat is easy to transpose to Satan. But at any rate, they claim that Lucifer came here

18 million years ago to help man up the evolutionary ladder from mineral to godhood."

"And so it just happened that Christians picked that name up and made up the evil being?"

"Right. The evil being. They claim that the word Satan never appears in the Bible and Lucifer only appears once."

"So much New Age stuff seems to come from Hinduism; is there a Hindu counterpart to this Lucifer who came here 18 million years ago from Venus?"

"Actually, Luciferianism is from the western tradition. You see, theosophical thinking that Hitler followed and the modern New Ager follows is actually a confluence of two things. One is Hinduism and Buddhism, the Eastern religions, but the other stream is what is known as the Western esoteric tradition. That's good old-fashioned western occultism. And I think the New Age idea of Lucifer is actually from the old gnostic ideas of two equal gods, Rex Mundi, the god of this world—the prince of this world is what they called him—and Demiurge, the other god of the spirit world. Gnosticism with a bit of the '60s flower children's influence.

"In fact, there's a direct link possible and that's what James Webb does in *The Occult Establishment* and *The Occult Underground*. You go back to the Bohemian culture in Paris and Vienna in the late nineteenth century and then you come to the New York and San Francisco Bohemian cultures of the '20s, the Beatniks of the '40s and early '50s and the hippies, they're all the same groups. If you read Jack Kerouac, after having studied New Age thought you say, hey, I've seen that stuff before. Go back and read Jack Kerouac. What do you think *The Dharma Bum's* all about? 'Dharma' is a seeker in Hindu.

"What is the New Age movement? It's an attempt to Hinduize the West. There's nothing new in the New Age movement.

"You can make a direct link to about all those Middle Eastern, those central Asian religions that grew out of Babylon. The mystery schools of the Hellenic world, the gnostics that arose and contended with the Catholic church, the alchemy of the Middle Ages which was nothing but the old gnosticism, the literature that grew out of the minstrel tradition was actually gnostic. Most of those traveling troubadours that sang those songs and did those epic poems in the medieval period were actually cathar bishops, were gnostic bishops, usually of episcopal rank, as one commentator put it. Then you get into freemasonry and Rosicrucianism. You can trace it on up, every 75 or 100 years, every century has its occultism. The question is, is this current occult movement a bigger manifestation than before or is it just scaled to our own ability to communicate? Maybe it's really the same old thing and of no particular harm except for the people who are in it."

We sit in the fire lane talking until I'm embarrassed to have kept Joe from his work so long. And the delivery trucks are piling up behind us.

"Thanks," I say. "And did anybody ever tell you you know too much for your own good?"

"My fourth grade teacher always said that," Joe climbs out of the car. "And so does my wife."

Suicide and Spirit Guides

Stopping for gas, I pull out the materials I've run across on the New Age link to occultism. A couple giveaway magazines I'd scrounged in L.A. look interesting, so I take them along to get a haircut around the corner at a mall at wherever I am in the District of Columbia.

The Afghan lady cutting my hair chatters politely about her aunt in a television production position in Afghanistan and would I greet her if I'm ever there? I say I certainly will next time I'm in Kabul in my next life.

"Do you believe in reincarnation?" she asks.

"No, it was just a joke, see. American humor?" —Which reminds me to haul out my New Age stuff—or Aquarian Conspiracy or New Consciousness, New Orientalism, Cosmic Humanism, Cosmic Consciousness, Mystical Humanism, Human Potential Movement, Mystical Health Movement or any number of other names the phenomenon goes by.

Two things bother me about New Age emphases and teenagers' interest in the occult. One is the reincarnation angle. Again, I worry about teenagers who aren't coping in this life being taught that after death comes a whole new chance at another life when you'll be different, better. The New Age Movement's mishmash of beliefs doesn't, of course, borrow from purely traditional Hinduism which preaches that a person may be reincarnated as a wooly worm or possum, depending on his karma. So teenagers hearing New Age doctrine may come to firmly believe that death is only a momentary doorway through which lies another try at life on a higher plane. Some New Age teachers even emphasize, as Linda Deer Domnitz does in an *L.A. Resources* article, that "there is no death." Such a view invariably cheapens life and makes "Should I end it all?" an easier question. So do me a favor; don't go New Age witchhunting, but keep an eye on the potential powderkeg of New Age teachings and teenage suicide.

The other thing that nags at me about the New Age Movement is its friendly teachings on communing through altered states of consciousness with your higher self, with the "God Force," with the ascended masters, with spirit animals—with spirit guides.

The altered state of consciousness—whether drug-, ritual- or meditation-induced, is a mentally vulnerable plane on which to be meeting spiritual entities, garnering the wisdom of the ages, traveling astrally or making significant decisions about life. And yet that seems to be the crux of the New Age experience.

In the September, 1988 *L.A. Resources*, for instance, I read through Lee Coit's article on "Inner Listening (Guidance) Made Simple": "About twelve years ago I became aware of a presence in my life. It took the form of an inner guide or teacher and was the second voice of a two-part dialogue going on in my head. As I have been willing to listen to this second voice and learn to recognize its presence, it has become more and more a dear friend and companion. A source of both inspiration and information, I rely now on it for all my decisions."

Coit tells how to contact an inner spirit in three easy steps:

The first step is to get past our upset and concern. . . . The second step is opening to all sources of inspirational support, contact a source beyond your own judgment and dedicate your efforts to that goal, the more clearly you will hear. Our inner guide ("second voice") is not pushy like our "first voice." It will not intrude or try to change you against your desires. Since your inner guide sees nothing out of place and you as unlimited and perfect, his voice is quiet, calm and supportive. He has no need to shout since he knows all is well.

I wonder at the personal pronouns in the article. Coit talks of the inner guide as an "it" for most of the piece, then here switches to "he." Up until now, everything he's said could be construed to mean an inner guide is simply your own intuitive thinking. Then I notice a footnote to this switch from "it" to "he": "The reference to my inner guide," writes Coit, "using the male pronoun is strictly for convenience. I do not experience my guide as sexual." But it bothers me how similar Coit's description of these inner voices is to the descriptions I've been hearing of satanists and dabblers describing their alleged personal demons.

The article goes on to answer a subtitled question: "How Do We Tell When It Is Working?" Coit begins to answer with method number one: "We will have a warm glow." I flip to other pages in the magazine.

There are ads for trance channeling ("Kevin Ryerson, Trance Channel, Expert Intuitive. Personal Consultations $250"), for locating roommates by Numbers and Stars. I see another article, "Tuning in to Your Inner Voice," I'll come back to after flipping through the August/September 1988 *Conscious Connection* freebie magazine I picked up. The ads have a little more pizzazz: "How to Supercharge Your Brain and Meditate Like a Zen Monk in 28 Minutes! Astounding sound technology induces altered mind state, intensifies psychic functioning, and causes peak experiences. Some are calling it the 'lazy path' to enlightenment! It meditates you—no mantras, no hypnosis, no concentration!"

As far as I can tell from the ad, this cosmic Zygon product is basically a cassette tape—all for $55.94. The Connection advertises local seminars for $18–$325; you can have a Crystal Dreamtime weekend, a shamanic initiation with author and teacher Lynn Andrews. You can attend a 13-week Psychic Development Class with Rev. Anita Profumo for $130. You can order The Crystal Oracle "do-it-yourself fortune-telling kit" for just $24.95. Or get Astral Octave Tuning Forks for $27.50 each. You get the idea.

Other offers in the Conscious Connection deal with getting help from the experts to contact spirit guides. Bill Pinckard, hypnotherapist, advertises, "Meet Your Spirit Guides." Omega Seminars founder Matt Schoener promises to do this to you during application of "The Complete Shakti System": "During the attunement process, which is a short ceremony, the OMEGA teacher, assisted by a Deva and OMEGA Masters on other planes, anchors within you high cosmic frequencies."

Alexandria, Psychic Master, advertises as a "Clairaudient Channel— Telepathic communication with your higher self, your personal spirit guides, and 2000 other spirit guides called the Hierarchy."

Sean Michael, medium, suggests: "Listen to ARONK speak, and a number of spirit energies in an intimate atmosphere."

Trance Channel Taryn Krive's ad: "Through Taryn, a number of Spirit Guides bring forth their teachings and messages. They will answer your questions regarding this life and other lives. Spirit Guides and your Higher Self, fulfill your life plan and advance to your next level of development . . . . Learn to communicate with your Spirit Guides, Master Teachers and Higher Self."

A particularly interesting article by Magzcha Westeman discusses "Spiritual Healing" on page 18. The piece describes psychic surgery going on at the Spiritualist Center in Los Angeles.

"The theory holds," writes Westeman, "that highly-evolved spirit intelligences, with medical expertise and a desire to alleviate suffering, work through certain individuals to perform healing and provide information otherwise unknown. This healing is of 'divine origin,' coming from God but carried out by 'His intermediaries'—those who once lived on earth, but are now on the highest levels of spirit; who continue to do medical research while in spirit." The discussion reminds me of the book, *The Beautiful Side of Evil*, by Johanna Michaelson.

Johanna, with a background of occult abilities and interest, established her connection with her spirit guides through a Silva Mind Control program in Mexico. She subsequently used her psychic abilities to assist Panchita, a spirit healer who performed miraculous psychic surgeries with a rusty knife. One of Johanna's spirit guides was Jesus Christ, whose psychic image in the "laboratory" of her mind sporadically switched from a loving Christ figure to a bloodied monster. Yes, it's just one more bizarre story, but one that's well worth reading—particularly for its insider-style narrative on the topic of spirit healing and spirit guides.

How can the curious contact their own spirit guides? That Linda Deer Domnitz article, "Tuning in to Your Inner Voice," tells how:

> Now let us look at how to contact a guide in a meditative state . . . . This can be done with the aid of a commercial spirit guide tape, a self-made tape or under the direction of a channel or therapist. Once the initial connection and rapport are established, you can continue doing this with practice.
>
> Through the visual channels, guides may be experienced as pulsating or swirling light, color, or energy, as well as having a definite structure, shape or form. The voice of the guide may be heard through auditory channels. A pressure or pulsation may be experienced . . . .
>
> After making the connection and feeling rapport with the guide, it is important to ask for their name.

I pull from the middle of the magazine a couple of references I'd stuffed in there from previous reading. From *Love, Medicine and Miracles* published in 1986 by Harper & Row, Doctor Bernie Siegel on page 19 shares how he met his spirit guide at a visualization seminar:

> I approached this exercise with all the skepticism one expects from a mechanistic doctor. Still, I sat down, closed my eyes, and followed directions.
>
> I didn't believe it would work, but if it did I expected to see Jesus or Moses. Who else would dare appear inside a surgeon's head?
>
> Instead I met George, a bearded, long-haired young man wearing an immaculate flowing white gown and a skullcap. It was an incredible awakening for me, because I hadn't expected anything to happen.

Occultism and the New Age

Is there a New Age link to the occult? If there is, it's in this particular area of the New Age emphasis on open-minded, altered states of consciousness and the expectation of meeting spiritual entities.

Do teenagers gravitate toward these teachings? Frankly, I haven't met enough avowed New Age kids to tell since the movement is so firmly rooted in the Baby Boomer-30-40-ish age groups. In the Huntington Beach Church of Religious Science worship service I attended a few weeks ago, however, the youth group of well over a hundred seemed genuinely delighted to be part of a church teaching reincarnation and altered states of consciousness.

I amble back to the car and head north out of Washington toward Baltimore. A radio spot comes on announcing a "Be All You Can Be" seminar offered this weekend in DC; it reminds me of the "Course in Miracles" seminars offered by New Age groups around the country. Needless to say, most popular are actress Shirley MacLaine's seminars stemming from her *Out on a Limb* book and TV miniseries. After her ABC special, the actress went on a ten-city seminar tour with a $300 fee for each participant—"$100 for mind, $100 for body, and $100 for spirit," MacLaine was heard to quip.

A week later I'm in Oklahoma chatting from a phonebooth beside a Stuckey's: "Ms. Bridgeman?" I yell over the roar of refrigerated trucks parked next to the store.

"Yes, it is." Her voice is frail.

I explain the book project and ask her about a rumor I heard. "Was it the same voice?"

"Yes, it was. I'd know the voice; just as you'd know your father's voice or the voice of a close friend. I remember all those years so clearly. It was during the depression and my family I think survived on the money that came from our seances."

"Were there any particular incidents you remember?" I ask.

"Oh, my, yes. There were several incidents such as when I lay beside my dying grandmother. The house was dark and all we had for lights were globes and gas jets. And while I was lying there next to her deathbed the gas light was lit without anyone turning on the gas or striking a match."

"But what about the voice in the seances?" I ask.

"Yes, when my family had seances in the '30s, my grandmother seemed to mostly contact one particular spirit. The trumpet would float up around the ceiling and people would ask questions around the table. We held seances right up until my brothers left for the service in World War Two. My father did defense work. But I remember the days of the spirits, I'll tell you."

It's a dusty, windy day on Interstate 40, the major highway that cuts across the middle of the state; the phone keeps crackling, obscuring some of the elderly lady's comments. Dust devils reel across the highway. "And then when you were watching Shirley MacLaine's special?" I prompt.

"Yes," she says. "I had wanted to watch Shirley MacLaine with that 'Out on a Limb' special since I'd heard so much about the new rash of spirit guide interest. Well, you know what happened. I was watching the show and on it the medium Shirley was consulting went into a trance for the camera. And when he spoke I nearly fell out of my chair!"

"And why was that?"

"The same voice. The spirit's voice. It was the same voice as I heard during our seances 50 years ago. Just like anyone's voice you'd know—I knew that voice! I couldn't believe it and was still amazed the next day when a dear friend of mine said she'd seen the actor who had played the medium on that series. But he wasn't an actor; he actually was a medium."

"So what is it you think about this, then, Ms. Bridgeman?"

"Well, that the spirit my grandmother contacted in our seances who I since have found was a demon was the same spirit that spoke through the medium on Shirley MacLaine's TV special."

I try to think of some better response than "That's interesting"—which is what usually comes to my lips after I've heard a bizarre story. I can't think of anything else. "That's interesting," I say.

"How kind of you to say so," says Marie Bridgeman. She would like to chat further.

But I've got a date to meet a witch.

▶ *15* ◀

The Wiccan Witch

The little town of Tahlequah is capital of the Cherokee Indian nation, crouched in the oaks, elms and loblolly pine forests of what the Oklahoma Tourist Board calls Green Country. Just northeast of Tenkiller Lake I cruise the main street in early evening; the sun is red in Oklahoma haze. I pull into the Calico Cafe as I wait to meet a witch.

Neo-pagan/Wiccan Witchcraft

She's wearing Levis and a yellow cowboy shirt, carrying a bookpack like a college student. Her hair is black, cut in a page-boy. In her mid-twenties, she clumps into the Calico on rattlesnake skin Tony Lama boots. "I'm Heather," she says.

She's obviously nervous.

I flip open my stubby yellow notepad to the list of questions I wanted to ask a witch—a real witch. "You wouldn't consider yourself a dabbler?"

"We go back generations," she says. "Centuries. Here. I brought some things you might be interested in. This coloring book is something Sasha just loves."

Sasha is Heather's four-year-old daughter who lives with her in a house along a side street in Tahlequah. Sasha's father, according to Heather, is an alcoholic and has been prohibited by the courts from visiting.

"Sasha isn't really a witch yet," Heather says. "Of course, anyone who wants to call herself or himself a witch simply can; and Sasha does. But basically she's just a sweet little girl who's being raised as new pagan. You'll find most witches don't call themselves witches because of the religious prejudice and superstition. Most call themselves pagans."

Heather explains the basics of neopaganism, wiccan and traditional

144

witchcraft—The Craft. First she reads some selections from Margot Adler's *Drawing Down the Moon.*

Generally, she explains, witchcraft falls into categories of wiccan and satanist. Wiccan, from the Old English "wiccian" then divides into Gardnerian, after the famous English occultist Gerald Gardner, and traditionalists. "Gardnerians are generally wilder," she says. "I'm more of a traditionalist myself," says Heather. "Although you can't really group witchcraft into categories since there are thousands of traditions and thousands of interpretations of those traditions."

Most modern witches are young women, many of them feminists, who are mostly concerned with taking care of mother earth. Many wiccans feel their religion is the spiritual element of the ecology movement. Novice witches come from every level of society, from every religious tradition.

Wiccans believe that the world is currently under the rule of the "Sky Father," although the earth once enjoyed a time when disciples of the earth mother, the goddess, predominated. Under the goddess' rule, the world was filled with peace and harmony; compassion was valued more than power and intuitional energy wasn't squelched by institutionalism.

"The pop witch these days is probably Laurie Cabot," says Heather. "She's the official witch of Salem in Massachusetts who's organizing the Witches' League for Public Awareness and legal defense funds to help witches fight religious discrimination. But there's no actual organization at all. There is a group in Idaho Springs trying to build a temple to the goddess. If that happens, it will be a rallying point."

"Idaho Springs?"

"Yeah, in Colorado." She explains that wiccans don't really want to organize, although there are more national groups loosely forming lately such as the Witches Anti-Defamation League and the Pagan Action Alert Network.

Witches just want their common bond to remain a basic neopagan devotion to their religion of nature. The cycles of nature orchestrate practitioners' ritual schedule, and they feel that the energies of the earth, wind, air and fire are programmed by the season and the moods of nature.

Like Hinduism, Wicca is polytheistic, accepting all the "gods," teaching that being devoted to just one god is contrary to the powers obvious in nature. Tapping into those gods' powers through ritual is the key to solving both personal and the global problems.

Basic Witchcraft

Basic beliefs? "And ye harm none, do as ye will," she says. "We believe that what you do comes back to you multiplied—which stops wiccan witches from playing too deeply in curses and negative magic. Let's see," Heather taps the side of her nose and reminds me of the old Elizabeth Montgomery figure in

TV's "Bewitched" series. "If you're willing to pay the price, you can get anything. And respect all of nature; attune to all of nature. That's about it as beliefs. Oh, some believe in reincarnation, some don't. There's no creed, no hierarchy to take orders from. There really aren't any special powers—it's just understanding and using the powers that are already in nature. There's no black or white witch; it just depends on how you use nature's power. You can worship Diana or Isis or Mother Nature or make up your own."

"How about rituals or spells with steaming potions?" I ask.

She laughs. "Potions, yes. We mix herbs for certain ceremonies. And we chant certain phrases—poetry, actually. Wiccan witches lay on hands for healing, pray for world peace, share rituals with others for problem-solving, and celebrate the earth mother goddess' blessings in ceremonies of joy," Heather says.

She shuffles through her stack of books and begins reading selections on the occult views of psychologist C. G. Jung, who stated that the many archetypal memories in the unconscious mind of individuals are actually a mass human consciousness. And that mass human consciousness, suggests Heather, is not only the source of all our potential powers. It's also the inner voice that monitors whether we're acting, thinking and believing in accordance with all the forces of nature or whether we're violating those forces.

She closes the Jungian booklet and tells me that most wicca groups are loosely organized into circles of nine to 13—small groups that resemble modern support groups more than some spooky version of a religious church. Some people only call satanic groups "covens," and Heather is one. She refers to groups of witches as "circles." Much of what happens is a combination of group rituals and instruction of younger members by specially designated practitioners. In many areas the circles or covens are affiliated in "groves." Groves often join in regional conferences and festivals which sometimes include actual "competitions" in magical prowess.

"Do you believe in the devil?" I ask.

"Of course not. Satan is just Christianity's scapegoat for irresponsibility and guilt."

"But I've read that most of witchcraft's basic belief—Wiccan or otherwise—is based on Aleister Crowley's work. Have you any of his books?"

"Well," she says. "Yes, I do, as a matter of fact. But just because he was loony toward the end of his life doesn't mean his earlier writings weren't inspired. And you don't have to go along with any of the dark side of his work anyway. He just had some interesting insights. Like in any pursuit, you take the good and ignore the bad. He simply believed in a being called Satan just as Christian preachers do. Yet I don't have to believe everything they do to glean some good insights from Crowley or preachers or you, for that matter." Her real hero, she tells me, is Victor Anderson of "the faerie tradition."

By now it's completely dark outside the little Calico Cafe. "So thanks so much for your time," I conclude.

"More to come," she says and stands. "I wanted to show you a place just up in the hills near here where you might see some of what we've talked about."

Outside it's dark and mostly overcast. Heather strides across the little gravel parking lot to a '66 Mustang with a huge, grizzly-faced man sitting in the passenger seat. "I didn't want to come alone, so I brought Uncle Throe along."

I lean over and grin with what I hope is a bit of an Oklahoma drawl, "Good ta meet ya, Uncle Throe."

He fills the passenger side of the car with his blue denim overalls. He waves and says, "T-H-R-O-E. Make sure you spell it right, fella."

Dance of the Faeries

I follow the taillights of her old Mustang out onto the main drag, past the Wal-Mart, up the hill from the tree-covered campus of Northeastern State University where Heather said she takes dance classes, east on Highway 62 to a turnoff about four miles out of town.

It's a dead-silent dirt road, and the trees arch over it like sides of a tunnel. It's dark. And in spite of the benign demeanor of witch Heather and her country uncle, I'm feeling a little spooked; who knows where I am right now? God, I think. And maybe Satan. I don't want to think about it. I follow the taillights.

Without wanting to, I start mulling over all the macabre things I've heard and read and dug into in the last weeks. I picture little Michelle Smith from my reading of her and Lawrence Padzer's *Michelle Remembers*: She's being groomed to be a special treat for Satan at the 1955 Feast of the Beast in Victoria, Vancouver. As a preschooler she's led into a room, strapped down on a table and a doctor-type sews ears and a tail on her in preparation for a ritual. She's abandoned by her mother, taken charge of by a demonic woman who dresses like a nurse. She's kept in a cage and let out for grisly rituals and brain-warping sessions such as—hypnotically or actually—she's strapped to a stretcher, forced to watch the construction of a body as satanists sew together different limbs from different bodies. Then they attach electrodes to the monster and with electric shocks make it flop around as if alive. Then they attach the electrodes to her.

I don't want to think about it. Or about the videotape of a woman being exorcised, or, as clinicians now term the process, dispossessed of a demon. She is dispossessed of several demons who speak in booming male voices, twist her face into demonic grins, thrash her around on the floor as if she's paper maché.

I don't want to think about Dr. Rebecca Brown's accounts of counseling a family who had left a satanic cult and who were consequently dragged back as victims in a ritual. The parents allegedly were tied down and forced to watch as one of their daughters was skinned alive.

I don't want to think about the two counselors I uncovered who are alleged satanists and who in different cities are treating teenagers who've come out of a satanic-abuse background. Or the prominent religious leaders —one an administrator and one a priest—who again in different cities were identified as ritual abusers of children and recruiters of teenagers. Or the California satanist who's a psychiatrist. Or the two camps identified as satanic playgrounds in different sections of the country. And I don't want to think of Lynn, the woman who calls Tricia in Kansas City regularly with horrifying tales of being, like Cassandra Hoyer in Richmond, beaten and raped and terrorized to rejoin a satanic cult in the South.

I don't want to think about how frustrating it is to beat this hydra with its many and elusive heads. I don't want to think about the ire I may have stirred up by nosing around. I don't want to believe it. Any of it. Especially right now.

We pull into a sort of logging road just past a decaying barn and Heather and Throe shut off their lights. She comes back to my window. "This is it. Aren't you going to get out?"

I feel the old I'm-no-chicken feeling that's probably got more people than you could shake a wand at involved in eerie situations they'd just as soon avoid. "Sure," I say, and shut off the car and headlights. It's pitch black.

Throe stays in the Mustang and Heather leads me by the sound of her voice down a path toward what sounds like a stream. She sits on a rock at the edge of what she says is Fall Creek and tells me to find a comfortable rock.

"Now just relax. I know you're nervous; I can see it in your aura. Just relax and listen."

I look around for my aura and try to relax. Above the circle of black trees and brush, the sky is lightening up and there are a few stars blinking through the clouds. I forget to listen.

"Listen," she says again.

I hear nothing.

"Look there," I can see her yellow shirtsleeve pointing upstream.

I see nothing.

"You don't see them, do you?"

I swallow. "Who?"

"Relax. Look."

I look upstream into black blackness. I close my eyes to see if it makes any difference. I think about what I'm seeing with my eyes closed and realize I see little specks of light and patterns—the harder I squeeze my eyelids closed, the more specks and patterns I see. Then I realize I'm playing third grade and open my eyes. I look upstream and see little specks of light and patterns.

"They're my friends," Heather says.

"Do you have many others?"

"Sprites you mean? Faeries?"

"No, I mean other friends."

She pauses and says, "No."

"Are you a happy witch?"

"Oh yes," she says too quickly.

"Are you ever a sad witch?"

"Most of the time," she says.

"How about a mad witch?"

"They're gone," she gestures upstream. "I knew there'd be the negative questions. No, I do not practice black or even gray art. That's always the insinuation, isn't it? That these kind witches only claim to be good and they can conjure up hell anytime they want to? I and every witch I've ever known has never played with black magic."

"Ever?" I ask.

"Never. Now tossing a curse or two is certainly within my powers. Like once I was going with this guy. Not really going. We'd dated a few times and one night I walked in on him in bed with some floozy. So I grabbed a woman's hairbrush on the table and ran out."

"Why the hairbrush?"

"That way I got some of her hair and dug out some little used incantations," Heather says.

"You cast a spell on her. Did it work?"

"It was a hefty curse, too. I don't know. I never found out who she was, not from around here. So I couldn't find out if it worked."

My rock is getting uncomfortable. "What was supposed to happen to her?"

"Her hair would fall out."

Heather wants to stay at the creek—"My friends will come back after you leave. So 'blessed be,' Jerry Johnston," she says in wiccan/neopagan blessing.

I say good night, stumble up the path to the cars, say good night to Uncle Throe and head back out to Highway 62.

Driving through the Oklahoma hills of Cherokee country, I'm reminded of the many animistic traditions of native Americans, wondering how many youth in those ethnic groups are buying back into the historical spirit-worship of their ancestors.

I remember reading about a recording done by anthropologist Richard Preston in Rupert House, Quebec. During a two-hour "shaking tent" ritual recorded by Preston, the shaman conjured up eight "mistabeo" or spirits that spoke in different voices. It took place at night inside a tent. Cigarettes were passed into the tent and bystanders later told the anthropologist they had seen their glow above the tent as the spirits smoked the offering of cigarettes. The article had stated that every Eastern Cree in Canada believes he has an attending mistabeo.

I wonder how many strange religions, variations of voodoo or spirit worship we could research. Too many. Let's look at the basic roots of the group we're basically interested in: the satanists.

The Victorian Vortex

Victoria. I flew into the Esquimalt airport and have spent most of the summer day strolling around the inner harbor—that's "harbour"—area. The granite balustrades sprout white, ornate iron lampposts with hanging planters of blazing red and purple fuchia, topped with old fashioned globes. The Parliament Buildings reflect sunlight from windows, from the rows of lights lining the edges of each building, from the gleaming statue of Vancouver on top of the dome. The harbor itself is bustling on this beautiful afternoon, deep blue sky splotched with clouds that look like foam.

Victoria on Vancouver Island, British Columbia, is one of the major centers for religion, witchcraft and the occult in the world. Every major religion in the world is represented; for instance, Saltspring Island has one of the largest Buddhist monasteries in the western hemisphere. The island has the highest percentage of Transcendental Meditation practitioners per capita of any place in the world. Every cult you can imagine has a representative office or headquarters here.

Tarot card reading and table-strolling fortune-telling of all sorts is expected in Victorian restaurants. Major tourist attractions such as the Crystal Garden routinely offer seminars in ESP. The native Indian population is particularly dedicated to traditional spirit worship and spirit dancing. The northern end of Vancouver Island was one of the major New Age sites of prayer during the much-touted "Harmonic Convergence" of 1987. Victoria is, like Sedona down near Flagstaff, Arizona, a major "energy vortex" to mystics. Victoria was the site of the 1955 Feast of the Beast ritual recounted in Michelle Smith and Lawrence Padzer's *Michelle Remembers*.

I'm wishing I had some time to nose around and make some contacts, but I have just a few hours before the ferry steams off from Swartz Bay over to Vancouver where I'm to speak tonight. But I decide I've got some study time; I wander into the Library wing of the Parliament Building—colorful mosaic tiled floors, Southwell murals, marble-finished walls—and plop my bookbag and bulging notebooks on a huge wooden study table in a room off the main Legislative Library. The room is paneled in mahogany decorated with elaborate carvings. It's a good spot to ruminate through a lightweight history of satanism and an overview of the groups who worship a god that most of us would rather think of as a cartoon character with red pajamas and a pitchfork.

The history of the black end of the occult fills volumes. So this is definitely not the tome in which we can concentrate in detail on the origins of satanism as an historical phenomenon. But at least a quick overview suggests that a history of satanism is defined by your version of just who Satan is.

Satan and Christianity

One version of who Satan is comes from traditional Christian beliefs. He is a created angel. As the "lightbearer" Lucifer, he was perhaps the highest angel. He rebelled against God and was tossed out of heaven before the creation of man. A third of the angels in heaven had rebelled with him and, banished to the earth, now form his demonic mafia.

In this view, then, satanism has existed since prehistory. It is a belief system that incorporates:

1) continuing demonic rebellion against God and anything godly,
2) man as an expendable pawn in that spiritual battle,
3) denial that the death and resurrection of Christ—God in a body—foiled the satanic plan to spite God by dragging mankind into the Hell prepared for Satan and his angels, and
4) the ultimate banishment of Satan to what he chose—a place or dimension completely removed from anything having to do with God.

According to this traditional Christian version, then, satanism has existed throughout history in various forms of religion—for example the Babylonian worship of Nimrod and the Queen Mother of Heaven, or the Canaanite Moloch or Baal religion which involved child sacrifice and sexual ritual.

Modern satanism is seen as simply an extension of the age-old Garden of Eden insinuation that God is not to be obeyed, that the forbidden fruit is fair game if you've got the nerve. Further, when He is not obeyed, the result will be physical pleasure (the fruit was "good for food" and a "delight to the eyes" according to Genesis 3:6), wisdom ("your eyes will be opened" and "the tree was desirable to make one wise," verses 5–6), and divinity ("you will be like God," verse 5).

Of course, if this is the scenario, then Satan must be deceptive. He's got to lie about his origin as just another angel, about his promises of pleasure, wisdom and divinity since they lead to eternal death, and about his plans for man.

So Satan is an actual spirit being, he rules a horde of demonic spirit entities, and he offers pleasure and power to those bound to him. But he's bound for Hell. Perhaps this overview explains why those taking their perspective on satanism from traditional Christianity are more concerned about the deceptive, mystical dangers of satanic worship.

Other pseudobiblical views of who Satan is define other histories of satanism. For instance, the Bulgarian Bogomile sect which originated in the tenth century held that Satan and Jesus were both created as brothers. The antagonism of the two didn't begin, then, until Jesus was chosen over Satan to save mankind. Satanism's goal is therefore to wreak revenge on Jesus and His followers.

The Jewish Kabbala, a mystic philosophy incorporating legend, numerology and the stories of apocryphal literature, simply sees the devil as the enemy of Yaweh. Most orthodox Judaism relegates the existence of a personal devil to this mystical tradition and the influence of Christianity rather than to actual revelation from God.

Satan as Symbol

Still others hold that Satan is not a being at all but is a personification, a symbol of the evil in the world. This rational view, obviously popular since the era of The Enlightenment in Europe and North America, is espoused today by most occultists, wiccan witches, and anyone who denies the existence of a spiritual dimension.

If Satan is not an actual being, satanism is therefore simply a mindset.

For example, Dr. Herbert Modlin, forensic psychiatrist at the Menninger Foundation in Topeka, Kansas, says that "we can't ignore the fact that there is evil in the world. The devil makes these diffuse and hard-to-grasp feelings more manageable." Symbolically, the devil personifies the id, the darker drives of human nature. And therefore, Modlin says in the *New York Newsday* of December 1, 1987, satanism "legitimizes sin. It gives people license to do things they would not ordinarily do."

The *Newsday* article by Jamie Talan goes on to suggest that "this may explain why people, many of whom are confused adolescents, dabble in black magic and devil worship." Talan quotes Dr. David Halperin, assistant clinical professor of psychiatry at Mount Sinai School of Medicine in New York: "Devil worship focuses on spells, incantations and magical symbols. It gives people the feeling of power over others. [Also] these people are angry at a society that made them feel powerless. What better way to lash out than through the devil, the ultimate evil?"

Many satanists come from dysfunctional families, where they were given no distinct sense of right and wrong, where they had no control over their treatment which often swung from doting kindness to horrific abuse. The devil, then, becomes a character that incorporates the amorality and fear the child grew up in—he's the "god of this world" so that's the way the world is. And that same devil endows the power to survive in such a world—power over circumstances and over other people.

How does this view of who Satan is define a history of satanism? If Satan is a symbolic characterization of evil, he therefore will appear and be worshiped in periods of pronounced, perceived evil. In this view, then, the history of a culture's unrest is the history of satanism—regardless of Satan's namesake in the culture.

An August 30, 1982, *Newsweek* article on page 72, "Giving the Devil His Due," suggests that the devil's return to "haunt our cultural and social psyche is not hard to explain. In times of great social unrest and political instability, observes Northwestern University historian Josef Barton, the individual's feelings of impotence tend to elicit a sense of overwhelming evil at work. 'The devil is an ancient way to symbolize the existence of such evil and people are groping about for that suppressed image.'"

That suppressed image is, according to historians such as Barton, a myth drawn from several ancient sources such as Kabbalic traditions or the myths of the Persian god Ahriman. The ancient Persians worshiped this Prince of Darkness who was the equal and opposite of the good god Ohrmazd. Modern Kurdish Yezidis still worship these opposites, appeasing the dark god Shaitan with sacrifices at the Temple of the Black Serpent at Sheikh Adi in Iraq and petitioning the god of order and light.

The Gnostic Satan

Belief in equal and opposite gods is, of course, based in Eastern mysticism. For example, Shiva, the destroyer, has for millennia been worshiped equally with Brahma and Vishnu in India.

This belief in dualistic deities was and is the basis of another history of satanism. Gnosticism, from the Greek word for "knowledge," was a philosophy combining basic Christian elements with a dualistic worldview. The Gnostics believed God was good, but the created world was evil and under the domination of Satan, an eternal force of evil. Much of the scholarship of early Christian church fathers was devoted to refuting the heresies of Gnosticism; yet the philosophy grew throughout the Dark Ages as a viable explanation for the rampant evil in the world.

Gnostic traditions formed the base of the beliefs of Europe's Cathars, an influential sect that flourished from the eleventh to the fourteenth centuries. The Cathars were perhaps the first group to actively worship Satan. Cathar traditions include belief in the equality of Satan and God, encouragement to choose Lucifer or Satan as the god to be worshiped, and the development of satanic ritual from the reverse of Christian liturgy.

As early as 1022 an organized sect of satanists was discovered in Orleans and burned at the stake. In the thirteenth century a satanist movement called the Stedingers rose in the northwest of Europe. Pope Gregory said of them: "The Stedingers, seduced by Satan, have abjured all laws, human and divine; they have derided the church, insulted and horribly profaned the sacraments; consulted with witches to raise evil spirits; shed innocent blood like water; burned and plundered and destroyed; they are in fine enemies to all good, having concocted an infernal scheme to propagate the cult of the Devil, whom they adore at their secret sabbats," as quoted on page 106 in Frederick Tatford's book *Satan: The Prince of Darkness.*

In the Middle Ages, the Order of the Knights Templar, a group of knights originally formed to protect the properties of the Roman Catholic Church, was rumored to worship Satan in their secret society gatherings. Based on traditions called "The Ancient Wisdom" or "The Ageless Wisdom," the Templars' rites and beliefs influenced several secret occult societies throughout Europe up through the eighteenth century. The Luciferians, one of these groups, became popular throughout Switzerland, Italy and France.

The Luciferian philosophy suggests that Satan has been given a bum rap by Christianity, that Satan isn't actually evil. For example, the late-nineteenth-century Theosophist leader Helena Blavatsky says in her entry under "Lucifer" in *The Theosophical Glossary*: "Lucifer (Latin). The planet Venus, as the bright Morning Star. Before Milton, Lucifer had never been a name of the Devil. Quite the reverse, since the Christian Savior is made to say of himself in Revelations [sic] 16:22 'I am the bright morning star' or Lucifer. One of the early Popes of Rome bore that name; and there was even a Christian sect in the fourth century which was called the Luciferians."

This Luciferian philosophy is espoused today by New Age shamans such as David Spangler. On page 41 of his *Reflections on the Christ*, he writes: "Lucifer, then, is neither good nor bad in his true essence. He is completely neutral."

The occult revival of the late 1800s spawned other groups who believed that Satan was indeed an equal and opposite god from Christianity's God. But to these groups, Satan was no mere neutral force; he is evil and should be worshiped as such. This slant, labeled the Palladist philosophy, is the root of today's black witchcraft and true satanism.

Palladists believe Satan will eventually overcome the Judeo-Christian God, reclaim heaven and rule forever.

The man most reknowned for promoting this version of satanism is Aleister Crowley, a name I've heard over and over by teenagers who began dabbling by reading Crowley's works. I pull out the Encyclopedia of Occultism and Parapsychology to get a bio on the satanist popularly dubbed in the early twentieth century as "the wickedest man on earth."

▶ *16* ◀

Satanism Today

Aleister Crowley was born October 12, 1875, as Edward Alexander Crowley, son of strict Plymouth Brethren parents. In his memoirs, Crowley recalls loving to shock his fundamentalist parents by detesting their dogmatic Christianity. His mother apparently called him "The Beast"; and in later years he "proudly claimed this title."

The encyclopedia reveals that young Crowley in 1898 joined the Hermetic Order of the Golden Dawn. After being expelled from the Order, Crowley published the secret rituals of the Golden Dawn and formed his own society called The Order of the Silver Star, also known as A A.

After marrying in 1903 and moving to Ceylon, Crowley found his life mission through the revelations of his spirit guide, Aiwass, who dictated the book *Liber Legis, The Book of the Law.* The book, says encyclopedia editor Leslie Shepard, proclaimed a new magical era of the world's history to be ruled by the Law of Thelema—"Do what thou wilt shall be the whole of the law."

Thereafter Crowley devoted himself to the practice of magick—the "k" added to signify occult ritual. Crowley discovered and elaborated on the techniques of ancient Tantric Yoga sex magic, establishing his Ordo Templi Orientis or OTO to preach his doctrines.

After the bizarre ritual death of his grown son, Crowley allegedly spent his last years in senility. A Black Mass commemorated his death on December 1, 1947. After cremation at Brighton, Sussex, his ashes were sent to disciples in the U.S., where especially in California, significant numbers of satanist groups follow his works and some propagate his Order of the Silver Star and OTO.

The Law of Will

Crowley's significance in the history of satan worship is seen in the influence of his writings. The satanic principles he taught in 1920 at his Abbey of Thelema—which means "will" in Greek—near Cefalu in Sicily still touch a nerve in the occult-leaning youth of the 1990s. Imagine today's disaffected teenager hearing this religion's laws:

—Do what thou wilt . . . .
—Good is evil and evil is good.
—Thou hast no right but to do thy will. Do that, and no other shall say nay.
—Man has the right to live by his own will . . . , eat what he will . . . , think what he will . . . , love as he will. Man has the right to kill those who would thwart these rights.

With these and other Crowley mandates as bylaws, with worship services designed to conjure power over circumstances and people, is it any wonder satanism is growing as a pop "religion" among North American youth?

Crowley's Palladist version of satanism grew covertly in Europe in the affluent '20s. In the '30s, Paris was a center of satanic worship, with more than 320 satanic covens known to be practicing in the city.

The Twisted Cross

As we learned talking with Joe Carr in Washington, the decades of the '20s and '30s also saw the rise of a ruthless political machine that was apparently powered at least in part by the occult and satanism: the Third Reich with its twisted cross swastika, an occult symbol from ancient times.

"Occult beliefs and practices, however weird," writes Dusty Skylar on page 2 of his book *Gods and Beasts: The Nazis and the Occult*, "played a major part in the irrational history of the Third Reich.

"Original Nazi depositions taken for the Nuremburg Trials but never included in the record, told of periodic sacrifices wherein a fine Aryan specimen of an SS man was beheaded and the severed head made a vehicle for communion with Secret Masters in the Caucasus. These beings, presumably, were not believed to be earthly, and were looked to for guidance."

In that interview with Joe Carr, I had asked, "How about Hitler? How'd he get into dabbling?"

"Hitler got his occultism probably in Vienna, although it's interesting to note that the headmaster of the place where Hitler went to secondary school was a gnostic and was excommunicated by the Church for his beliefs. So Hitler had gnostic beliefs when he moved to Vienna in 1909. And Vienna in 1909 was a theosophical city. It was just as occultic as possible."

"Joe," I had said, "I was talking with my mom a couple weeks ago about a newly released bunch of film footage as the British came into the Dachau death camps at the end of World War Two. Afterwards she had bad dreams, and as we talked about it she mentioned how incredibly demonic that had to be. Were the Nazis actually into satanism?"

Joe had said, "In 1949 a study was performed by the World Jewish Fund on the psychology of the SS men. The scary part is that these guys were not what you might call congenital criminals. They looked at their family backgrounds, they looked at their careers. The SS was an elite military unit. They had no place for misfits. A military unit like the SS has a primary requirement, discipline.

"And that primary quality is what the criminal element doesn't have and what the military unit needs the most. The horror of the SS is that they were normal people who were corrupted. Think about that for a moment. They found these people from normal Roman Catholic and Lutheran backgrounds. Their families were utterly normal.

"In fact, Himmler's—head of the SS and an avowed occultist—Himmler's family was utterly boring. His father was a respected civil servant who retired after 47 years. His mother was a matron of the church. Everything about these people was utterly normal. They had no room for the misfits. Some of them became misfits later on, but they were not misfits to start. They were simply well indoctrinated in the theosophical version of the occult.

"For example, there's a thing called the Theosophical Doctrine of Races. That was the excuse for Auschwitz. It goes something like this:

"According to the theosophical variant, mankind is evolving from mineral up through animal, vegetable up through animal, and finally there will be seven races. Northern European man is the fifth race. He will soon make the leap, the evolutionary leap, to the sixth race who Hitler and Nietzche called the Superman.

"According to Nazi doctrine, the capital crime of the Jew was to try to prevent this through blood poisoning, blood mingling, rapes and intermarriage. Furthermore, the SS salved their own conscience by claiming to themselves that, by forcing a Jew to die a violent death now, you help him work off some of his bad racial karma so that he can come back as an Aryan next time.

"Now, words like Aryan, the swastika, are all of Hindu origin. In fact, you can see temples in India today that are decorated with swastikas. Even the word, swastika, comes from salvastika which is a Sanskrit word. But basically, what Naziism was, was an attempt to Hinduize Germany with the occult."

On page 87 of *The Twisted Cross* Joe writes that it is "in the occultic connection that we find some of the most vivid evidences of the true nature of Naziism. We know that Hitler and his top luminaries were either dabblers in the occult or outright satanists. It is no wonder the Holocaust happened;

the seeds of disaster were sewn in fertile, well-tilled soil by men who were thoroughly evil."

The Modern Era

A major figure in the more modern chronicles of the black arts is the Englishman Gerald Gardner. Spokesman for the Museum of Witchcraft he established on the Isle of Man in 1936, Gardner became probably the most famous advocate for witchcraft in Europe. After the repeal of the British fortune-telling law in 1951, which effectively legalized witchcraft, Gardner published his *Witchcraft Today*, a textbook still carefully studied by aspiring witches.

Gardner's teachings maintained a religious respectability for The Craft, and he was and is usually associated with "white" forms of witchcraft. However, his own rites and off-the-record discipleship apparently featured the more satanic aspects of black witchcraft with ceremonies involving sado-masochism, sex, magic and drugs.

Like Gardner and Crowley before him, the next figure in modern satanism popularized satanism with shock theatrics. Pop religious satanism was the 1960s brainchild of Anton LaVey.

The Religious Satanists

The groups we're calling the religious satanists are the ones that have gone public—which makes them a bit suspect as true satanic devotees. The well-known showman for religious satanism is Anton LaVey, who organized the first Church of Satan in San Francisco in 1966. Neither his activities as a satanist nor his "church" itself are, frankly, significantly threatening compared to the antics of hardcore satanic cults. The Church of Satan boasts a conveniently secret membership roster of 10,000 names, but from my investigations seems to be barely active two decades after its founding. He's been overrated.

But his writings are significant; nearly every satanically oriented teenager or adult I've read of or talked with either started on the highway to Hell through LaVey's writings or studied them en route.

His 1969 Satanic Bible outlines his philosophies of "white" or what we've seen as wiccan witchcraft's relation to satanism's black witchcraft. LaVey writes, "White magic is supposedly utilized only for good or unselfish purposes, and black magic, we are told, is used only for selfish or 'evil' reasons. However, for the satanist there is no such dividing line. Magic is magic, be it used to help or hinder.

"During white magical ceremonies, the practitioners stand within a pentagram to protect themselves from the 'evil' forces which they call upon for help," LaVey says. "To the satanist, it seems a bit two-faced to call on these forces to help while at the same time protecting yourself from the very powers you have asked for assistance. The satanist realizes that only by putting himself in league with these forces can he fully and unhypocritically utilize the Powers of Darkness to his best advantage."

LaVey defines magic as "the change in situations or events in accordance with one's will, which would, using normally accepted methods, be unchangeable."

Satanic magic falls into two classifications, ritual and manipulative. Ritual magic, referred to as "greater magic," is highly emotional, while manipulative magic, the "lesser magic," is the "wile and guile obtained through various devices and contrived situations, which, when utilized, can create 'change in accordance with one's will.'"

The nine satanic statements that form the basis for its dogma are, from page 25 of *The Satanic Bible*:

1. Satan represents indulgence, instead of abstinence!
2. Satan represents vital existence, instead of spiritual pipe dreams.
3. Satan represents undefiled wisdom, instead of hypocritical self-deceit.
4. Satan represents kindness to those who deserve it, instead of love wasted on ingrates.
5. Satan represents vengeance, instead of turning the other cheek.
6. Satan represents responsibility to the responsible, instead of concern for psychic vampires.
7. Satan represents man as just another animal, sometimes better, more often worse than those that walk on all-fours, who, because of his divine spiritual and intellectual development, has become the most vicious animal of all.
8. Satan represents all of the so-called sins, as they all lead to physical, mental or emotional gratification.
9. Satan has been the best friend the church has ever had, as he has kept it in business all these years.

LaVey himself has stated: "We feel a person should be free to indulge in all the so-called fetishes that they would desire, as long as they don't hurt anyone that doesn't deserve or wish to be hurt. This is a very selfish religion. We believe in greed, we believe in selfishness, we believe in all the lustful thoughts that motivate man, because this is man's natural feeling. This is based on what man naturally would do."

Members of the Church of Satan follow nineteen mystical incantations which supposedly produce fulfillment of their every desire. They speak the ritual Enochian language during parts of ceremonies. This is an ancient occultic language first published in the 1659 biography of two well-known seers and astrologers, Joen Dee and Edward Kelley.

LaVey claims to have translated these Enochian keys himself and says, "The meaning of the words, combined with the quality of the words, unite to create a pattern of sound which can cause great reaction in the atmosphere. The barbaric tonal qualities of this language give it a truly magical effect which cannot be described."

The last incantation of the nineteenth Enochian key commands the "gates of Hell to open wide," demands that the heavens serve the petitioner. It commands those who are reciting the words to "arise and move and appear before the covenant of His [the Devil's] mouth, which He hath sworn unto us in His justice." It demands that the "mysteries of His creation be unfolded to those who follow Satan and they be able to partake of the undefiled wisdom."

An elitist mindset is probably the most obnoxious feature of the public, religious satanist. One satanic snob told Walter Martin in his 1970 book, *The Occult*, "Practitioners of white witchcraft, also referred to as the old religion of witchcraft, are no different in our eyes from Christians or Buddhists or any religion per se. It really doesn't matter whether they worship Jupiter, Juno, Diana, or the horned god, or any other figure; the fact is that they are trying to avoid their own personal sense of responsibility. By postulating that there is a god that they bow down and worship, as far as we can see it, they might as well pray to Jehovah or Jesus Christ."

Are religious satanists actually worshiping a personal devil, a being called Satan? Most say no. The satanic snob continues: "No satanist or black magician will ever pray to Satan or any form of the other devils for anything at all. The names are used as symbolism of various parts of the human ego. Satan represents the complete human ego. The other names represent other parts of the ego. We are struggling toward all aspects of this total human being."

Religious satanists claim that Satan can actually appear as a being, but the appearance is just that—a projection of the mind. "It's a psychological playing with the senses," one Church of Satan member said. "It is an actual image. There is a force within yourself, and when you psychologically are able to free yourself, these things happen. It is not anything supermagical and mysterious; it is just when you discipline yourself so that you are able to release your inner forces, you allow them to actually manifest themselves like some type of abstract projection."

So religious satanists actually fall into the category of, perhaps, occult humanists rather than Palladian devil-worshipers. Why do people—who for the most part are middle-aged, intelligent and even intellectual adults— become Church of Satan members? "We are just a very minute part of a very large universe," a member said. "Man just happens to have control of this planet. That isn't because god gave him any capacity to raise himself up, but simply because he raised himself up. Man fought very hard to evolve, but it's as much chance as anything else that you and I are around today.

"So once we take man, the animal, and give credit to man the animal for what man the animal did, we try and see what we can make of man, whether we can lift him above animal status and turn him into a god. This is what the Church of Satan eventually wants to do."

An offshoot of LaVey's group getting presstime these days is Michael Aquino's Temple of Set. Aquino has a doctorate in political science, two master's degrees, and has studied at the U.S. National Defense University. A purported expert in international relations, he's served in the military in Viet Nam and Germany, was a Defense Intelligence Agency attaché, and taught political science on university levels. Without giving him more attention than his group of satanists—which reportedly number only around 100—deserve, we probably should look at his writings. These, like LaVey's publications, have far more effect on the dabbler and self-styled satanist groups than does the Temple of Set organization. Kids from California to Maine to Victoria to Key West read these materials, interpret them as they will, and base their own covens' philosophies on Setian tenets.

The Crystal Tablet of Set, written by Aquino, asserts that "while the Temple of Set as an organization was formally incorporated in 1975, its magical and philosophical roots are prehistoric, originating in mankind's first apprehension that there is 'something different' about the human race—a sense of self-consciousness that places humanity apart from and above all other known forms of life.

"Ancient religions," Aquino writes, "of which those of Egypt are generally acknowledged the eldest—either exalted or feared this self-consciousness. Those who exalted it took the position that the human psyche is capable of opposition to and domination of the forces of nature.

"While all philosophical schools embraced the psychocentric consciousness to some degree, there were very few that made it avowedly and explicitly the focus of their attention. The divine personification (gods) of such schools have come down to us as symbols of what worshipers of non-consciousness consider the supreme evil, the Prince of Darkness in his many forms. Of these, the most ancient is Set, whose priesthood can be traced to predynamic times. Images of Set have been dated to ca 3200 B.C.E. with astronomically based estimates of inscriptions dating to ca 5000 B.C.E."

Here again, this version of religious, public satanism smacks of little more than intellectual egotism; Aquino's message, in case you missed it, is that his group is tough enough to take on the forces of nature while the rest of us are wimps—"worshipers of non-consciousness."

Aquino drones on: "In ancient Egyptian mythology, Set is represented either as an animal with a long nose, stiffly upraised ears and a forked tail or as a male human body with the head of the aforementioned animal. The Temple of Set uses this image because of its traditional symbolism of the god—or more precisely Neter, in Egyptian hieroglyphics—meaning one of the key principles of the cosmos. We conceptualize Set as a center of intelligence far more abstract. It's what Plato would call the form of the independent self-aware psyche. While we perceive this entity as quite real—as real as your own sense of self-contained being—we don't envision it as an anthropomorphic creature any more than you would represent your own psyche in such a manner."

Like LaVey, Aquino sneers at witchcraft as he does the purveyors of any other religion that backs down from self-exaltation: "White magic as practiced by primitive pagan and modern institutional religions offers devotees the illusion of 'reinclusion' in the universal scheme of things through ritualistic devotions and superstitions.

"The Black Magician on the other hand rejects both the desirability of union with the universe and any self-deceptive antics designed to create such an illusion. He has considered the existence of the individual psyche—the real you of the conscious intelligence—and has taken satisfaction from its existence as something unlike anything else in the universe. The Black Magician desires this psyche to live, to experience, to continue. He does not wish to die or to lose his consciousness and identity to a larger universal consciousness. He wants to be. This decision in favor of individual existence is the first premise of the Temple of Set."

The Temple of Set, according to Aquino, is organized under the Council of Nine, which appoints both the High Priest of Set and the Executive Director. Initiates are recognized according to six degrees based on the Western Magickal tradition and incorporating features from many Black Magickal societies: Setian I, Adept II, Priest or Priestess of Set III, Magister/Magistra Templi IV, Magus/Maga V and Ipsissimus/Ipsissima VI.

The Crystal Table of Set continues: "The Temple of Set enjoys the colorful legacy of the Black Arts and we use many forms of historical Satanic imagery for our stimulation and pleasure. But we have not found that any interest or activity which an enlightened mature intellect would regard as undignified, sadistic, criminal, or depraved is desirable, much less essential, to our work. Under no circumstance is any life form ever sacrificed or injured in a Black Magickal Working of the Temple of Set. Violation of this rule will result in the offender's immediate expulsion and referral to law enforcement or animal protection authorities."

The Non-Publicized Religious Satanists

Remember the little old lady dressed in white we met on the plane from Memphis? She had jotted down the number of a Don Blythe as leader of the Brotherhood of the Ram in Los Angeles. I contacted him on a trip out to L.A.

The head of the Brotherhood of the Ram is a congenial, articulate 62-year-old who says:

"I always had a philosophy, Jerry, that as long as it's not at the expense of someone else. I don't mind people getting kicks just so long as they don't do it by stepping on others' heads. Or victimizing people."

"What is your background in the occult?" I ask.

"Well, frankly, Jerry, I prefer to call my interests metaphysical." In his eloquent discussion on religions, Don mentioned what he sees as the distinction between devil worship and satanism: "The devil worshipers—I don't know if they really believe in anything. I think they assemble the whole thing to permit themselves kicks. As a cover story to rationalize their way of life. I've known people who call themselves satanists and they're actually rather plain people. They don't go around cursing people and so on. The name of one of the group's leaders is Roger, and his satanic group is basically one that meets for fun times. They have costume parties and I think it's simply a rationale for wearing outlandish outfits and going through rituals. Rituals is the name of the game for them. They'd probably be as scared as you would be if anything really showed up.

"These groups in Southern California at least are very much into their own organizational lines and programs; I don't think it's very structured." He talks about his group: "We actually had a store in Hollywood; I myself never had much to do with it. Some Big Brother came along one night and torched it. We used it for our meeting place. Now our meetings were terribly unstructured. And that's probably the norm."

"So are they just taking some of the literature on satanism such as the writings by LaVey—?" I ask.

"Jerry, isn't LaVey pretty much of a self-confessed fraud?"

"I don't know if he's self-confessed; but I gather everybody else thinks he is."

Don says, "Again, I think he's just used satanism as a cover. I don't know if he's even still active."

Another black magician is Sam Webster—claiming ties to the amorphous but basically public neopagan movement. Among most of the adults I talked with who were deeply into occultism and who were referred to by others as satanists, the terms "metaphysician" or "neopagan" seem to be more comfortable than "satanist." So Sam claims to be a black magician-neopagan. But his philosophy seems to closely resemble the other public religious satanists we've seen. "The risk in occultism is obsession—turning the mind down a particular path and not being able to get it out of the groove. A properly trained magician does that intentionally but when you walk into one of those grooves intentionally, it's much easier to step out. When you or a teenager tumbles down into one it's like falling through the rabbit hole in Alice in Wonderland; it's not possible to come back all that easily.

"It's less dangerous than they say. Of course, the real trick is to see the sociopathic side of it. That's where I see the real danger. What the children are really rebelling against is that we do not give children a religion of experience in our culture. We only give them a religion of thought and of social responsibility. That's all well and good, but when you're an adolescent, you have so many hormones running through your body, you are drugged. And you need something that will take this ecstasy, this anguish and channel it, focus it, put it to use. In other cultures, this is done. In our culture, we've forgotten how to do this; our culture is bereft of ritual."

Sam used the example of aboriginal cultures in which village men take boys of the proper age out into the desert to be circumcised, and this is a definite ceremony giving their youth passage, rituals of growth. "They're different when they come back into the village. The ritual is very intense, and with that kind of pain under controlled circumstances, they know they're adults. The line has been drawn and they've stepped over it.

"In a sense the Western hermetic tradition provided this for me, but since I had very little external guidance, the price I paid was very high," says the Brotherhood of the Ram leader. "Without the shamanic class, or with its being driven underground, our culture's children have no guidance in occult ritualism. So they dabble."

"Speaking of underground," I said, "are you involved in a group now?"

"Oh, several," Sam said. "There is a very large network across the country. Many people tend to see us as homogeneous; we're far from it. Network idea is more the fact that this person knows this person and so on. There are a couple of formal organizations, but it's mostly a subgroup, a core group that maintains the lines of communication and promotes a few events, and this keeps the flow of information going."

"Do you know of a group called W.I.C.C.A.—not as in wiccan witchcraft but an acronym for something like the World International Council of Covens? They supposedly met in Mexico in 1981."

"Life span on these kinds of organizations runs ten years and less. We're watching some of the major ones in their death throes now."

"Such as—?" I ask.

"Oh, Covenant of the Goddess."

"In her final death throes, hmm?"

"But the neopagan community has grown and mutated immensely in the past ten years. It's matured, and now it's in its adolescence. It needs to shrug off its child's clothing and step into a new arena. And we'll see what arena that is."

"Will you have any say in that?" I ask.

"Only in my own subtle way. I'm more known in the magickal community rather than the wiccan community, although I'm respected among the wiccan. Most of the magicians seem to be more stodgy; I'm not one of those—much more hierarchical, designed to endure. So in the magickal community I have some say."

Are these groups dangerous? In the glare of publicity, they'd be completely deranged if they were to attempt any sort of animal mutilation, human sacrifice, drug running or pornography dealing. And since membership in most of these groups is simply a matter of being over 18, filling out several forms for background checks and proof of mental stability, and about $10 annual dues, long ago these public groups have been infiltrated by law enforcement informants. If they step over into occult crime or the recruiting and endangerment of minors, they'll be hung. And they know it.

So again, the danger of the public religious satanist is primarily in the dissemination of their leaders' writings. These writings are gobbled up by dabblers and self-styled groups that make the Church of Satan look like the local women's missionary society.

Self-styled Satanist Groups

Compared to LaVey's theatrical style and Aquino's genteel intellectualism, the typical self-styled satanic group is helter-skelter and messy. A good example is the strange group uncovered some time ago in Waco, Texas.

"When law enforcement officials peered into an eerie walk-in closet in the home of a suspected drug manufacturer in Waco, they stumbled upon something scarier than old shoes and outdated clothes. It was an altar to Satan . . ." reads an article in the June 5, 1988, Waco *Tribune-Herald*.

"Drugs and satanism were linked in Waco . . . when David Zell went on trial in Federal Court on charges of drug manufacturing. Testimony in that trial linked Zell to a cult called 'The Circle,' which a Department of Public Safety Officer described as a satanic cult . . . . Among the materials collected from the group were robes with inverted pentagrams, or five pointed stars, and a horned skull and large horns mounted on a plaque, both marked with slightly askew pentagrams.

"On an altar, flanked by red and black candles, was a crude black disc with 'satan,' 'lucifer' and 'beelzebub' lettered on it."

On that disc sat a black-painted, animallike head with string for hair.

"In related searches, agents discovered [things] such as a demonic mask, tarot cards and pewter figurines of wizards and satanic symbols . . . . The group, involved in drugs, was armed with as many as eight machine guns. It came out in testimony that Zell commanded the group to carry weapons to protect themselves against the police or the street.

"According to Assistant U.S. Attorney Bill Johnston, 'It was a tightly knit group, dangerous to law enforcement. The satanic aspect tightened the group's bonds.'

"Eight of the group pleaded guilty to drug charges. On May 26, a Jury found Zell, 41, and Wells, 33, guilty of conspiracy to manufacture drugs and possession with the intent to distribute methamphetamine. Group members said they feared Zell, according to a special agent with the Federal Drug Enforcement Administration who worked on the case. 'They said they believed he could hurt them spiritually and physically,' he said.

"The Department of Public Safety Narcotics Agent who worked on the case and also asked not to be named, added: 'The 'master' could enter their body and tell whether they were lying or not.'"

What is the philosophy of a self-styled satanic group? "Whatever thou wilt." These groups apparently take their basic creeds and incantations from writings by Crowley, LaVey and other classic black artists. A group then refines its belief system and ritual by borrowing freely from any black magic author commercial enough to have books in an occult bookstore.

Each group shapes its teachings and ceremonies to its common interest, of course, which makes it "self-styled" in the first place. That is, if the main interest of the group is sexual experience, then oddly enough most of their beliefs and ritual relate to sex. If the interest is hatred of Christian organizations, the group organizes according to that focus. Whatever the interest, a satanic coven is the perfect setting for doing whatever thou wilt and for the most part ensuring that thou canst get away with it—whether it's dealing drugs, producing pornography, selling illegal weapons, kidnaping, or whatever.

As seen in the Waco drug-ring satanic group, a charismatic leader can demand dedicated loyalty to perform even illegal tasks and expect absolute secrecy. The viciousness of satanism guarantees obedience—one of Jacquie Balodis' patients had had a four-inch patch of skin removed from her stomach by her satanist group leaders as a small sampling of what would happen to her if she ever crossed the group. Further, the belief that evil spirits monitor a member's every move and thought guarantees loyalty even when others of the group aren't around.

And this is the type of criminal group that's geared to recruiting teenage dabblers, the adult version of the kind of group teenagers organize themselves into. This can be a self-styled satanic group knit together by terror, with vague "religious" justification to do anything, or a group almost as insidious as the well organized, generational satanic cults that have always been with us.

▶ 17 ◀

Satanic Rituals

Self-styled satanic covens are impossible to categorize according to philosophy, identity or number simply because they're purposely autonomous and often short-lived. The primary, underground satanic cults are equally hard to pin down in terms of identity of groups and numbers involved—but for a different reason. They're totally, diabolically secret. Is the "Son of Sam"/Charlie Manson Process Church cult termed a traditional satanic cult? Is The Brotherhood? The Illuminati Brotherhood? How many are involved? Exactly where are they operating?

Traditional Satanic Cults

Not too many researchers actually want to find the answers to such questions. Including this one.

But a little insight into the hardcore satanic cults comes occasionally through purportedly authentic writing such as the following description of a traditional cult structure. Produced in Victoria or possibly Vancouver, this information was given me apparently copied from an old, yellowed clipping:

To become a satanist, a worshiper, once he has overcome the initial difficulty of being admitted to a coven, he becomes a First Grade Satanist, called a Neophyte. He is required to pass a revolting test of nerve and if he passes, he is given a hooded robe of a plain brown material, belted at the waist with a thin, black cord.

After a suitable probationary period, provided he has shown certain required mental capabilities—a latent psychic power is considered most important—he is again submitted to a test of nerve. If he passes, he is given a black, hooded robe.

Blood is taken from his left wrist and two daubs of blood are placed on the left breast of the robe, signifying he is of the Second Grade, called an Acolyte. There are seven grades a satanist can reach, but few rarely ascend beyond the Fourth Grade. To proceed higher calls for unusual mental capabilities and many years of intense study under an Ipsissimus, a Fifth Grade level. Such study is made available only to those of outstanding ability.

A Sixth Grade Satanist is an Adept, but such men are rare. There have been only nine Adepts in the past 200 years; most covens are led by an Ipsissimus. An Adept has the power to see and converse with Satan himself and to command the lesser Dark Legions to do his bidding without question. Aleister Crowley was probably the most famous Adept of this century; Rasputin the most famous of all.

The Seventh Grade Satanist is even rarer. Since 1745, there have been only three: a Hungarian, an American and an African. As far as I know, the African is the only Adept alive; the American died around 1800.

What, actually, do these largely generational, traditional satanic cults believe? Jacquie Balodis, director of Overcomers Victorious and a satanic cult survivor, says the basic cult philosophy hinges on the concept of opposites.

From my notebook, I pull out a section of an unpublished manuscript she shared with me down in California. She writes:

Satanic cult philosophy centers around healing defects in the individual's spiritual and psychological core personality. The cult, of course, determines what is considered a defect. Healing is accomplished by reconciling opposites and establishing a balance between the opposites. A healthy person allows both sides to exist and fosters growth to both sides. For example, the following opposites should have equal manifestation in a person's thoughts and actions: love and hate, good and evil, spiritual and material, freedom and bondage, reason and passion, and pain and pleasure. Whenever possible, opposites should be in balanced combination to promote the fullest human potential. Ritual liturgies are designed to mobilize and unleash the animal driving forces from the depths of human personality. To bring man to the power of infinity, one must equally manifest and combine his qualities of man the civilized thinker and man the raving beast, according to Cavendish and LaVey. Satanists believe that a person is capable of experiencing and enjoying emotions to the fullest only after venting both opposing forces. For example, if a person can experience full hatred during a ritual, only then is he more capable of expressing the deepest kind of love.

The sexual act is an important element of many rituals. Sex incorporates the opposites in humans—male and female, adult and child, and humans and animals. Sex, considered one of the most powerful human drives or energies, should incorporate both gentleness and discomfort. To enjoy sex without pain would not be reconciling the opposite forces in man, according to Cavendish. In ranking order, the highest degree of sexual reconciliation, producing the greatest magick is between: mother and son, father and son, mother and daughter, father and daughter and father-mother-child.

—Which, disgustingly enough, leads us to wonder just what these black arts groups do in their satanic rituals.

The Legislative Library in the Parliament Buildings in Victoria is wonderfully antique, horrifically stuffy on this beautiful summer afternoon. I gather up my trashy briefings—I'm always a little embarrassed to be seen poring over articles with headlines like "Satan Stalks the Heartland" and books like *What Demons Can Do to Saints*. But it keeps me humble.

I walk a few blocks back toward the Empress Hotel in the fresh breeze coming off the harbor and settle down on a bench in what's called Thunderbird Park. I think we endured an adequate overview of who these satanists are; now I'm wondering just what they do.

Satanic Ritual

What do satanists do? Although the specific ritual activities are either too self-styled or atrocious to describe, most of the information I've seen on the religious, self-styled and traditional satanic rituals suggests ceremonies involving an invocation to the spirits, the presentation of petitions, sacrificial offerings and ultimately an orgy of celebration.

In the public religious satanic groups such as the Church of Satan, the satanic ritual is highly emotional. According to Anton LaVey's writings, three different types are performed. The first, the sex ritual or love charm, is used actually to put a "spell" on someone, "or create a desire on the part of the person whom you desire," *The Satanic Bible* says. However, the Church of Satan will not condone sex unless both partners consent.

The second ritual, one of compassion, is performed to help someone else in situations such as health, finances, happiness, education, or material success.

The hex, the third force, is used to destroy. The person to whom the destructive forces are aimed does not have to be a believer in magical forces of any kind, or even know that any curse is being put on him.

According to LaVey's writings, most of these rituals are performed in the early morning hours, or about two hours before the "target" person awakes, when the subconscious mind is active in dreaming and more susceptible to outside influences.

Dabbler/Self-Styled Rites

Dabblers, particularly teenagers, make up their own rituals. Mature dabblers and self-styled groups aren't very sophisticated as they follow a few instructions from Necronomican, the Satanic Bible and Satanic rituals, and the Witch's Bible.

Suzanne Bourret, a Canadian writer based in Windsor, Ontario, described her invitation to a teenagers' satanic ritual in an article I photocopied from the Canadian Magazine/*Star Weekly*:

It's a typical Saturday night in any city across Canada with any group of teenagers gathering to find their kicks swinging at a local dance or in a friendly coffeehouse. But a group of Windsor teenagers meet on a lonely road outside a wood 18 miles from the western Ontario industrial city, to get their kicks from a weird and ancient practice.

The time is about 9 on a biting November night but the group, all dressed in light black clothes, don't seem to notice the cold, as we leave our car and make our way silently towards the wood. With only the moon for light we turn off into a tangle of trees and underbrush until finally we reach a clearing where our eyes do a double-take. At the far end stands an altar with candles burning on it in antique candelabra, while one or two earlier arrivals stand by a fire that is burning in front of the altar.

This is the setting for my introduction to the black mass ceremony as practised by a coven of proclaimed witches, all Windsor high school students who with their leader Asmodeus—a term for Satan—say that they find in witchcraft an alternative to drugs. With a photographer present they will perform only part of the mass.

I discovered the practice of witchcraft among Windsor high school students while doing a series of articles on the rising popularity of the occult sciences, from old-fashioned tealeaf reading to experiments in ESP—extrasensory perception. I met Asmodeus and found him to be an intelligent 18-year-old who formed the coven two months ago "to see if it was possible to get power from it."

"Kids today are looking for an experience of belonging to something," says Asmodeus. "Witchcraft brings you together in a group physically and mentally whereas drugs bring you together physically but not mentally."

He thinks that more adults are getting interested in reviving witchcraft too. "There is a rise in the supernatural beliefs because there is nothing left for man to wonder about, even the moon."

Asmodeus and his followers practise a type of black witchcraft that believes that bad is more powerful than good, and that to achieve power over your fellow man you must worship and pray to Satan instead of God. Their service for the worship of evil is called a black mass. Asmodeus and his closest associate both say they derive a feeling of power out of this antireligion, and that their prayers to Satan have been answered. "We prayed for money and we got it," says his friend. Some of the others admit they don't understand witchcraft well, but find it fascinating.

During the last two months the group, which now numbers 17, has held several black masses with Asmodeus acting as the priest. The ceremony starts from the time they walk in silence to the grounds. "You have to get in the mood and if you talk Satan will be scared away."

When they get to the grounds the unbaptism of each member takes place and they revoke all ties with Christianity. Following this is the pre-ceremony feast, usually lasting for one to two hours. "Ideally, lots of raw meat should be eaten and blood should be consumed for the mind to be in a state of confusion. We eat steaks cooked but without salt, because salt is a symbol of purity and goodness."

Finally the black mass—the old Catholic mass inverted—starts with a creed beginning: "I believe in one god, Satan almighty," followed by the consecration, during which black wine and black wafers are consumed.

After the mass occurs what Asmodeus calls the height of the ceremony, when the group all join hands in a circle around the fire and chant, "Sangeue super nos et filios nostros," meaning "his blood be upon us and our children."

Asmodeus and his followers take the whole thing very seriously and he insists that there is no fooling around. "Although nothing tangible has happened as yet during the mass the presence of the spirit has been very tangible. We had the feeling that we were the most feared thing anywhere. It was a feeling of intense evil."

Several members of the group claim to have experienced mystifying incidents without any plausible explanation that they feel are signs that Satan is accepting them. One member, Arcularis, says he was sitting in a room meditating when a book of matches on the middle of the table ignited for no apparent reason. When he put them out he noticed that the matches had started burning from the bottom, not from the head.

At a recent session in the woods several members claim to have looked up in the sky and seen a burning cross. Asmodeus says it was no plane or radio tower and that one friend who is "superstraight" saw it too.

Asmodeus says he knows that satanism "can be extremely dangerous even if you don't believe in it. A psychiatrist told me not to get involved in it because of the mental implications. It can freak you out simply because it renounces God and brotherhood and every good concept that is natural in a person."

But at the same time he likes the power he feels he has attained through it. "I've found I have more power over people from it. You can con them and play games with them. It's an excellent ego trip."

Especially on such a wonderful summer day in one of Victoria's flower-strewn parks, I pack away the photocopy of the Windsor group's story with a definite sense of weariness. Do you know the feeling yet as we've come this far in tracking what Satan is doing in the new generation?

The seriousness of the Windsor teenagers' rituals and attitudes reminds me of an experience recounted in *Jay's Journal*, that book that has impressed me with what I think is a realistic odyssey of a young man recruited into a self-styled coven. Jay gives his account of an initiation ritual:

December 8

All 13 of us cut school this afternoon and went up the canyon to Dell's uncle's cabin. We had stashed the blood and things in the cemetery shed on our way home, now we had to sneak them out into our cars. Unbelievable!

I tried to take the whole thing lightly until we had all the drapes drawn in the cabin and rugs and stuff pinned up over every opening that let in the barest amount of light. It was going to be like a club initiation, I told myself, dumb but dangerous . . . . I didn't know then about Tina's and Mel's intensity, their insistence and seriousness.

I tried to pass when Tina offered the little vial of blood, having thrown it up once made me cringe. But Tina and Mel demanded that each thing be done with precision and exactness. Dell and Brad sitting next to me gagged when they took their tastes, but at least it was just a sip this time.

Minutes after accepting the offering my eyes began to roll around in my head and a new kind of lightness lifted up my body . . . .

All the blood was dumped into the tub and one by one we were baptized in it, washing the sins and imperfections of our pre-O [pre-Satan] life away! Our heads were anointed with a few drops of the urine we had milked out of the bull as he was laying there.

What amazes me most of all, as I look back, is that I wasn't repelled by all the ghoulishness, but rather intrigued . . . .

I was stoned crackers. I would have to have been to have taken part in any of that crazy nightmare movie madness.

After we'd cleaned up every drop of blood, Tina passed us another "potion." Again part of me tried to fight her off but I couldn't! It was like I'd been given sodium pentathol or something. I couldn't stop myself from saying and doing things I didn't want to say and do. I couldn't hold back! I remember feeling like a prisoner of war or something, that they had taken my will away.

I fought until I literally could fight no longer and fell weeping to the floor . . . I find myself saying:

> Our Father which art in Hell
> Hallowed be thy name
> Thy kingdom come, thy will be done
> on earth as it is in Hell
> Give us this day . . .

Of course, since Crowley's rule for true satanists is to do whatever you will, dabblers and self-styled groups can make up their own rituals in any way they choose. And often, apparently, the self-styled satanic covens can call even a psychotic homicide a "ritual."

I pull out Larry Kahaner's excellent book, *Cults That Kill*. On page 141 Darlyne Pettinicchio, a deputy probation officer in Orange County, tells the story of a thirteen-year-old girl:

Her parents were divorced. Neither one is really interested in the kid. The mother is involved in some lesbian relationship, and the kid is always running off.

From her house, she would look down the hill and see a bunch of kids. They looked like they were always having fun. So she ended up running away and meeting up with them.

They had a little cult. The cults I deal with are not formal satanic cults. They're kids who get together, take a little from this book and that book, and add a little of their own. They get a nineteen-year-old to be the high priest, and they dabble. In this instance they had a twenty-one-year-old high priest.

She said one night they brought in three kids who were loaded, and they were going to have a ritual. She said that she was always loaded when she was with this group. She couldn't stand to do it otherwise. I asked how loaded they were. I was trying to get an idea. She said they had to carry them in.

They brought them in and apparently these three had ripped off the little satanists in a dope deal. They started ritual: They rang the bell; they did an invocation to Satan. Then they went out to the hills—she drew me a map—where there was a chain and some trees. They had cans of gasoline, and they did the ritual and brought one guy out and threw him in the middle. They all had candles, and the high priest threw the candle on him and he was torched like that. The girl said he wasn't so loaded that he wasn't screaming and yelling. They just let him burn.

Satanic Cult Worship

Self-styled covens may be simply helter-skelter, but as we consider the rituals of the primary traditional groups, the rituals become more organized. And the ultimate ritual of the organized groups is, of course, the Black Mass.

I'm reading through Tom Wedge's discussion of black rituals in his 1987 Daring Books publication, *The Satan Hunter*. With the plethora of do-it-yourself satanism groups practicing a plethora of rituals, I remind myself to check Wedge's descriptions against that of others.

Wedge writes that the Black Mass, held as seldom as four times or even only once a year by some covens, is considered the ultimate ritual to Satan. Following the basic structure of a Roman Catholic mass, the Black Mass perverts the liturgy, culminates in a blood sacrifice and is followed by an orgy. The Black Mass, then, isn't an ancient rite of paganism but arose as a Middle Ages denunciation of the church by renegade priests under the influence of groups such as the Cathars and the Knights Templar.

The Black Mass had its precursors, of course. Historians point to the seventh century Council of Toledo as the first Roman Catholic mention of the dangers of perverted mass rituals. The council denounced the Mass of the Dead, in which a priest consigned the soul of a man to death. The Mass of Saint Secaraire was mentioned in later literature as a ceremony performed by a priest and a female server with whom he'd had sexual intercourse. The St. Secaraire host was triangular and black; the wine was water from a well in which a baby has drowned.

The only ex-satanist I've come across who is willing to talk about an actual Black Mass is "Elaine," a friend and prominent character in two of Dr. Rebecca Brown's books—*He Came to Set the Captives Free* and *Prepare for War*—by Chick Publications.

I decide to call and see if Elaine can share her story. From a phone in the Empress Hotel, I call Dr. Brown in Encino, California: "Any way I could interview Elaine on that account of the Black Mass she attended as a teenager?"

Dr. Brown was personable yet firm. "The kind of pain it took to dredge up those memories for her—she had nightmares for weeks after we did that chapter—is something I just feel I need to protect her from. You can use the story as long as you attribute the reference; but no, I won't let her be put in a situation where she has to tell that story again."

Eyewitness at a Black Mass

So, sitting comfortably on a red velvet loveseat in the lobby of the quaint and beautiful Empress Hotel in Victoria, British Columbia, I'll share with you from *He Came to Set the Captives Free* by Rebecca Brown (Encino, CA: Chick Publications, 1986). We'll simply take this account on a Studs-Terkel basis and let her tell her story without comment from me, although I have edited parts of it. A definite "Believe-It-Or-Not" entry, here is what Elaine, an ex-high-priestess in a highly organized satanic cult called The Brotherhood, writes:

The customs and ceremonies involved in human and animal sacrifice differ somewhat in different areas.

There are eight "holy days" out of each year when human sacrifice is performed. Human sacrifices may also be performed on other days for other reasons such as discipline, fertility rites and so on. Smaller covens who do not have the necessary facilities usually join with the larger covens nearby on these occasions. The holy days are Christmas, Easter, Halloween, Thanksgiving, and as close as possible to the first day of spring, summer, fall and winter.

Halloween has, since its inception by the Druids in England, been a special holiday for human sacrifices to Satan. It continues the same in our day. The epidemic of harmful substances—razor blades in apples, poison in candy—placed in the various Halloween treats for trick-or-treaters is no accident. It was a planned effort by Satanists. The children injured by these treats are sacrifices to Satan.

The purpose of the sacrifices as taught to cult members is to "purify" them so that they can receive Satan's blessings. Also, anyone who drinks the victim's blood or eats their flesh gains new demons and therefore greatly increased power. The drinking of blood is an important part of all satanic activities.

Human sacrifices, as with all cult meetings, are never held in the same place twice. Most members do not find out the location of the meeting until a few hours prior to its start. Sacrifices are always held in the most hidden and isolated areas possible. In large cities this is sometimes a problem, but there are usually enough vacant or abandoned warehouses and buildings available. Rarely does The Brotherhood hold a human sacrifice outside except when very secluded and isolated country or swampy areas are available. This is not true with the younger, bolder people tripped out on drugs. They are not overly concerned with security and because of this The Brotherhood sees to it that many of them are discovered by the police and arrested, or are simply exterminated to prevent trouble. They are always declared to be insane; The Brotherhood sees to this so that a serious connection with satanism is not made.

Specific committees are appointed and maintained within The Brotherhood to set up the necessary equipment and to provide clean-up afterwards. Satanists who are also policemen are almost always on these committees. Their function is to prevent any interference from law enforcement agencies. The equipment, such as the altar or in large cities, Satan's golden throne, is transported in plain vans. It can be quickly set up and taken down. The bodies are almost always disposed of by cremation. Babies are rather easily ground up—even in a garbage disposal, and are often disposed of in this manner. Occasionally the body is cremated at the site of the sacrifice. When this is not practical, there usually is no difficulty in using the facilities of a nearby mortuary. Also crematory facilities at veterinary hospitals or animal shelters are frequently used. The highly disciplined and carefully planned work of both the setup and clean-up committees have been responsible for keeping the practice of human sacrifice out of the public eye for many years.

Security at such ceremonies is always tight and police radio frequencies are continuously monitored throughout the ceremony. Anyone who has witnessed such a ceremony of human sacrifice and then tries to pull out of the cult does so at the cost of his or her own life. The only way to get out is through the power of Jesus Christ and even then it is not easy. The demons monitor everyone who has ever been even slightly involved with such a practice.

I will describe here a Black Sabbath—also called the Black Mass—that I was forced to attend. I was, at the time, a minor, not yet a high priestess and was literally a captive. Black Sabbaths take place once per year. Always at the time of the full moon and on Easter weekend.

I was very young at the time of that horrible weekend, still a child actually, but the memories of it torment me still and always will. I had been a member of the cult for less than a year. I was not permitted to go alone but was taken by my master—the high priestess—and several other witches.

The meeting was held in a very large isolated barn which had been roughly remodeled for the purpose. I suppose that there were a couple thousand people there. Most had already been taking drugs prior to coming and all were given potions to drink containing drugs and alcohol at the beginning of the meeting. The higher members of the cult never partook of these drugged drinks and despised those who did so.

It was a Friday night—Good Friday. The meeting was to run through that Sunday. I saw that the barn had a platform across one end. Above the platform sat a throne made of what looked like pure gold. That throne was for Satan.

As the high priest and high priestess came out onto the platform an absolute silence fell over the crowd. A silence so intense you could hear a pin drop. The silence was one of fear. Each one was afraid that he or she might be chosen to be the sacrifice. At that moment Satan was no longer a glory to anyone, no longer an honor. A ripple of relief went through the crowd when the victim was dragged kicking and screaming through a side door and up onto the stage. The main Easter sacrifice is always a man. Occasionally additional sacrifices of women, children or animals are made, but the ceremony centers around the sacrifice of a man. Often a hitchhiker is picked up some days before the ceremony and is carefully guarded until the time of the meeting. In the eyes of the crowd, that man becomes Jesus and Satan's supposed victory over Jesus at the cross is celebrated.

I watched in utter horror as a crown of huge long thorns was driven into the young man's head, the thorns going so deep as to pierce his skull. Then he was stripped and beaten with whips tipped with metal studs, and tortured with spikes and red-hot pokers. Finally he was nailed to a wooden cross which was then picked up and put in a hole in the ground just in front of the middle of the platform. I will never forget the stench of the burned and tormented flesh, the screams of the victim, his writhing agony, his pleas for mercy. The crowd roared like a pack of wild animals, the inhuman voices of many demons from within the crowd joining in. They jeered and cheered as the cross was raised into place and dropped down into the hole. The high priest urinated on the victim and members of the congregation threw feces at him while everybody cheered Satan's supposed victory and then bowed down and worshipped Satan.

. . . Finally the high priest drove a long spike through the man's head, pinning it to the cross, killing him. The crowd went crazy, screaming and shouting and dancing in crazed ecstasy at the "victory." They loudly proclaimed all victory and power and honor to their father Satan.

The meeting then turned into a sex orgy. Every type of sexual perversion imaginable was practiced . . . . The victim's blood was drained off, mixed with drugs and alcohol, and was drunk by the high priest and high priestess and passed through the crowd. Many of the crowd went up to desecrate the body. The night hours passed while the drugged, demonic drunken frenzy of the crowd continued. Eventually the body, separated from the head, was ground up and portions were mixed with drugs and other substances. Those who wanted more power ate some of the mixture. The third day, as people began to come down from their drugged state, they left for home in two's and three's—all proclaiming that their great and glorious father Satan had won yet another victory over the enemy Jesus Christ.

The Formal Satanic Rites

Few other accounts of the secret rituals of the organized satanic cults seem to be as convincing as those from Canadian writer Alan Jay whose undated account of a satanic cult Grand Sabbat was published by the Vancouver *Columbian*:

It is late October and the night is cold. A numbing wind blows in from the sea and causes the torches on the crude stone altar to hiss and flicker angrily. Their uncertain light throws leaping shadows across the clearing in a lonely wood, now filled with 200 or so men and women clad in black, hooded robes.

They murmur restlessly, rub their hands and stamp their feet. The cold is beginning to eat into their bones, for they are naked beneath their thin robes.

They have travelled from many countries to be in this spot, for this is the place of the Grand Sabbat, or Black Mass, the third of the thrice/yearly major Satanist celebrations. They are here to renew their pledge of devotion to the Master, Lucifer, Prince of Darkness, to advance to the grades they have earned and to be rewarded with gifts of abnormal power, life after death and even immortality from the Dark Host.

Suddenly, a hooded figure steps from the darkness into the circle of light before the altar. Like everyone else present, he is clad in a long robe. A hood covers his face. On the left breast of his robe, five daubs of blood stain the thin fabric. This indicates that he is an Ipsissimus, a Satanist of the Fifth Grade and a leader of the Satanist cult.

He raises his hand and expectant silence falls on the waiting worshipers. They move closer to the altar. He greets them in Latin, giving the Satanist greeting said to have been written in the legendary book "The Clavicle of Solomon" by Solomon himself.

The worshipers answer with the traditional reply, in Latin, and the Grand Sabbat begins. It is being held in the middle of a lonely wood on a private estate. The owner is said to be a Satanist of the Fourth Grade, but as Satanists rarely know the identities of each other, nobody is sure.

The Ipsissimus turns to face the altar. It is a crude pile of stones about 10 feet long and three feet high. On its flat surface rest two candlesticks containing black candles, a curved sword, a crucifix placed face down and an ornate silver chalice. Nearby, a black rooster struggles vainly to free itself from the leather thongs that bind its feet and wings.

Speaking in Latin, the Ipsissimus calls on Lucifer to witness that his children are gathered to worship him. He lists the titles of the master and takes the worshipers through an involved chant and response litany that takes almost an hour. Then, at a signal, two Acolytes, or Satanists of the Second Grade, hurry forward. One hands the sword to the Ipsissimus, the other holds the rooster in both hands above his head as he kneels before the altar. As the Ipsissimus takes the sword in his left hand, the other Acolyte picks up the chalice, again with the left hand, and holds it below the bird's head.

Chanting in Latin, the Ipsissimus slits the bird's throat with the sword and a gush of blood spurts in the waiting chalice. When it is almost full, the Ipsissimus tosses the dead rooster into the darkness and turns to face the worshipers. And as he recites the traditional litany, again in Latin, both arms raised high, the Acolyte passes among the worshipers bearing the chalice of blood. Each worshiper pledges his being to the wishes of his Dark Master, sealing the spoken pledge by drinking from the chalice.

When every worshiper has made his pledge, all kneel before the altar. In some Black Masses, a female member of the coven lies naked on the altar and the chalice is placed on her stomach.

As the Ipsissimus reiterates the basic belief of Satanism, that "we are the vassals of Beelzebub; our physical bodies belong first to him and then, by his gracious consent, to each other, for his and each other's enjoyment. By devotion shall we live; by the Lefthand path will we join the master," other Acolytes hand chalices of wine and platters of dark, spicy bread to the worshipers.

The Satanists eat the bread, drink the wine and shout the praises of Lucifer. More wine is handed around and all drink except the Ipsissimus and the serving Acolytes. Several hours pass. The satanists are now intoxicated and some have started to dance before the altar. Others join in and soon, everyone, with the exception of the Ipsissimus and the two Acolytes, is gyrating wildly to the throbbing music of a strange stringed instrument and the beat of a small, cowhide drum.

The Ipsissimus turns to gesture at the two candles. Inexplicably, they burst into flame and this is the signal for the dancing satanists to tear off their robes and toss them in a pile in the center of the whirling circle of dancers.

As the music reaches a crescendo, one of the Acolytes brings forth a semi-circular gong, hidden until now behind the altar. He holds it high above his head and the Ipsissimus picks up the sword and strokes the gong with the flat of the blade. As the brassy sound reverberates through the clearing, the satanists cease dancing and, hurriedly selecting partners, vanish into the bushes. The Ipsissimus and the Acolytes leave, vanishing into the darkness.

As the night wears on, the worshipers gather in the clearing and fall asleep. And for the next three days, this scene will be repeated time after time. Then, they will leave and resume their everyday lives in other cities, other countries until the time of the next Grand Sabbat comes around.

How often do these incredible rituals occur? I've found that groups from occultists dabbling in the paranormal and divination right down the spectrum to the traditional satanic cults generally observe the same cyclical round of occult holy days. Let's look at them briefly, keeping in mind that these dates are significant times to watch for satanic-related crime, significant times to monitor the activities of teenagers who might be dabbling in satanism.

The Satanic Calendar of Brainwashing Ritual

When do satanic rituals occur? Whether the group is pagan, wiccan or satanic, the dates of the spring and autumnal equinoxes are significant, as are the winter and summer solstices.

Although it appears that the specific holydays mandated in various groups depend on that group's tradition, most satanists observe four major holidays in addition to the equinoxes and solstices. Five weeks and one day from each of those seasonal dates is a "grand climax" celebration, with the "High Grand Climax" celebrated on Christmas Eve, December 24th.

The high point of the satanic calendar is Halloween. Notes from a browse in the library's encyclopedias remind me that the source of Halloween celebrations is the old Celtic festival of Samhain. Samhain was worshiped as the Celtic god of death about 2,000 years ago in what is now northern France, Britain and Ireland. The Celtic new year began November 1, and since these tribes began their "day" in the evening, the night of what the Romans dated October 31 was the festival of Samhain.

It was thought that Samhain would allow the spirits of the dead to return to their homes before the long winter season of the new year began. Some legends have it that the souls of the wicked dead of the preceding year had been condemned to live in animals throughout the 12 months, and food set out in honor of Samhain would free these spirits from their condemned status. If a spirit returned to his home and found no offer of food, an evil spell would be cast over the house—sort of a macabre prototype of "trick-or-treat," I would guess.

The October 31 celebrations were orchestrated by the teacher-priest Druids. Huge bonfires of sacred oak branches were kindled to burn sacrifices of crops, animals and apparently humans in honor of the god of death. The people dressed in animal skins and wore animal headdresses as the priests predicted the coming year's fortunes by examining the remains of the sacrifices.

After the Romans conquered the Celts in 43 A.D., the festival of Samhain incorporated a Roman festival of the dead and a festival honoring Pamona, the Roman goddess of fruit and trees.

In the ninth century, the Roman Catholic Church shifted its traditional All Saints' Day from May to November 1 to counter the pagan festival of Samhain. The November 2 All Souls' Day, when one could pray for the dead, became a holiday in itself as poor people went "a-souling," promising to pray for dead souls in exchange for "soulcake" pastries.

So today we have millions of dollars of retail sales in costumes and candy and fake wax fangs climaxing on October 31; and in every source I've encountered in this quest of satanism we have satanic groups celebrating the high point in their year on October 31. Halloween is considered by most occultic groups to be the best time of year to contact spirits as they're unleashed to roam the earth for the night.

Other holidays have similar backgrounds in pagan and medieval religious tradition. Pagan and wiccan groups tend to observe the four seasonal dates, Halloween, and three other holidays:

Candlemas—February 2—is a celebration of the coming of spring.

Beltane or Walpurgis Night—April 30—is a festival centering around the planting of crops and fertility.

Lammas—July 31—signals the beginning of the harvest season.

Satanism, of course, isn't so concerned about the cycles of nature as it is the machinations of evil. Think through an overview of a satanic ritual calendar compiled from several sources:

RITUAL CALENDAR		
January 7	St. Winebald Day	Blood rituals
January 17	Satanic Revels	Sexual rituals
February 2	Satanic Revels	Sexual rituals
February 25	St. Walpurgis Day	Blood rituals
March 1	St. Eichatadt Day	Blood rituals
March 20	Equinox Feast Day	Sexual rituals
April 26–May 1	Grand Climax	Blood rituals
June 21	Solstice Feast Day	Sexual rituals
July 1	Demon Revels	Blood rituals
August 3	Satanic Revels	Sexual rituals
September 7	Marriage to the Beast	Sexual rituals
September 20	Midnight Host	Blood rituals
September 22	Equinox Feast Day	Sexual rituals
October 29	All Hallow Eve	Blood rituals
November 1	Halloween	Sexual rituals
November 4	Satanic Revels	Sexual rituals
December 22	Solstice Feast Day	Sexual rituals
December 24	High Grand Climax	Blood rituals

In addition to the above dates, a satanic group member's birthday is considered a special holiday. Also, as mentioned in the context of stories like *Michelle Remembers*, the satanic calendar revolves every 28 years, culminating in a year-long series of celebrations called the "Feast of the Beast." The next Feast of the Best will occur in the year 2009.

Brainwashed Beliefs

But doesn't all this—the types of groups, the rituals they devotedly perform—seem almost silly? Imagine trying to schedule a normal-appearing life around your satanic datebook of ritual holidays!

I sit in the Empress Hotel, watching delicate, elderly folk shuffling along the carpet and stopping to rest periodically, and I think: *Just to do all this crazy stuff, to coordinate it within a group, and to keep it all secret with alibis and with meticulous security measures to eliminate evidence must take an amazing amount of energy! How can they possibly believe this idiocy is worth it?*

Jacquie Balodis' work provides the answer: They believe it's worth it because they're brainwashed. In her excellent paper on satanic brainwashing, she writes:

There is evidence that the cults perform human sacrifices, burying of children underground in animal carcasses, sexual acts with children, drinking human blood, eating human flesh and torturing animals and humans. Most adults and children simply could not participate willingly in such events without having been first programmed or brainwashed by the cults.

The cult promotes its philosophy by both performing its magick rituals and teaching its doctrine. Thus, initiates learn through both experiential and intellectual exercises. Criticism of others, self-criticism, esprit de corps, favorable thought conclusions and learning by doing are ingredients that facilitate brainwashing and eventual acceptance of the cult's philosophy.

Jacquie writes about satanic cults' expertise at breaking down defenses with threats. The greater the perceived threat, the faster is the attitude change toward acceptance of the cult's belief. This acceptance is enforced by periods of hunger, fatigue, tenseness, threats, violence, mind-altering drugs or hypnotism. Most adult and child survivors describe these reinforcements as part of their cult experience.

This negative reinforcement is, of course, balanced by positive reinforcement in the forms of having one's life spared, receiving affirmation for a well-done ritual, gaining a trusted cult position and receiving other cult benefits such as free drugs, and a place to act out sexual fantasies and aggressive behavior.

Jacquie explains that a person needs to be placed within a psychological fog in order to accept what would otherwise be unacceptable. Consider your reactions if, in an atmosphere of total terror, you were consistently subjected to:

HUNGER: Satanic cults practice depriving their initiates and slaves of food until they are weak. When food is given it is often putrid, in the form of fecal matter, or raw human or animal eyes, organ parts, or other unidentifiable substances.

FATIGUE: The rituals are usually performed at night between 10 p.m. and 3 a.m. The cult's victim is usually tired before the rituals begin and becomes even more exhausted by high energy demands during the rituals, which sometimes last 24 hours.

Tension also produces fatigue as the victim is taught that Satan and his cult know everything about him. Rituals incorporate "Satan's seeing eye" and the assignment to the victim of a familiar spirit who will report to the cult all the victim's activities and thoughts.

THREATS AND VIOLENCE: Threats and violence occur constantly during rituals and meetings. For example, a victim might be forced to help skin or decapitate a living animal or person. He is then told that if he reports to anyone anything about the cult, the same thing will happen to him or his family. To reinforce this threat, the cult often gives or sends the victim an object such as a decapitated doll, a bouquet of color-coded carnations, a death mask, a dead bird, black feathers, or notes written in the satanic alphabet. The victim may also be programmed to observe other "not talk" cues such as police or medical uniforms, or hand signals from cult members.

DRUGS AND HYPNOSIS: Other agents used in brainwashing are hypnotic substances, psycho-surgery, mind-altering drugs and hypnotic trances.

Drugs, obtained from members who are doctors or pharmacists, are sometimes used to increase a victim's heart rate. This heightened state allows a person to be more receptive to exhibiting aggressive behavior, and to accepting suggested imagery and cues to forget.

Jacquie then discusses some interesting insights into why satanic victims firmly believe as true certain memories that are absolutely impossible:

Children who are trance-induced and then asked to roleplay are highly susceptible to accepting that which was roleplayed. If cued to remember the roleplay after the hypnotic state, the child will remember and defend the hypnotically induced suggestions as factual. For example, the child may have roleplayed a scenario where he is bathed by a person dressed in a Micky Mouse costume. Under hypnosis, he is given the cue that when he hears a given sound, he will see Micky Mouse. Later, the non-hypnotized child is sexually molested while the given cue is sounded. He recalls the hypnotic suggestion and thinks that Micky Mouse—the cartoon character—is the actual perpetrator.

Mind-altering drugs are often combined with goal-directed imagery to program victims. Either before or during a drugged experience, a person is shown pictures and given suggestions. During a trance state either induced by drugs or hypnosis, the person believes that he is accomplishing behaviors or feeling sensations that he expected to occur. The experiential expectation was produced as he viewed the pictures and listened to the suggestions. For example, a person might have viewed a sketch depicting someone leaving his body and flying around the room or having sex with demonic entities. He is then induced into a trance, and while under the trance, believes that he experiences the directed goal imagery. This process renders the victim unable to distinguish between the events of the ritual and the programmed fantasy.

For example, children in a daycare center might take a field trip to Sam's meat market. There they might observe the cutting and packaging of meat into various cuts.

Their attention is directed to the freezer with sides of beef hanging from meat hooks. After they return from the field trip, they may be induced into a mind-altered state and forced to remember the hanging carcasses. While in the altered state, they are guided to replace the animal carcasses with human bodies. Once this new image has been programmed in, the child is made to participate in a human sacrifice. The human sacrifice ritual is intermingled with the programmed imagery, making the victim believe that after the ritual, the corpse is taken to Sam's market and hung with the other bodies, the programmed imageries. Brainwashing techniques that include controlling the mind with programmed imagery produce mental distortions and psychological distress. People do not believe the victims nor do they accept as fact any of their experiences because some of the related details cannot be validated or are impossible to have occurred.

Hypnosis is also used to instruct a victim to forget selected items or events. During a hypnotic trance, victims might be instructed not to remember the events and/or the names of persons involved in the rituals. Kihlstrom has found that it is difficult to retrieve information that was forgotten during hypnotic amnesia. For example, Jill, a survivor of satanic ritual abuse did not remember some events that she had been cued to forget. Only after Jill had undergone therapy using body work did she recall being trained to feel guilty and worthless whenever lying on her right side, even while asleep. Frequently, she had awakened at night crying and depressed with no apparent reason.

The cult had programmed her to believe that her right side was evil and her left side good [as part of the satanist "left hand path" mythology]. During body work, she could actually feel the two opposing feelings in her body. As she worked through deprogramming the right side from feeling evil or bad and to feeling good, other memories surfaced. One of these memories was the programming of another survivor by the cult. Jill remembered the other survivor lying on an altar; her left side was stroked and told it was good. Jill was forced to beat and cut the other survivor's right side and at the same time tell it how bad it was and that it needed to be destroyed. After the right side was punished for being bad, an older cult member told the survivor that she would not remember being told why she hated her right side.

Do these sick-minded satanists actually believe they can successfully brain-wash children to accept satanic doctrines? Do they even believe these tenets themselves?

When properly programmed in self-styled groups by fear and drugs or in cults by all the methods Jacquie mentioned, a satanist will answer, "Yes." They believe Satan is their god, that opposites need to be experienced to reach their full potential, that power comes from blood—the more undefiled the victim, the more power.

They believe in the presence and power of evil spirits.

It's time I head north of the city to catch the Vancouver Island ferry.

Several hours later, I'm sitting in the Vancouver hospital room of a minister's daughter named Julie. She tried to commit suicide today. She had quit eating regularly back in March, her father tells me. He remembers the date specifically because it happened to be the same day on which a colleague, Karl Klassen, had exorcised demons in a man they both knew.

From the boggling study of the afternoon, I'm convinced most true satanists—even the dabblers—resolutely believe in the existence and power of Satan and his demons. I'm also convinced that plenty of nonsatanists believe this just as resolutely. And it is a question we probably have to consider: Is there any spiritual power in satanism? Do these people actually deal with demon entities? Is he really there?

Part Four

◀▶

The Power of Darkness: Is He Really There?

Few people now believe in the devil;
but very many enjoy behaving as their
ancestors behaved when the Fiend
was a reality as unquestionable as his
opposite number.

Aldous Huxley

An 18th century copper engraving by Chodoviecki depicting St. Walpurgis Night (Witches' Sabbath). The Bettman Archive.

▶ 18 ◀

Occult Phenomena—
Paranormal to Possession

Dallas. Central Expressway, snaking with two jam-packed lanes from Plano south, is neither. Neither central to the Dallas megalopolis nor an expressway. So I bide my time watching the bumper of the cream and rust-colored—with real rust—'76 van in front of me; the back of the van is all I can see and at two miles per hour I figure it doesn't matter. I'm also listening to the mellow jazz fusion on the local New Age station called "The Oasis." In L.A. the New Age station was called "The Wave"—as it was in Kansas City. New Age music is a hot slice of the music industry pie these days; and well it should be. Anita Baker, George Winston, Manheim Steamroller, an occasional piece by Sting; the good music makes me wonder whether the hardcore New Age occultic types think they're lulling us Old Agers into a reincarnating altered state of consciousness wherein we'll meet mysterious ascended masters who speak with other tongues about life on other nebulae—

I slam into the van in front of me when he jams on his brakes. I stop, jump out and begin to run up alongside the van.

A young Mexican with a wispy mustache and black Bon Jovi hair sticks his head out of the van window and says, "It's okay. Sorry I stopped so quick."

There's no damage to either vehicle, so we again begin putting down Central Expressway. I determine to keep my head on the traffic situation, but within minutes find myself wondering the old question that's haunted me since the beginning of this trek in search of Satan. Maybe you've been wondering it too.

Is he really there?

The opinions on just how to answer that question, of course, depend on the respondent's predisposition. Strict, naturalistic materialists will predictably

187

say no. But surprisingly, supernaturalistic religionists say no as well as yes. From a disgustingly nonscientific straw vote poll I've been conducting in my interviews with experts and conversations with cabbies, I find that religious folk differ on their answers about the reality of Satan as they differ on their answers about the value of the Bible.

That is, a religious person who believes the Bible to be a good book of divine, ancient wisdom but not the actual Word of God doesn't seem to believe in a personal devil. Obviously I'm generalizing, but I've yet to meet a Jewish, mainstream Protestant or Eastern-oriented mystical religionist who believes the devil is anything more than a symbolic personification of evil.

However, the Roman Catholics, fundamentalist Christians and evangelical Christians I've met have said, yes, they do believe in a personal devil and demon entities. They based that answer on their face-value belief in the Bible. And the Bible teaches the reality of these dark entities.

"Is he really there?" I had asked Father Michael J. Flannery whom I met on a flight out of LaGuardia. Father Flannery and several other Roman Catholic priests I talked with basically affirmed the classic biblical view of Satan. "We believe in a personal devil," said Father Flannery in between his stories of flying over Turkey and Iran as an Army chaplain. He's a huge, friendly 62-year-old, and he knows his doctrine. "Satan was once Lucifer and with his host was cast out of heaven. He now actively intervenes in the affairs of men, though not, I think, with all the power that's usually attributed to him. Yes, we believe in the power of the devil."

As I'm inching along the "expressway" I put in a cassette of the interesting conversation I'd had in Los Angeles with Don Blythe.

In my chat with the leader—he didn't call himself a high priest—of the L.A. Brotherhood of the Ram, Don Blythe, I had asked, "Is there anything to it? Any real power there?"

"Oh, Jerry," he said. "If you believe in anything there will be power in it. You make it work. If you're dramatic enough and influential enough and you can brainwash people enough, it'll work."

"Do you have an example of 'something that worked'?" I asked.

"Well, in any consideration of an experience, there are three criteria. First, is it historically valid? Secondly, is it logical? Thirdly, does it work? And if something works, that working supersedes the first two considerations. I don't care where it came from or how old it is or what the form is, if it's workable, it's like a person giving me the combination of a lock. If the numbers open the lock, I don't care about the rest of it.

"Have I ever seen anything abnormal? Yes, I have, in fact." Don tells an intriguing story of becoming a specimen of scientific study because of his abilities in muscular control. UCLA has films of some of his anatomical feats, he said. In one particular study, Dr. Norman Herr at a university in Cleveland ordered the room housing embalmed bodies in vaults to be locked, filled with chlorine gas and sealed during the summer recess. Months later the seals were broken, the gas was allowed to seep out, and the professor of anatomy entered by himself to ensure that if there were traces of the gas left, there'd be someone still breathing at the door to pull him out.

Don finished his story: "He walked into the room, turned, stopped; then as he came out he asked me, 'Did you wash the blackboard by the door as I had asked before we sealed the room?' I told him, 'Chief, you know I did; you saw me do it.' And he said, 'We know nobody has been in there, don't we?' I agreed. But written on the board, Jerry, were the words, 'Oh merciful Father—' Now I'm a pretty skeptical person—I have a background in metaphysics, philosophy and science and I'm pretty hard to delude."

Head of the Brotherhood of the Ram discounts most fortune-telling schemes as not reading crystal balls or tea leaves but reading people. "Eight out of ten insights and predictions are totally off but those two that hit—people think, that's amazing; and the others go right down the drain.

"Now, as far as the evil connected with the occult," Don goes on, "can we compare it with the Jim Bakker problem or the Oral Roberts scheme of 'God's gonna take me home if you don't give three million dollars' or the Jimmy Swaggarts? There's good and bad in everything. I've seen everyone from abject occultists right on up to hootin' and hollerin' evangelists using—for good or evil—a sort of mass hypnosis. And I frankly think that's as far as it goes."

Paranormal Power

Duke University's J.B. Rhine began his scientific investigations into the paranormal way back in 1927 on the premise that much of the unexplained is due to unrealized potential in the human mind. With general acknowledgment that modern man uses only a fraction of his brainpower—estimates vary from 10 percent down to 2 percent—it's entirely possible that the 90 percent of mental capabilities that lie latent have something to do with paranormal phenomena.

However, organizations such as the Committee for the Scientific Investigation of Claims of the Paranormal, chaired by State University of New York philosophy professor Paul Kurtz, insist that all paranormal experience can be explained on the bases of hallucination, tomfoolery, magic tricks, autosuggestion and simple superstition.

But explanations of latent brainpower or superstition seem inadequate when faced with case after case of various manifestations of the paranormal. For instance, public libraries' occult shelves are stuffed with volumes written by people entranced. "Automatic writers" such as Jane Roberts with her "Seth materials" have published books which were rapidly dictated to them, they claim, by other intelligences.

Pearl Curran, an eighth-grade-educated St. Louis housewife, claimed to record in automatic writing the literary efforts of seventeenth-century Patience Worth of Dorsetshire, England. Pearl's writing—more than a million words in poetry and historical novels—included a 70,000-word piece rapidly produced by Curran in a nonstop automatic-writing trance. The piece was analyzed by Professor C.H.S. Schiller of London University. Schiller's analysis? *Gnosis* Magazine on page 11 of its fall 1987 issue quotes the good professor: "The vocabulary contained not a single word to have originated after 1600. When we consider the authorized version of the Bible has only 70 percent Anglo Saxon, and it is necessary to go back to Lyomen in 1205 to equal Patience's percentage of over 90 percent, we realize we are facing a philological miracle."

The point is, there's no way poorly educated Pearl Curran's latent mental powers or her best efforts at tomfoolery could without pause produce such a massive amount of historically dated vocabulary in her Patience Worth writings. There seems to be another intelligence operating in such paranormal cases.

I've researched this further in Carl Jung's *Psychology and the Occult* published by Princeton University Press, 1971, and *Memories, Dreams, Reflections* published by Pantheon Books in 1963.

Carl Jung, a remarkable influence in much of modern psychotherapy, felt that the intelligence which much paranormal phenomena tap into is called the "collective unconsciousness." But Jung's private, occult views on the source of that collective intelligence is rarely mentioned. For example, it isn't readily acknowledged that his *Septem Sermones ad Mortuos* or *Seven Sermons to the Dead*—an early work outlining his basic outlook—was itself a product of automatic writing: "[It] began to flow out of me, and in the course of three evenings the thing was written," Jung wrote. In 1948 he said, "Those who are not convinced should beware of naïvely assuming that the whole question of spirits and ghosts has been settled and that all manifestations of this kind are meaningless swindles."

Jung did not teach that spirits were external beings, but rather "exteriorizations" of the unconscious which "somehow or other . . . manifest themselves outwardly." But near the end of his life, Jung admitted that one of the "exteriorizations" who had stuck with him since 1912 was the spirit-being-like "Philemon." On page 183, Jung writes, "Philemon represented a force which was not myself . . . . It was he who taught me psychic objectivity, the reality of the psyche . . . . At times he seemed to me quite real, as if he were a living personality. I went walking up and down the garden with him, and to me he was what the Indians call a guru."

The other "father" of modern psychology, Sigmund Freud, seemed to admit that his earlier break with Jung's psychical concepts was perhaps premature. Toward the end of his life Freud wrote, "It no longer seems possible to brush aside the study of so-called occult facts; of things which seem to vouch-safe the real existence of psychic forces"—according to Nandor Fodor's quote on page 220 of his *Freud, Jung and Occultism*, a 1971 University Press release.

Let's take a break to remind ourselves that we're not out to prove anything about the paranormal. But we do need to listen to the possibilities that our kids, in dabbling with curses and conjuring and pacts with the devil just might be closer to the edge of evil than we dare think. Faddish satanism obviously can slide into drugs-sex-violence. That's documented because it's documentable.

But we might consider that the danger is even more diabolical: the demons they all talk about, the power that they say they can feel, the Satan that they worship just could be real. Or should we simply close our minds to that possibility because we know better?

But do we know better? Or are we only predisposed to insist that there is really no "bump in the night"?

Fathers LeBar and Flannery say that from the Roman Catholic position, there is supernatural or preternatural power in satanism and in much of the occult.

A half hour later I drive south on the cleared expressway past the Coke truck on my way to the Dallas Theological Seminary, a nondenominational school in the heart of old downtown Dallas.

The library is old; it creaks. The book stacks are packed into two stories with a small study area on the first floor. I find an annotated New American Standard version Bible called the Ryrie Study Bible. The notes are provided by Dr. Charles Ryrie, a longtime professor at the seminary. Thumbing through his notes at the back of the book, I find his outline on the biblical doctrines of Satan and demons:

The Doctrine of Satan

I. THE EXISTENCE OF SATAN

A. The Teaching of Scripture. The existence of Satan is taught in seven Old Testament books and by every New Testament writer.

B. The Teaching of Christ. He acknowledged and taught the existence of Satan (Matt. 13:39; Luke 10:18; 11:18).

II. THE PERSONALITY OF SATAN

A. He Possesses Intellect (2 Cor. 11:3).

B. He Has Emotions (Rev. 12:17)

C. He Has a Will (2 Tim. 2:26)

D. He is Treated as a Morally Responsible Person (Matt. 25:41)

E. Personal Pronouns Are Used of Him (Job 1)

III. THE DESIGNATIONS OF SATAN

A. Names 1. Satan (adversary) 2. Devil (Slanderer) 3. Lucifer (son of the morning). 4. Beelzebub (Matt. 12:24) 5. Belial (2 Cor. 6:15)

B. Titles 1. Evil One (I John 5:19,ASV) 2. Tempter (I Thess. 3:5) 3. Prince of this world (John 12:31) 4. God of this age (2 Cor. 4:4) 5. Prince of the power of the air (Eph. 2:2) 6. Accuser of the brethren (Rev. 12:10).

C. Representations. 1. Serpent (Rev. 12:9) 2. Dragon (Rev. 12:3) 3. Angel of light (2 Cor. 11:14).

IV. THE NATURE OF SATAN

A. His Character. 1. He is a creature (Ezek. 28:14). 2. He is a spirit being (Eph. 6:11–12). 3. He is of the order of angels called cherubim (Ezek. 28:14). 4. He was the highest of all angelic creatures (Ezek. 28:12).

B. His Personality Traits 1. He is a murderer (John 8:44). 2. He is a liar (John 8:44). 3. He is a confirmed sinner (I John 3:8) 4. He is an accuser (Rev. 12:20) 5. He is an adversary (I Peter 5:8).

C. His Limitations. 1. He is a creature and therefore not omniscient or infinite. 2. He can be resisted by the Christian (James 4:7). 3. God places limitations on him (Job 1:12).

V. THE ORIGINAL STATE AND FALL OF SATAN

A. Satan's Privileges (Ezek. 28:11–15).

B. Satan's Sin (Isa. 14:12–20).

    1. The Person (vv.12,15–20)

        a. his name (v. 12)

        b. his power (vv. 15–20)

    2. The Sin (vv.13–14)

        a. "I will ascend into heaven."

        b. "I will exalt my throne above the stars of God." (Either actual stars or other angels.)

        c. "I will sit on the mount of the assembly in the far north" (either assembly of angels or of Israel under Messianic rule).

        d. "I will ascend above the heights of the clouds" (usurp the glory of God).

        e. "I will be like the most High." (Satan wanted to be the possessor of heaven and earth.) His sin is called pride in I Timothy 3:6, and it may be characterized as counterfeiting God (like the Most High).

C. Satan's Punishment (Ezek. 28:16–19).

VI. SATAN'S JUDGMENTS

A. Cast Out of His Original Position in Heaven (Ezek. 28:16)

B. Judgment Pronounced in Eden (Gen. 3:14–15)

C. Judged at the Cross (John 12:31)

D. Cast Out in the Midst of the Tribulation Period (Rev. 12:13)

E. Confined in the Abyss at the Beginning of the Millennium (Rev. 20:2)

F. Cast into the Lake of Fire at the End of the Millennium (Rev. 20:10)

VII. THE WORK OF SATAN

A. In Relation to the Redemptive Work of Christ. 1. Prediction of Conflict (Gen. 3:15) 2. Temptation of Christ (Matt. 4:1–11). 3. Satan used various people to attempt to thwart the work of Christ (Matt. 2:16; John 8:44; Matt. 16:23). 4. He possessed Judas' body for the betrayal (John 13:27).

B. In Relation to the Nations. He deceives them now (Rev. 20:3). 2. He will gather them to the battle of Armageddon (Rev. 16:13–14).

C. In Relation to Unbelievers. 1. He blinds their minds (2 Cor. 4:4). 2. He snatches the Word from their hearts (Luke 8:12). 3. He uses men to oppose God's work (Rev. 2:13).

D. In Relation to the Christian. 1. He tempts him to lie (Acts 5:3). 2. He accuses and slanders him (Rev. 12:10). 3. He hinders his work (I Thess. 2:18). 4. He employs demons to attempt to defeat him (Eph. 6:11–12). 5. He tempts to immorality (I Cor. 7:5). 6. He sows tares among believers (Matt. 13:38–39). 7. He incites persecutions against them (Rev. 2:10).

VIII. THE DEFENSE OF THE BELIEVER AGAINST SATAN

A. The Present Intercessory Work of Christ (John 17:15).

B. The Purpose of God May Include Using Satan for Beneficial Purposes in the Life of the Christian (2 Cor. 12:7).

C. The Christian Should Never Speak of Satan Contemptuously (Jude 8–9).

D. The Believer Should Be on Guard (I Peter 5:8).

E. The Believer Should Take a Stand Against Satan (James 4:7).

F. The Believer Should Use His Armor (Eph. 6:11–18).

It's beginning to get dark outside the seminary library. One wall of the study area is completely glass, and between campus buildings the beautiful architecture of the Dallas skyline glint reflections of the sunset. One of the skyscrapers is completely outlined in green neon lighting. And it's hard to believe that any of the seminarians get much studying done here. But back to demons. Ryrie also has a section on biblical demonology:

Doctrine of Demons

I. ORIGIN OF DEMONS

A. Souls of Departed Evil People. A heathen Greek view.

B. Disembodied Spirits of a Pre-Adamic Race. The Bible speaks of such a race.

C. The Offspring of Angels and Antediluvian Women (Gen. 6:1–4).

D. Fallen Angels. Satan is an angel, and is called prince of the demons (Matt.12:24) indicating that the demons are angels, not a pre-Adamic race. Furthermore, Satan has well-organized ranks of angels (Eph. 6:11–12), and it is reasonable to suppose that these are the demons. Some demons are confined already (2 Peter 2:4; Jude 6) and some are loose to do Satan's work. It is thought by some that the reason certain demons are presently confined is that they participated in the sin of Genesis 6:1–4.

II. CHARACTERISTICS OF DEMONS

A. Their Nature. They are spirit beings. Note that the demon in Matthew 17:18 is called an unclean spirit in the parallel account in Mark 9:25. See also Ephesians 6:12.

B. Their Intellect. They know Jesus (Mark 1:24), their own doom (Matt. 8:29), the plan of salvation (James 2:19). They have a well-developed system of doctrine of their own (I Tim. 4:1–3).

C. Their Morality. They are called unclean spirits, and their doctrine leads to immoral conduct (I Tim. 4:1–2).

III. ACTIVITY OF DEMONS

A. In General. 1. Demons attempt to thwart the purpose of God (Dan. 10:10-14; Rev. 16:13-16). 2. Demons extend the authority of Satan by doing his bidding (Eph. 6:11-12). 3. Demons may be used by God in the carrying out of His purposes (I Sam. 16:14; 2 Cor. 12:7).

B. In Particular. 1. Demons can inflict diseases (Matt. 9:33; Luke 13:11,16). 2. Demons can possess men (Matt. 4:24). 3. Demons can possess animals (Mark 5:13). 4. Demons oppose the spiritual growth of God's children (Eph. 6:12). 5. Demons disseminate false doctrine (I Tim. 4:1).

IV. DEMON POSSESSION

A. Definition of Demon Possession. Demon possession means a demon residing in a person, exerting direct control and influence over that person, with certain derangement of mind and/or body. Demon possession is to be distinguished from demon influence or demon activity in relation to a person. The work of the demon in the latter is from the outside; in demon possession it is from within. By this definition a Christian cannot be possessed by a demon since he is indwelt by the Holy Spirit. However, a believer can be the target of demonic activity to such an extent that he may give the appearance of demon possession.

B. Effects of Demon Possession. 1. Sometimes physical disease (Matt. 9:32-33), but physical disease and demon possession are distinguished in Scripture (Acts 5:16). 2. Sometimes mental derangement is due to demon possession (Matt. 17:15) but not always (Dan. 4).

C. Extent of Demon Possession. 1. As to persons, only unbelievers may be possessed. In the time of Christ, most instances of demon possession were among non-Israelites.

2. As to time. Usually there is an outbreak of demon activity when truth and light are the strongest (e.g. time of Christ).

V. DESTINATION OF DEMONS

A. Temporary Destiny. 1. Some free ones were cast into the abyss (Luke 8:31; cf. Rev. 9:11). 2. Some confined ones will be loosed in the Tribulation (Rev. 9—11; 16:13-14).

B. Permanent Destiny. Eventually all demons will be cast with Satan into the lake of fire (Matt. 25:41).

Heady stuff, this biblical view of Satan and his minions. Apocalyptic stuff. It's dark outside, but Dallas downtown looks like the Emerald City with dazzling skyscrapers looking like tall crystals and searchlights winding across the sky announcing some new car dealership.

I decide to go ahead and plow through this topic that frankly is a little uncomfortable: demon possession. Through the afternoon we've seen how the Roman Catholic Church believes in Satan and his demons and their activity on earth. Protestant fundamentalists and evangelicals believe in the same. And from our perusal of Ryrie's biblical outline, apparently so does God.

Hardcore scientific types, of course, do not. But then, what can a philosophy based on the empirical repetition of experiments say about something as elusive as "spirit"? Nobody—we included—is going to prove or disprove the existence of Satan or of God for that matter. Or of demons.

But as we have in the rest of our inquiry, we can simply see what is said. Let's focus on this unnerving matter of demon activity, of demon possession.

In the seminary library I find a copy of *People of the Lie.* Psychiatrist Scott Peck, author of the popular *The Road Less Traveled,* began his personal investigations into the "psychology of evil" after serving as chairman of a committee studying the atrocities at the My Lai massacre during the Viet Nam War. He was gripped by the evil evidenced. In his 1983 Simon and Schuster book, *People of the Lie,* Peck discusses his experiences in trying to understand the power of evil. He says on page 188 he has "personally met Satan face to face." On page 196 he shares this story of an exorcism he attended:

When the demonic finally spoke clearly in one case, an expression appeared on the patient's face that could be described only as Satanic. It was an incredibly contemptuous grin of utter hostile malevolence. I have spent many hours before a mirror trying to imitate it without the slightest success.

When the demonic finally revealed itself in the exorcism of [another] patient, it was with a still more ghastly expression. The patient suddenly resembled a writhing snake of great strength, viciously attempting to bite the team members.

More frightening than the writhing body, however, was the face. The eyes were hooded with lazy reptilian torpor—except when the reptile darted out in attack, at which moment the eyes would open wide with blazing hatred. Despite these frequent darting movements, what upset me the most was the extraordinary sense of a fifty-million-year-old heaviness I received from this serpentine being.

Almost all the team members at both exorcisms were convinced they were at these times in the presence of something absolutely alien and inhuman. The end of each exorcism proper was signaled by the departure of this Presence from the patient and the room.

But is demon possession too easy an answer for complicated psychological disturbances—such as multiple personalities?

▶ 19 ◀

Alter Personalities?
Spirits? Or Both?

Many psychiatrists, of course, dismiss the concept of demon possession as archaic superstition. This position is bolstered considerably by the surge of recent study in multiple personalities. An Institute of Noetic Science newsletter I picked up at Dr. Bennet Braun's office back in Chicago overviews the amazing findings of psychiatrists such as Braun as they work with dissociative disorders.

Multiples and Alters

Many of the patients providing insight into multiple personality disorders have been satanically terrorized. In fact, Jacquie Balodis in the L.A. area suggests that hardcore satanic cults have perfected methods that, applied to children, purposely produce multiple personalities.

I pull out of my book bag a yellow marker and the packet of materials Braun gave me. Let me highlight some of the Institute of Noetic Sciences information on multiple personality disorders, keeping in mind it's a possible explanation for what people view as demonization.

The Investigations research bulletin, volume 1, number 3/4 begins its discussion of the multiple personality phenomenon with John Milton's "Paradise Lost" insight into the satanic mindset: "The mind is its own place, and in itself can make a heaven of Hell, a hell of Heaven."

In the article, "Inner Faces of Multiplicity," the bulletin explains, "Multiple Personality Disorder or MPD is an extraordinary syndrome in which two or more integrated alter selves co-exist simultaneously in a single body.

"Alter personalities may differ in terms of voice, posture, physiognomy, handedness and—if preliminary research studies are correct—numerous physiological features such as brainwave patterns, immune status, and skin electrical responses. Behavior patterns, reported life history and [subjectively perceived] sex and age also tend to vary. Different personalities have often mastered different physical abilities, interpersonal skills, and intellectual subject areas. Some may command entirely different languages."

The article has an inset: "The average number of alter personalities in a multiple is 8–13, although super-multiples may have more than 100 alternates."

The history of the study of dissociative disorders, the bulletin says, goes back to antiquity. "Transformations of personality such as those occurring in multiple personality have occurred throughout history in societies around the world. In many such cultures, . . . such transformations are interpreted as possession by a spirit or by another species. Ninety percent of societies worldwide have records of such possession-like phenomena."

Modern interest in personality transformations is largely credited to Dr. Cornelia Wilbur's work at the University of Kentucky School of Medicine as she identified the role of severe abuse in MPD's development in Sybil Dorsett. The book and movie *Sybil* popularized the notion that some people can exhibit more than one personality.

Daniel Keyes' book, *The Minds of Billy Milligan*, furthered the general public's knowledge of MPD. Milligan exhibited 24 distinct alter personalities including a Serbo-Croatian-speaking karate expert of enormous strength, Arthur who is the British physicist able to read and write fluent Arabic, Adalana the 19-year-old lesbian and three-year-old dyslexic Christene.

Throughout the history of psychiatry, MPD has "been considered extremely rare. Yet known cases of MPD have mushroomed during the last 15 years, and some authorities in the field now think that MPD may be more prevalent than ever suspected. At the First International Conference on Multiple Personality/Dissociative States, Dr. Frank Putnam called cases that have been seen to date 'just the tip of the iceberg.'

"The trend in the number of diagnosed cases of MPD," the Institute of Noetic Sciences bulletin continues, "is clearly upward . . . . Dr. Martin Orne . . . estimated that at least two to three times as many cases . . . have been reported in the last 10–15 years than in the entire 100–150 years prior to 1970."

The methodology of satanic cult abuse of children is designed, according to Jacquie Balodis of Overcomers Victorious, to produce splittings of the child's personalities. Why? The Noetic bulletin suggests that "splitting" or the creation of alter personalities "involves the polarization of emotional identifications so that the child fails to integrate experiences of 'good' and 'bad' in developing mental representations of the self and others." In other words, satanists adept at ritual child abuse can "create" amorality in a multiple-personality child. And a growing child who doesn't distinguish between good and evil is prime material for satanic cult recruitment.

Multiplicity is often seen in more than one generation of a family, and psychiatrists are actively arguing whether this phenomenon suggests a genetic susceptibility to MPD or a simple chain of cause and effect: "It has been found that the violent personalities of adult multiples attack their children."

Multiple Physiologies

Some of the elements of MPD are nothing short of amazing: The bulletin reports differences of brain electrical activity among alter personalities; there is apparently a "structural reorganization of the nervous system" when personalities switch.

Implications for study of the mind-body problem seen in MPD are intriguing, to say the least. Ilya Prigogine in "Multiplicity and the Mind-Body Problem" on page 19 of the Institute research bulletin points out that even standard traits such as handedness, color-blindness or allergies can vary according to which alter is in control of a multiple's body. "The evidence is strong . . . that persons with MPD undergo dramatic shifts not just from one personality to another, but from being left-handed to right-handed and from being allergic to non-allergic." There can be "shifts in the status of the immune system." Prigogine states that "the fact that these people can make such switches 'at will' after therapy opens up new avenues for the study of the mind-body problem that promise to tell us things about the connections we never knew."

Doctors have substantiated changes in brainwave patterns; Dr. Robert deVito reported at the First International Conference on MPD "changes in regional cerebral blood flow in multiples as they switched personalities."

In the American Journal of Clinical Hypnosis Dr. Braun described cases in which multiples are allergic to citrus or animals in one alter personality but not in others. Dermatologic reactions are also remarkable: Dr. Braun "reports on the case of a female multiple who was tortured by both her mother and brother. One form of this abuse involved putting out lighted cigarettes on her skin. When the personality that received burns took over during therapy sessions, the burn marks would reappear on her skin and last for 6–10 hours."

Prigogine's article continues: "In many cases, . . . there are reports of multiples with alternates that are either anesthetic and don't feel pain at all or cases where there are special personalities whose 'job' it is to take the pain. . . . The extent to which multiples seem to be able to use this mechanism appears to be exceptional."

Apparently multiples heal more rapidly than other people. "The anecdotal evidence here comes from cases discussed separately by Dr. Frank Putnam of the National Institute of Mental Health and Dr. Cornelia Wilbur and Braun and includes cases where third-degree burns healed with extraordinary rapidity. . . . Wilbur suggests that multiples don't seem to age as rapidly as other people."

The incredible effects of MPD are further catalogued in the bulletin—for instance, Dr. Braun has reported on the case of "a woman who is diabetic in one personality and not in another."

The bulletin concedes that "scientists still know remarkably little about dissociation." Dr. Richard Kluft, Braun's colleague, said, "We do know that it appears that dissociation is a psychophysiological event, the dynamic contents of which do not explain its essential structure and process."

The remarkable, mysterious aspects of MPD do apparently lead some clinicians to consider more than the biochemical reactions of the syndrome. Dr. Ralph Allison, the bulletin states, "who with Dr. Cornelia Wilbur is one of the pioneers in the modern treatment of MPD, says bluntly that many of his multiple personality patients have exhibited symptoms of possession.

"Repeatedly, [Allison writes] I encountered aspects of their personalities that were not true alter personalities. . . . In many of these cases, it was difficult to dismiss these unusual and bizarre occurrences as mere delusion. In the absence of any 'logical' explanation, I have come to believe in the possibility of spirit possession."

Allison recounts numerous cases of apparent spirit possession in MPD in his 1980 book, *Minds in Many Pieces*. He has developed a conceptual scheme which distinguishes five levels or types of possession—ranging from simple obsessive compulsive neurosis on one end to full demonic possession on the other—and says that he has "corresponded with many professionals who have come to similar conclusions about the origin and purpose of alter personalities."

Multiple Spirit Guides?

In keeping with Myers' view that the mind is "open at both ends," Allison has also described benign spirit guides that therapists sometimes encounter in multiples, which he calls Inner Self Helpers (ISH). Unlike genuine alter personalities these beings have no specific date of origin, serve no ordinary function such as handling anger or expressing sexuality, and "know the patient's past history and can predict future actions with great accuracy." They expect to work with the therapist, and "serve as conduit for God's healing power and love."

Jacquie Balodis, whom we met in Garden Grove, California, emphasizes the validity of explaining much "demon possession" as dramatic manifestations of split and multiple personalities. She herself had more than 100 alters when she fled the satanic cult she'd grown up in. But she also asserts that in some cases, strange manifestations of varying voices, personalities and abilities such as inhuman strength are demonic in nature.

Robert Karman was another therapist I'd met in Los Angeles. His counseling of several patients who had in various ways dabbled in the occult or been raised in a satanist family led him to acknowledge the presence of demonic forces. I pull out the booklet he's published through his Suntelo counseling practice in Whittier, a town tucked into the middle of the Los Angeles area sprawl.

Robert's first lesson occurred in the very room in which we sat when a patient said in characteristically schizoid fashion, "I hear voices most of the time."

Robert said that his usual response as a therapist to this common statement is to ask if he can talk with these voices. The schizophrenic will then have to admit that no one else can hear them—which is a step in confirming to the patient that the voices are only auditory hallucinations.

He had asked the patient, "Well, can I speak with these voices?"

Surprisingly, the patient had said, "Of course."

The psychologist had then groped for words to tell me how he felt the patient "retreating" somehow and another being altogether stating in another voice, "Well, shall we talk?"

I found Robert's position on demonization interesting as he intelligently articulated the rational balance of psychological and spiritual therapy needed in these cases. Robert, dark-haired, comfortable in early middle age, slouched back in a soft chair and offered me the booklet he'd published. I'll share some of it with you:

One patient, a graduate of a Christian university, had five years of productive psychological therapy before coming to my office. During those five years she had worked through most aspects of a number of early traumas including several incestuous relationships, being branded as a young child in a satanic ceremony, and so forth. Although the previous therapy accomplished a great deal, an underlying spiritual conflict remained covered but was not ready to emerge.

Initially, I had diagnosed her as having multiple personalities, which proved accurate and which had not been previously addressed in therapy. However, not all of the personalities loved or even knew about God. Based on techniques I developed and employed successfully with another case in which some personalities knew and loved God and others did not, I explained the gospel with the "atheist." She responded positively and started to love God.

A few days later I attempted to talk with another personality about God, but "voices" prevented her from accepting Christ's work on the cross. As I explored their nature I discovered that the voices were neither psychotic symptoms nor additional personalities, but a group of demons. Through subsequent therapy the woman gained sufficient strength to remove these demons herself, a difficult process but with permanent results.

In presenting an ever-changing kaleidoscope the multiple personalities diverted Satan from finding and stealing the soul. Once the demons departed the personalities fused together easily, for they were no longer needed to divert.

In this case spiritual problems were identified and addressed as part of an ongoing course of psychological care. When they are not, and Satan continues to work inside or from outside of the person, most traditional psychotherapy will fail, not because the psychological concerns cannot be identified, but because it does not address the underlying spiritual source. Spiritual damage can create, maintain, and resist psychological treatment by regenerating the psychologically damaged areas under treatment.

Put another way, I am suggesting that a major source of failure in psychological treatment of some persons is that most professionals accept the mind but either deny the spiritual bluntly or deny it by attempting to translate it into psychological terms.

Conversely, the other source of failure is those who never seek treatment because they accept the spiritual but then spiritualize the mind and consequently deny what psychology has to offer.

I look up at the faces of the dozen or so seminarians frowning over their studies. A black-bearded, pale-faced young man in a white turtleneck sweater; a very plain girl—no makeup, olive green skirt and blouse, hair pulled back in a pony tail, finger-smudged glasses; an attractive couple reading with arms linked—I wonder what their preparation is to head out into the world to battle the forces of evil. Do they think of themselves as being pitted in a cosmic struggle against actual evil entities? Or is their vision of ministry a coaxing of people from their hearts of darkness toward goodness, toward a commitment with no realistic acknowledgment of serious demonic opposition?

I fall back into a perusal of the stack of books on my study table and lose track of time till the librarian gives me a heart attack by yelling "The library will close in five minutes!" And I don't really have an opportunity simply to ask any of the students about their own views on demonology.

I use the five minutes to frantically run off photocopies of several pages of a Kurt Koch book, *Occult Bondage and Deliverance*—published by Kregel Publications of Grand Rapids in 1970. I recognize Koch as one of the names mentioned by nearly every theological contact I've made. The German theologian and a psychiatrist, Dr. Alfred Lechler, are a team that, according to a blurb, are "perhaps the best source of case histories and other factual data relating to the practice of occultism. [Koch] has devoted over thirty years to this study, and has personally investigated more than 20,000 incidents in which psychic and occultic phenomena were involved."

I suddenly wonder about the blurb's claim of 20,000 cases. Maybe I'm getting cynical about even the ministerial claims about this slippery topic.

Koch begins the section on possession by stating that "for the non-Christian psychiatrist possession just does not exist. At most it is only an advanced form of hysteria. But attitudes like this need not worry us. Possession is a religious and spiritual phenomenon which needs to be regarded and judged from a spiritual point of view."

He then lists symptoms of possession as seen in a New Testament story of a Gadarene demoniac in Mark 5:

Mark 5:2   The demoniac had an unclean spirit. In other words, he was indwelt by another being.

Mark 5:3   The possessed man exhibited unusual powers of physical strength. No one could bind him any more.

Mark 5:4   The third characteristic was the paroxysms (fits of rage). He had wrenched chains apart and broken his fetters in pieces.

Mark 5:6,7   The fourth sign is one of disintegration, the splitting of the personality. The demoniac runs to Jesus for help, yet cries out in fear.

Mark 5:7   The fifth sign is that of resistance, an opposition to the Christian faith and spiritual things. He tells Jesus to leave him alone. One meets this resistance to spiritual help quite often in counselling subjected people.

Mark 5:7   The sixth symptom is hyperaesthesia, an excessive sensibility. The Gadarene had clairvoyant powers. He knew immediately who Jesus really was.

Mark 5:9   The seventh sign is seen in the variations or alteration of voice. A 'legion' of demons spoke out of him.

Mark 5:13   The eighth characteristic is occult transference. The demons left the man and entered into the swine.

"It should be noted," writes Koch, "that the second, third and fourth characteristics we have just outlined are similar in many respects to the symptoms of certain mental illnesses . . . .

Koch then suggests that the remaining five characteristics are not psychiatric conditions. For example, clairvoyance (speaking in a voice or a language he has previously not learned) and transference don't occur as signs of mental illness. Koch then answers the question of how possession can be recognized. He says if one "meets a person who claims to be demon possessed, then he is not demon possessed. Anyone who is really possessed will neither realize nor broadcast the fact of his possession." Koch's characteristic signs of genuine cases of demon possession include a resistance and a trance-like reaction to prayer, clairvoyance and the ability to speak unlearned languages.

"There is one further striking factor to mention with regard to the counselling of possessed people," writes Koch. "If the counsellor is not a born again Christian, one finds that not one of the characteristics we have just mentioned will make an appearance."

A Spirit Battle?

In the car, I listen to the tape of Lyle Rapacki, a 6'5" ex-cop psychologist who counsels satanically traumatized kids and adults from his base in Flagstaff, Arizona. He also produces reports on deviant crime through his INTEL investigative agency. Lyle is a busy man and he firmly believes his counseling satanic victims and educating judicial system personnel is a spiritual battle. We had sat in the waiting room of his nicely appointed, Arizona-sunny office in Flagstaff:

"After eight years and about 175 exorcisms," Lyle says, "I'm still seeing things I had no previous understanding of, no previous experience with."

Lyle told me of specific cases of demon possession, of a boy whose "Exorcist"-type behavior prompted a psychiatrist-colleague to comment, "This is far more bizarre than I'm prepared to handle."

"Of course, there are people who are cynical out there about ever mentioning the power of evil, demons or Satan. But it's mostly due to the fact that they've been hurt by the church. They've been hurt because the God they were introduced to through their church or through Christians is either a pussycat or he's Santa Claus.

"A lot of people have grown up with these theologies, and they're finding when things go bump in the night in our homes, in our communities, who can they call on? You see, God has lost his identity, so we don't know who to call on in the face of evil; so we're forced to deny the whole thing. Of course there are no spirits beyond ourselves; and if there are, of course they're only kind and good or fully under our control. Because we don't have a real God to turn to, denial is the name of the game.

"And yet here I am getting calls daily from law enforcement since that's my background saying, 'Will you help us out? We've got a situation here we're not prepared to handle.' I get calls saying, 'Can you help me—my five-year-old has just been taken and sacrificed and nobody will believe me.'"

He concludes, "Law enforcement is getting swamped with the stuff; it hasn't hit the epidemic stage, but it's coming. And I'd be a liar if I called it anything than what it really is. It's spiritual warfare. I have more witnesses than you can shake a stick at—my secretary is one—who've heard the demons scream."

I remember asking his secretary Lori Mountjoy on my way out if this is a wild office to work in. "Undoubtedly," she said.

When I arrive back at my Dallas motel room, I decide to call the professor I'd missed up in Chicago, Fred Dickason of the Moody Bible Institute.

"And so you got the ghostbusting work," I say.

"Right. I really didn't ask for it, but it came my way, so I thought I'd better shore up my education in this area. I did some research and I eventually developed a book called *Angels, Elect and Evil*. I counseled people as they came along—counseled very carefully, cautiously, I should say."

▶ 20 ◀

The Exorcism

Back in my Dallas motel room, I read through an interview with Raul Reis, pastor of Calvary Chapel of West Covina, California. Raul's story begins:

"It was the last night of a pastor's conference at a facility in the San Bernardino mountains. As the final speaker was preparing to deliver his message, a couple of the other pastors and myself were approached by a police officer and told that there was a problem at a small church a few miles down the road which his department was unsure how to handle. He asked if we could help. Four of us quietly left the conference center and went with the officer to the church.

"When we arrived, we saw a young woman, maybe in her late twenties, about five feet, three inches, weighing no more than 105 pounds, sitting on a small stone wall in front of the church. Around her a safe distance away stood a circle of police officers, each one measuring at least five-eleven and weighing 190 pounds or more. None of them took their eyes from the woman sitting on the wall. She, too, maintained eye contact with the officers.

"The police officer, who was a Christian, told us the woman was brought to the church by her husband because he had thought she was demon possessed. After the first officers on the scene were unable to contain her violent behavior, they called for backups, but even all of the officers together were unable to subdue her. She had just tossed them around with superhuman strength. That's when they came for us.

"After talking calmly with the young woman and her husband, we were finally able to persuade her to come inside the church building with us, although she wanted no one to touch her.

"The other pastors and I went inside ahead of the woman and watched as she entered after us. As soon as she stepped foot inside the church building

204

her body tensed up as stiff as a board and she took each forward step as if her legs were 100 pound weights. She only made it halfway up the aisle before she stopped; something violent seemed to be going on inside her.

"One of the other pastors walked up to her and spoke in a calm, firm voice, 'In the name of Jesus Christ, I command you to come out of her.'

"In an instant the woman's face changed to a demonic snarl as she sprang at the pastor, her hands like claws, trying to gouge his eyes. There was no doubt in my mind that she was going to kill him, so I jumped on her back, applying my full weight to slow her. She didn't slow. I reached around her neck and applied the strongest chokehold I have ever used in all my years of kung-fu training. She slowed down some but still would not quit, turning her head from side to side, trying to bite my arm. I managed to come up tight under her chin with the inside of my elbow, locking her jaw shut. And then, as if I were on the back of a bucking horse, I wrestled her arms and legs down while I maintained the chokehold.

"Over the next three hours many demons were cast out of her, one at a time. It was a long, tiring process in which the woman repeatedly spoke in a man's deep voice, her face contorting, her eyes rolling back in their sockets. The demons fought viciously not to leave the woman's body, screaming and convulsing as the name of Jesus Christ forced them out. A putrid yellow and green ooze flowed from her mouth every time a demon left her. It was the foulest odor I have ever smelled in my life."

The Exorcism

It's nearly midnight, probably an appropriate time for such a story. I had sent the cassette tape with this story to a transcriber near Kansas City. When I didn't get any confirmation that the transcriptions were ready, I called to find out that her computer was on the blink.

Switching to another computer, she'd completed the transcriptions and Federal Expressed the floppy disk to me. I'd put the disk in my computer, noticed that this file labelled exorcism contained 28,000 characters, then pulled it up onscreen.

There were two rows of little face symbols, then about thirty blank pages. She transcribed it again, sent another disk and hard copy to me, and told me her husband had put his foot down. That was it; she would not be doing any more of this devilish computer keying for me. "Hey, maybe my next project will be on cultivating petunias," I had said.

But tonight, after mulling all day on the bizarre possibility that there really is something hiding in the closet waiting till you turn off the light, this tape doesn't seem anything but sinister.

I'll play the tape; it was given to me by Karl Klassen in Victoria, British

Columbia. It records the voices of Archie Huewright, of Ann, a teenager, and of several other entities whose names are legion. I'll let you read the transcript. Archie Huewright introduces the tape:

Ann was introduced to us through one of the ladies from our church who works with the Fernwood Street Girls' Hostel. She has had very little knowledge of her mother, her father is an alcoholic, and so she had very little love as a girl. Apparently she was kicked around more or less from pillar to post and no one ever really seemed to care for her. She said that when she was a girl of about 8 or 9 she spoke in tongues, and that when she did begin to speak in tongues again at a particular Pentecostal church here in Victoria she said it was very disappointing because it was the very same tongue, as far as she could tell, that she spoke when she was a child.

The first interview I had with her was at the Fernwood Home; I explained to her some of the basics of salvation and living the Christian life. At the home of one of the Christians I spoke to her further and experienced a good feel that there was a real presence of another spirit there.

Reverend Harwood of the Evangelical Union of South America came and spoke at our church, and I asked him if he would join me in speaking to this young lady and testing the spirit. When we spoke to this spirit in the English language it reacted violently, but when we spoke to it in the German language it reacted very violently.

The tape then breaks to Ann, sounding like any older teenager, saying: "Yeah, that was really weird because I said, 'Okay, devil, if you're real, you know, I want you to show me some kind of a sign, right this minute.' And then all the power went off in the house. And I said, well that could be a coincidence. And I said, 'If you are real, show me another sign.' And it went right on again. And I said, now this is—I don't know, that could have been a coincidence. I've never had anything really spectacular happen."

Archie then asks, "Along with this there is this depression, making you feel miserable? As you said a while ago you feel guilty?"

"Yeah."

"A depressive feeling that gets you down as though you were tired in some way? Darkness over you somehow? That's the way it is?"

Ann says, "Yeah. I'm very depressed even though it doesn't really show. People don't—I've been depressed for such a long time that—"

"It's almost a part of your life, like."

"Yeah, really. Awfully. I was depressed even before. Yeah, I guess it started about the time I started speaking in tongues but I don't know because, as I say, I stopped for a while, for a few years, but I was still depressed. But it might have been the circumstances of what was going on at home."

Rev. Harwood asks, "Do you have sort of inward weeping, sort of a pressure and a weakness?"

"Yeah, it's in my stomach. It is."

Rev. Harwood continues: "And sort of a weeping as if you'd like to cry but you can't really cry? I mean, that it's sort of, oh, if you could only cry it out of your system, but you can't really cry it out?"

Ann adds, "And even if I do cry, it really doesn't make any difference; it's still there. And sometimes I can feel this screaming inside of me. And sometimes sort of like baby talk is coming out. It's different from the tongues."

"Garbled, sort of?"

"Yeah. It's not the same all the time. There's a variation in it. Well, the tongues is I guess more or less the same. But then as well as the tongues, I get feeling really funny sometimes. It starts right here, just like the tongues, and my mouth goes tense and it starts to go funny."

A Mrs. Sibble from the girls' home adds, "It goes sort of round, too. The other night when you spoke in tongues it almost sort of went round, like a fish's mouth."

"Yeah, it does that. Ooh, it's awful. And I don't know . . . ."

Archie asks kindly, "Have you ever found out exactly what this is?"

"I've been thinking if I do have—have a bad spirit. I don't know how on earth I ever got it. Because I used to, when I was a little girl I used to like to cast spells and stuff like that but I never really knew anything about witchcraft. I would read about it sometimes, but I never really—I didn't go to a devil's church or anything like that.

"So where it came from I don't know."

"Did your parents or your father ever have anything to do with a spiritualist church or anything like that? Any relatives go to a spiritualist medium?"

"I don't know," Ann says. "My sister did, but this was just a couple of years ago. I don't know. But, like I just know that there's something the matter with me and my psychiatrist said that there's nothing wrong. So if I can't get help from him because—"

"Because he doesn't believe in spirits, evil spirits."

"No."

Archie says, "If you take the Bible, the Word of God, it tells us that these things do exist, and it tells us what to do in cases like this. Now, we need to know a little about this. The spirits themselves will speak; they may use your voice to speak. I have talked with spirits before in this way. You said a while ago that you want to be saved. You want to get right with God so that Heaven is your home and here is this thing that is troubling you." Archie and Ann discuss salvation. Then Archie goes on: "Ann, dear, you said a while ago that you practiced casting spells and that kind of thing so much as play.

"The reality of that may be that you lent yourself to it. It may have given leeway, an opening for the devil to come in with deceptions, even though you didn't realize what it was. People who are caught in these types of things often don't realize what they're doing once they get into it.

"The devil is deceptive, he's a sneak, he's a liar and he does these things to hinder one from being right with God. To ruin their life and their soul and everything possible. Well now, do you want to make the move right now to get rid of this thing, right this afternoon at any cost? Now, I'll suggest that, see, it's the spirit or spirits that have been bothering you that we have to deal with. Not with you, yourself. Any spirits. Now we need to use the power and the authority of the Word of God with these. Will you do that now?"

"Yeah." Ann is silent for a moment; then begins softly mumbling in "tongues"—in a repetitive lilt that to me sounds Middle Eastern, like Farsee. With this in the background, Archie asks five questions:

—"Spirit or spirits, how many are you? Are you one or are you more?"

—"Spirits, in the name of Jesus Christ, answer. Is there one of you alone or more?"

—"Spirit, in the name of Jesus Christ, answer this question. Are you one or more?"

Ann continues to mumble, speaking in tongues. Archie continues:

—"Now, spirit or spirits, will you confess that Jesus Christ has come in the flesh?"

—"Spirit, in the name of Jesus Christ, will you confess that Jesus Christ is come in the flesh? Speak in English and answer me now."

Suddenly the babbling stops and a huge voice wails, "Nooooo! Nooo—"

"No?" Archie sounds as if he has to gulp to ask. "No?"

"No!"

Archie says, "Spirit, in the name of Jesus Christ we ask, come out of her; leave her alone. In the name of Jesus Christ leave her now."

Rev. Harwood says, "Yes, in the name of the Lord Jesus Christ. Christ is victor, Christ is victor. God, Oh Lord, in the name of Christ we call on You now. By Your great power, cast out this spirit from this girl. Set her free. In Christ's name. Spirit leave her now, in the name of God."

The moaning wail continues.

Archie says, "Spirit, leave her and bother her no more. In the name of Jesus Christ, leave now and be gone. Oh, God, in the name of Thy Son, take over now this one and set her free. Deliver her now from this demon that has hold of her and set her free right now, Lord, in Christ's name."

The voice breaks feverishly into what seems to be Latin. It cries and moans.

Rev. Harwood says in German, "*Ist Jesu Christus in die Fleisch gekommen? Antwortete. Komm arousch, komm arousch. Arousch. In the name of Jesu Christus, komm rousch und niemald hierein segein? Komm arousch in name Jesu Christus.*"

The growls and moans crescendo. In my bare-feeling Dallas motel room I reach over to the tape player and turn down the volume.

Rev. Harwood says, "Same thing when I spoke German last time. Really reacted violently."

Archie asks, "In the name of the Lord Jesus Christ, are you German? How do you spell your name?"

The voice says slowly, "It's J-R-E."

"Have you other associates?"

"Ten."

"There are ten. Are they there with you now?"

"Yes."

"Do you command them?" Archie asks. "And they, you?"

"Unfortunately, yes."

"Will you come out now and the others of the group?"

"You're smart, aren't you?"

"In the name of the Lord Jesus Christ," both men say together, "we command you Jre and all that come with you, come out of Ann and go to the pit right now. Amen."

The tape breaks as it's turned off, then on again:

"Who are you? What is your name?" asks Archie in a distinguished Canadian lilt. "How do you spell your name?"

"L- U-."

"I said, how do you spell it?"

"You don't frighten me," says the voice. "You care nothing about us. You're putting us off balance, you know. It's L-U-F-E-R."

"And where did you come from?"

The reply is unintelligible.

Archie says, "Who sent you?"

The sing-song baby voice says, "Oh, the devil sent me, he sent me from the pit."

"All right, Lufer, you're uncovered; we know who you are. And we know you've caused Ann to look like a fool."

The voice sneers: "Funny, isn't it? You make us sick."

"You didn't succeed," says Archie. "You're beaten, aren't you? You're defeated, aren't you?"

"Christ can fool her all the time," the voice says.

"Yes. And so you are defeated by God."

"You know his reputation; he makes me so mad. He loved her; we hated her."

"Now then, you're beaten. All right, Lufer—"

"Wasn't that nice of us?"

"Do you have any associates?"

"They're out. Remember last year?"

"All right, now. Do you have any associates left?"

"I don't think so."

"You tell me the truth right now in the name of the Lord Jesus Christ."

"No, we don't. I said we don't, remember; I didn't say I."

Archie's voice is getting raspy. "Who are 'we'?" he asks.

The voice is sing-song, mocking again: "Here I am; where are you, Oscar?

Oscar, come here; oh, you've gone to the pit. You see, there are two of us, we didn't tell you, we should have told you."

"I see," says Archie. "Two by the same name. You've been uncovered, you've been uncovered. God uncovered you. He's the One who uncovers all the darkness; and do you admit that you're beaten now?"

"Beaten?"

"Yes. Do you realize that you are defeated now?"

"Yes, I suppose that we do."

"All right, Lufer. We bind both of you Lufers together, as with an unbreakable chain and we command you to come out of Ann right now and go to the pit. In the name of the Lord Jesus Christ."

The tape breaks to Archie asking if there are any more spirits.

"Don't forget me. Now you mustn't forget me, because I'm here too. My name is Lister, L-I-S-T-E-R."

"When did you come in?" Archie demands.

"Four years ago. We were in her before she was saved. Yes, so Ann gave herself to Christ, but we got back in. We know how it is."

"All right, you're being uncovered. We know you are. We—"

"Yes. I know, you know. We got Ann in Hollywood, you know . . . . So we could torment her. We have to tell you this." The voice whines in mockery: "We didn't tell you; we should have told you."

Archie says, "Now, then. Now, you four. We bind you together with an unbreakable chain and I command you to come out of Ann right now and go to the pit in the name of the Lord Jesus Christ."

The tape is stopped and started as the voice grinds into "Meer, and my associates. Don't forget Meer and don't forget Morr. Yes, Mere and Muir, and—"

"What's the next one?" Archie asks wearily.

"Mure and Murr."

"What association do you have with these other three?"

"We hate them."

"Why do you hate them?" Archie asks.

"Because they try to abuse her and we try to abuse her and so we have to compete against them, that stupid idiot—"

"All right. How many of you are there?"

"—And so are you."

Archie perseveres: "Mere, how many of you are there?"

"I'm not going to go," says a voice.

"Yes, you are. You obey what Christ tells you."

The voice mocks, "I have to."

"And so you are coming out?"

"Christ loves Ann."

"Do you love her?"

"I'd throw her into the pit and say suffer, suffer, suffer."

"How many of you are there?" says Archie.

"There's fourteen of us; there's three of us, Meer, Mere and Mure, that's all. Thank you very much."

"Now wait a minute. I want the truth from you and nothing but the truth in the name of the Lord Jesus Christ."

"There's only 14 left in there. All under my authority."

"Who told you to tell me that?" Archie says.

"Christ."

"And you have to obey Him. Then if these other 14 come out will that be the last ones?"

"Yes."

"Is that the truth?" Archie demands. "Is that the truth?"

"Yes. I've told you to tell you that under Christ's authority, you know."

"All right, Merr, Meer, Muir and Mure—"

"We're here."

"We bind you together in an unbreakable chain and we command you now in the name of the Lord Jesus Christ, come out of Ann and go to the pit right now."

The tape stops and starts again with Archie saying, "Now. In the name of the Lord Jesus Christ, tell me your name."

"My name is Greyer," the girlish voice sings. "Greyer had a little pony once—"

"All right. I rebuke you in the name of Christ. Do you have associates?"

"Two of them. Grayer, and G-R-A-Y-E-R-E; give me an O, give me an E—"

"Three of you," Archie says. "Are there any more in your group?"

"No. We tried to work through Ann's eyes, you know, so people would turn around and think Ann was looking at them but we were looking at them. So they would think, 'Oh, my goodness. What's wrong, dear?' But they still liked her; it made us sick." The voice begins to shriek. "Nothing worked with Ann, nothing worked. Nothing worked, nothing worked, nothing worked!"

Archie is obviously fatigued as he insists, "Now then, who is your master?"

"Satan."

"You belong to the pit."

"All of us? No we don't, yes we do, no we don't, yes we do."

Archie finally says, "In the name of the Lord Jesus Christ we command you three, come out of Ann right now and go to the pit. Amen!"

Listening to the tape has worn me out. I try not to think about the videotaped exorcism I watched some time ago. It'll be nice to get a good sleep tonight.

▶21◀

Demonized Christians

Demon Possessed Christians?

In his book, *Occult Bondage and Deliverance*, Kurt Koch gives his opinion on the question: Can genuine Christians be possessed?

Is there then any answer to the problem? We should wonder that there is such a difference of opinion among genuine born again believers. And yet there can only be one truth concerning the matter, and not two. This therefore means that either one or other of the two groups is wrong, or maybe the final answer lies elsewhere and both groups are right in their own way, but are only looking at the problem from different points of view.

One important thing to note, however, is that those who advocate the inflexible doctrine that Christians cannot under any circumstances be possessed, have usually seen no experience of possession themselves. On the other hand, those who have worked on mission fields where cases of possession have been in evidence, usually believe that Christians can be possessed.

Although personally I am more inclined to take the side of those who believe in the possibility of a Christian being possessed, I sometimes think that there may be a way of bringing the two sides together. But whatever the case, in heaven all our quarreling will cease. In 1 Corinthians 13:9 Paul writes, "For our knowledge is imperfect." It is only in eternity that we will fully understand. Realizing this therefore, we should be very hesitant in condemning a brother whose views differ from ours in certain points.

Another couple of pages I'd photocopied under the eyebrow-raised glare of the librarian last night was a passage from *What Demons Can Do to the Saints*, published in 1977 by Moody Press. The book is by Merrill Unger, another biblical scholar often mentioned as an occult expert. He writes on page 59 about this question of demon-possessed Christians: "The truth of the matter is that the Scriptures nowhere plainly state that a true believer cannot be invaded by Satan or his demons."

Apparently, judging by the other perusal I did last night through several theological treatises on the subject, few scholars flatly state their position on this touchy topic. But Unger does, back on page 51. He tosses around some typical theological jargon in his pronouncement, but his position is clear to anyone:

"The Holy Spirit indwelling the believer ungrieved by sin (Ephesians 4:30) and unquenched by disobedience (1 Thessalonians 5:19) most certainly precludes invasion by a demon spirit. But who dares assert that a demon spirit will not invade the life of a believer in which the Holy Spirit has been grieved by serious and persistent sin and quenched by flagrant disobedience?

"The demon enters, it is true, as a squatter and not as an owner or a guest or as one who has a right there. . . . But come he does if the door is opened by serious and protracted sin."

Along with Koch, Unger, Karl Klassen, the retired minister from Victoria, British Columbia, apparently a host of fundamental and evangelical Christians believe believers can be possessed.

Other Christian leaders disagree.

I was given a tape of a message by Dr. John MacArthur, pastor of Grace Community Church in the San Fernando Valley in Southern California. Dr. MacArthur introduces his message on the idea that God allows evil spirits to demonize even believers as a sort of chastisement:

This morning I want you to open your Bible to 1 Timothy 1:18: "This charge I commit to you, son Timothy, according to the prophecies previously made concerning you, that by them you may wage the good warfare, having faith and a good conscience, which some, having rejected, concerning the faith have suffered shipwreck, of whom are Hymenaeus and Alexander, whom I delivered unto Satan that they may learn not to blaspheme."

As I began to look at Verse 20, I was struck by the statement, "whom I have delivered unto Satan." What does it mean to be delivered to Satan?

It is a startling thought that someone would be given over to the devil himself. But that is precisely what it says, that is precisely what Paul has done to these two men, and it is precisely what he is inviting Timothy to do as well to others who are worthy of such a fate. It is a portion of the ministry of the church as it is a ministry of God, Himself, to deliver people to Satan.

Now the word "deliver" in Verse 20 means "to hand over, to give over, to commit," or the best translation to get the sense here, "to abandon." To abandon. Hands off, is the idea. To remove protection and abandon someone to Satan.

One other passage which uses the same terms is in 1 Corinthians chapter 5. First Corinthians 5 speaks of a person who is guilty of a form of incest in the church, a person living with his father's wife in a fornication relationship. Verse five enjoins the church at Corinth to "deliver such a one to Satan for the destruction of the flesh."

There are some people who go around today and say there are no conditions under which any Christian should ever be subject to Satan. I hear that from charismatic people continually and that is not what the Scripture teaches. The Scripture clearly teaches that not only is it a possibility to be handed over to Satan but it is a ministry of the church to do that. There are times and places and circumstances under the plan of God in which individuals are definitely to be turned over to Satan. And there are times and occasions when God Himself does that very thing.

Being turned over to Satan in both of these references has the idea of being put out of the church.

Of being disfellowshipped, or in the old terminology, excommunicated.

The instruction to the church to turn someone over to Satan means that someone is not at that time fully in Satan's control. So we must, therefore, be talking about people who are in one way or another under the umbrella of protection provided by the church. So we're talking here about people who are under the care of the church or within the community of redeemed people. This could be true of believers or unbelievers.

Christians Possessed? No Way!

Another Christian leader who insists Christians cannot be demon-possessed is Skip Heitzig. Skip pastors one of the largest churches in New Mexico, the charismatic Calvary Chapel of Albuquerque. The building is a light green steel-sided structure just down Osuna Road from the Sunset Grill where I'd been interviewing Gino Gerachi.

Since neither one of us had any time to talk, Skip had handed me a cassette of his message "Demon Possession." The tape had recounted some of Skip's teenage occultic interests in automatic writing and astral projection. He tells of a vacation with a bunch of guys in Mazatlan, Mexico, during which, in an altered state, he'd received a written communique from the spirit world that the group wouldn't return alive to the United States. Later that night in bed, Skip saw a wavering light bouncing on the walls. It took some time to realize the light was only a reflection of the moon—on a 14-inch dagger that had appeared out of nowhere next to Skip's bed.

I remember Skip talking on the two dangers of first, not believing in a personal devil and second, of believing too much. He used to listen to a broadcast in California of a minister who billed himself as "God's Man of the Hour." He'd cast out demons left and right—demons of nicotine and afflicting spirits of lust or greed. These people believed demons were responsible for laundry stain problems. Skip tells how the preacher "would pronounce—" Here Skip mimics a dialect that's a cross between a southern evangelist and Lawrence Welk. "He'd pronounce, 'O thou deaf and dumb spirit, hah. O come out, hah.'"

Skip recalls once when he was caught off guard by a mother's phone call: "'Do you deliver?' she said. I thought she'd mixed up our number with Pizza Hut. 'No, I mean do you deliver from demons, do you exorcise demonic spirits?' I suggested she bring the daughter she was concerned about down for a talk. It was only later I thought I should have said, 'Sure we do. We make 'em do pushups, jog laps. We exercise demons . . . .'"

As part of the taped message, he reads a Christian psychiatrist's report that the thousands of patients he has had who've claimed to be demon possessed only demonstrated that apparently all the demons he was seeing were allergic to thorazine. "In nearly every case," Skip quotes the psychiatrist as saying, "a week or two on thorazine would drive the demons with their voices away, and would bring the patient to his real conflict. These demons were merely auditory hallucinations. To maintain their self-esteem, these patients were unconsciously amplifying their own unwanted thoughts so loud that they seemed like real voices. They felt less guilty when they could convince themselves that their thoughts were coming from external sources such as demons." The psychiatrist went on to insist that as a literal biblicist, he believed in the existence of Satan and his demons. But they don't operate in all the minutiae of everyday life the way some Christians believe.

The message takes a look at Job 1 in the Old Testament, which Skip suggests is an inside look at the fact that although Satan "walks to and fro on the earth," he's limited in what God allows him to do.

"God has set hedges on what Satan can do," Skip says. "There are limits."

Vulnerability

Whatever your position on the existence of Satan, the activity of demons, the possibility of demon possession in those devoted to or not devoted to the Christ of the Bible, maybe you're feeling a little vulnerable. Let me share an unusual conversation I had with the chief of the police department of one of our largest cities, with concentrations of satanic groups, crime, and evil.

Chief Robert Vernon was telling me about walking into a motel room murder scene where the body's throat had been slit, the blood drained, water glasses that had been filled with blood and obviously drunk from, etc.—the typical cop story of the horrors of occult crime.

In the middle of the account, I found myself again hit with the grotesque evil that law enforcement have to daily contend with, the potentially spiritual evil they're up against. "So how do you keep sane?" I asked. "With this satanic stuff, how do you keep from feeling vulnerable?"

"What I've found is that people unwittingly make themselves vulnerable—let's be direct, okay? People sometimes unwittingly make themselves vulnerable to demon or evil spiritual attack by either giving up control of their minds to drugs, alcohol—they don't control what comes into their minds. Or by purposely putting themselves in neutral state of mind in some kind of a meditative trance—"

"An altered state of consciousness," I suggest.

"Right. And the first thing I'd say to anybody who feels vulnerable to evil is don't give up control of your mind. Not to chemicals or trance state where you're opening yourself up to any kind of outside influence. That's danger-ous. So maintain control of yourself. That'd be one practical suggestion.

"Second," he went on, "I have found that with all the negative influence I have in my life because of my job I need a balance; I need some positive influence. And I've found the positive influence in my life is in establishing a personal relationship with God through Christ. I'm not forcing this on everybody; I'm just saying this is what's working for me.

"For instance, over the years during my work as a police officer I've taught a twelfth-grade Sunday school class. Now, all during the week I'm exposed to the things that tend to make me cynical about people, about teenagers because of my so-called limited perspective as a police officer by only coming into contact with negative aspects of people, of teenagers because of the nature of my job. And then Sunday, I go to church and work with 30 or 40 kids who really have their heads screwed on, who are there to find out what God has in store for them; it's added incredible balance to my life. I realize all is not lost to evil; there are good kids, and there are good people who are really trying to find out what the Creator of the universe has in store for them, trying to fit in, in harmony with His creation and His principles. This relationship with God has been a solid balance in my life."

The chief of the police department of one of North America's wildest cities then gives a third clue on how not to succumb to the despair of evil: "Prayer has been a powerful force in my life. I believe in prayer. I pray every day in kind of an ongoing dialogue. I begin praying as I jog in the morning; I pray spontaneously through the day—whether it's during a staff meeting or whatever the circumstance. At that point I don't close my eyes and begin mumbling; I just pray internally—God hears me. It may be a silent 'God give me wisdom.' But I go about life in an attitude of prayer. I think this protects me from evil influence. I think God responds to prayer.

"Another factor is being exposed to biblical principles. These are time-tested principles from the Judeo-Christian moral base. Here are some princi-ples that have been around for 4,000 years and they work. For instance, I've studied through the biblical book of Proverbs, and I've identified over 50 prin-ciples of management—practical principles that work. So my exposure to what I believe to be the Word of God—but even if you're not coming from my standpoint and just look on the Bible as time-tested principles—has been a great source of strength to resist any kind of negative spiritual influence.

"And then," he concluded, "being accountable to a group of people that you respect is vital. In my case it's a group of a few believers in a church setting. But regardless of your religious affiliation, letting others help you see yourself, opening yourself up honestly to others' criticism and support is often what you need to keep from being washed up in the negatives of life."

"The parents with problem kids I run into these days," I said, "are the ones who feel most alone in their struggles and yet seem to be the very ones who resist getting into or forming a support group. It's tough dueling with Satan on your own."

Bob added the Proverb: "'Better are wounds from a friend than kisses from an enemy.' That principle has been very important in my life; I have some friends who on occasion have to be brutally candid with me—"

"A few wounds here and there, right?" I said.

"I've had a few wounds all right. But those wounds have been very helpful to me. But you know, the relationship with the Lord, speaking as a Christian, is the most important thing. I have the power of the Holy Spirit in me who can handle any evil spirit. The Bible says that 'greater is He that is in you than he that is in the world.' I don't fancy myself that I have enough spiritual power on my own to in any way compete with the evil forces—but since I have the power of God in me, I'm more than ready to face them."

Whether or not you'll subscribe to Chief Vernon's stratagem for personal protection from the mystical forces of evil, you still may be feeling vulnerable to the practical wiles of devilish dabbler groups, to satanic cults' terrorism. You may still feel vulnerable when you try to devise a plan to keep your kids or other teenagers you care about from ever toying along the edge of evil. What can you do?

For starters, read through the material in the next section carefully—particularly the section on what a parent can do.

Contact one of the groups listed in the resources section. Go ahead and shock them: volunteer to help.

Help the teenagers you know to develop a hardy sense of critical thinking. Guide kids interested in the occult in a simple exercise:

1. "What about satanism or the occult mostly intrigues me?"
2. Answer:
3. Why?
4. "Because I want . . . ."
5. Why?
6. "Because I want . . . ."
7. Why? (At this level, a person is uncovering some heart-level needs and desires, so the answer may be verrrrry slow in coming.)
8. "Because I really want . . . ."
9. "Are there any sources—disciplines, activities, relationships—besides the occult that can realistically give me #8?" List in order of preference those sources.
10. Unless you're a bit unstable, #8 is probably a very positive goal. Now compare the down sides of the different ways you can reach that goal. Draw a line down the center of a sheet of paper. On one side, list the negative results of occult involvement which you hoped would give you #8. Then,

one by one, list any negative downsides of your other options—listed in #9. Then determine what route you'll take; discuss the practicalities of that route with a trusted adult.

Coaching a youth through such a heart-searching self-evaluation is valuable regardless of occult involvement or not. So if you care about kids, get used to asking a lot of why's, to helping even preteens think deeply about what it is they need in life. Guide them in figuring out how they can realistically, positively find those needs met in nondestructive disciplines, activities and relationships.

Let's do something—something rational. But something definitely positive about Satan's influence in our homes, schools and communities. Read on.

Part Five

◀▶

Resisting the Devil:
The Response

"All it takes for evil to triumph
is for good men to do nothing."
—Edmunde Burke

From a European woodcut, 1508. Witches brewing a charm. The Bettman Archive.

▶ 22 ◀

Believing Too Little, Believing Too Much

You wouldn't believe the stories I've been told—particularly the stories told by the children. From the envelope of information received from Believe the Children president Leslie Floberg, I sift through the materials and run across an article by Dr. Roland Summit, head of UCLA's school of psychology. The report is "Too Terrible to Hear." I find he pretty much answers my question of whether people would believe any of this satanic threat business. They'd believe it the way they believe children's reports of ritual abuse. And that is, they probably won't believe it because they don't want to.

Why We Don't Believe the Children

In the paper, Dr. Summit suggests that our culture doesn't want such stories to be real. He suggests seven reasons.

First, for self protection every individual is more comfortable believing in a happy childhood and in a just and fair society. To admit child abuse in the home or outside it is to have to admit we can't wholeheartedly trust child protection resources. We don't want to admit that perhaps our judgment is off as we select those resources—perhaps a daycare facility. We don't want to have to empathize with the terror and helplessness of a child who submits without question or outcry. Belief in these widespread demonic stories of ritual abuse forces a reappraisal of societal trust.

Summit's second reason for disbelief is that we seem to expect any legitimate crime victim to complain. "If a child fails to make immediate outcry, and if a child fails to describe a conventional, recognizable style of crime, then the burden of proof that such crime exists reverts to the child and on any adults credulous enough to support the child's tenuous complaint."

Third, we don't want to believe the children because of lack of conventional evidence. Current modes of investigation are inadequate to handle this type of crime. Says Summit, "There is not enough coordination to make sense out of the disparate efforts of investigative reporters, governmental commissions, customs and postal inspectors, missing children's services and federal, state and local law enforcement agencies." Botched investigations and dismissed cases only illustrate Summit's thesis: "Every unproved allegation seems to encourage the hope that nothing the child is saying is true."

Fourth, these horrific crimes against children "seem to require criminal conviction to justify public validation," says Summit. I reread the paragraph, deciding he must mean that unless a criminal prosecution takes place, we don't admit that anything happened at all. "The insistence of proof beyond reasonable doubt for an invisible and illogical crime almost guarantees suppression and repudiation."

As defense lawyers argue the case through pretrial motions, depositions, preliminary hearings and delayed adjudications, both the children and the parents have tried to put the crime away, contends Summit.

I try to remember the dates of the McMartin case; Judy Johnson's first complaint was in the fall of 1983. As of fall, 1988, the court battles were still raging. Imagine the children having to recount—to relive—their bizarre tales of abuse and mind-bending pain year after year.

Summit testified, "The ultimate obscenity, mutilating and killing children for the titillation of viewers, has been described by numerous children throughout the country. Descriptions of drinking blood or urine and eating feces are almost routine. The suspicion that such atrocities might be staged in a trusted neighborhood preschool is simply intolerable to anyone.

"In my informal and scattered overview of some 25 investigations involving reports of blood ritual, each has become hopelessly confused and deadlocked. Investigations are suspended. Charges are contrived to avoid the issue. Witnesses who talk of ritual are dropped from consideration. Many cases are simply never filed because of the inflammatory effects of the unprovable rumors. And those that go to trial may be dropped midcourse, acquitted or reversed on appeal. Each failed attempt at prosecution buttresses the logical and welcome argument that such charges are obviously ridiculous, and that adults who choose to believe them should be viewed with suspicion."

Fifth, the messenger of such atrocious tidings as occultic ritual abuse of children is unwelcome. "Anyone who participates in uncovering a suspected nest of exploitation may now be accused of coaching witnesses into false accusations," says Summit.

I wonder about such accusations myself, having thought through Debbie Nathan's expose of the El Paso case involving obviously leading questions posed by interviewers of the children. I dig through the bookbag and pull out my notes on Tom Jarriel's report on ABC's "20/20" May 16, 1985.

Loaded Questions?

Jarriel in a voice-over says, "These 12-year-old boys, with their parents' consent, demonstrated how they were taught to inflict pain on their enemies. They also claim they witnessed sacrificial murder by members of our third category of satanism, satanic cults. Police have found no proof, made no arrest. But that's no surprise, for, nationwide, police are hearing strikingly similar horror stories, and not one has ever been proved. Take for example this case, the mother of a young victim who asked not to be identified."

I tried to watch for leading questions, suggestions by Jarriel as he interviewed these people:

Mother of Victim: Usually they have the children kill the infants or the other kids.
Jarriel: Do they do this with knives?

So it's Jarriel who introduces the knife idea, I think. Of course, maybe he's just bringing up something discussed before the camera started rolling.

Mother: Yes, they were. And if they refused to do it, an adult, usually the child's father or mother, would actually take the child's hand and make them kill the child.
Jarriel: There's also this similar case that links child sex abuse with murder.
Grandmother of alleged participants: The children were given—were given knives and told to go and stab those bodies. And my grandchildren told me that they couldn't do that, that it wasn't possible, that they could only get the knives to go in about that far. And then the adults put their hands over the children's hands and shoved the knives in.
Jarriel: Was there any reference to the devil?
Boy: Yes.
Jarriel: Tell me what you were asked to do.
1st Boy: I was asked to stab him.
Jarriel: To stab him. And this was in front of the other people who were there? Were you given a knife?
1st Boy: Yes.
Jarriel: And were you told what would happen to you if you didn't?
1st Boy: Uh-huh.
Jarriel: Do you remember what they said?
1st Boy: "This will happen to you."
Jarriel: So you either stab him or you'll be stabbed, was about what it came down to? . . . So you were given the knife, and then what did you do?
1st Boy: I went like this.
Jarriel: Did you push the knife all the way in deep, or did you just touch the skin?
1st Boy: All the way in deep.

Jarriel: In deep. Were you in the room when this was going on? Did you see what happened to the child that was stuck with the knife?
2nd Boy: Yeah.
Jarriel: What do you remember?
2nd Boy: All blood.

I stuff the "20/20" notes back in my bag and finish scanning Dr. Summit's treatment of why we don't quite believe these bizarre tales. His point was that we want to accuse the interviewers of leading the children, of believing the children too much:

"Children who disclose to an empathetic interviewer may take back their allegations in the face of dismay from their parents or disbelief from more skeptical examiners," says Summit. "A child who is confident with one listener may be mute with someone who is more upset or unbelieving. His mother may believe, while the same stories fill his father with incredulous rage. Similar hierarchical barriers to credibility line the path of disclosure to police officer, prosecutor, media reporter, editor, juror and judge. In general the more authoritative the position and the less time a person spends in the company of a child, the less such a person can hear from a victimized child."

The report goes on to suggest that the more fantastic and controversial the stories, the more the defense and the media will tend to attack whoever was responsible for assembling the case. He notes that in the McMartin case, both the original prosecutor and her specialist interviewer had been blamed. I think back on Debbie Nathan's brand of "witch-hunting" on the El Paso YMCA case and acknowledge that a good part of her diatribe focused on the hysteria of certain obnoxious parents, the Joan-of-Arc stance of the prosecutor, the ineptness of the interviewers and finally the devil-may-care attitude of the presiding judge. "Throughout the nation," Summit contends, "specialist interviewers face massive civil suits. Many have retreated to less punishing work."

The sixth factor in why the public doesn't really believe in satanic crime —especially ritualized child abuse—is the result of deliberate deception. Summit says that most suppression of ritualized abuse cases comes from unintended denial and simple avoidance by the public—many parents refuse to let their abused children undergo the trauma of telling and retelling and the public is basically pleased with not having to deal with the issue.

Then there's the suppression of cases from the influence of what Summit calls "the treacherous decisionmakers and gatekeepers." A doctor, judge, attorney, police officer, writer, school administrator, preacher or parent can also be an invisible pedophile or cultist. Children typically describe trusted institutions and community leaders in multiple-perpetrator abuse cases. Policemen and police vehicles are described in several cases. A social worker—as well as parents and grandparents—was named among the perpetrators in the case dropped in Bakersfield, California. The abused kid and his advocate hardly know whom to trust; and even this seemingly paranoid insecurity can be construed as just one more reason the allegations are outrageously unbelievable.

Conceptual Chaos

Summit's final point in why we don't believe the children is headed "Conceptual Chaos." He says that unlike other fields of knowledge, awareness of these crimes against children has been "revolutionary rather than evolution-ary and self-contradictory rather than self-evident." Until a more developed base of what we're dealing with is established, concludes the M.D., "investiga-tors will be hopelessly outclassed by the cunning of practitioners."

A phrase in his summary sticks with me as I sling the book bag over my shoulder. Like any adult victimization of children, ritual abuse is "offensive to adult comfort." That's why I don't want to think about these stories, why I tell myself I don't quite believe them: They're offensive to my adult comfort.

But is that any reason to avoid nailing down the truth? To avoid doing something about such diabolical injustice as slashing a little boy's mind for life? And for what? For Satan.

▶ 23 ◀

Educating the Educators

I'm back in the mishmash of Los Angeles International, prepping myself for a return to the East Coast. It'll be a good time to review for you the information I've run across from various experts on what to do about the dangers of satanism.

Just before Southwest Air takes off, I call Tricia, the secretary in Kansas City who's been getting calls from the woman we're calling Lynn. "Has she called again?" I ask. "Did you get a name or her number this time?"

"She was low," says Tricia. "I hate the idea that you're telling me some of this story might be true."

"What happened?"

"Well, she called the office and I couldn't talk right then, so she left a phone number. And it is from Orlando, just as she's been telling me. Well—"

"Just tell me. What'd she say? Then give me the number and let me start checking on the possibility that's it's true. I can do it without her knowing or anybody being alarmed. Because if she's actually going through this terrorism by the cult she got out of, somebody's got to do something."

"I don't know how to say this," Tricia tells me. "She told me that two weeks ago was some big ritual."

"That would have been the fall equinox. September 22 or so, and it was a full moon. It's a feast-type ritual that's usually just a sexual ceremony. But then, I guess a few days earlier would have been the Midnight Host rituals that call for blood sacrifices." I'm appalling myself with such nonchalance about such grotesque information. Here I am leaning against a fingerprint-greasy phone partition in LAX asking, "What happened to her?"

"Okay," Tricia says with a big breath. "She says she had a baby when she was a teenager in the cult years ago. A baby girl that she hadn't seen now for years

226

since the girl was kept in the cult. And Lynn says that a couple weeks ago she was kidnaped."

"Who was?"

"Lynn. Lynn was abducted and taken to a ceremonial site out in the country and—"

"Yes?"

"She said she watched them sacrifice her daughter."

I don't want this to be quite so real. I want it to be just another story to which I can apply my rule of thumb to discount 80 percent of what's said.

Tricia continues, "And her daughter apparently had had a baby boy. And they took the boy."

I find myself chewing my lip. "Why doesn't her husband do something? She says he's a minister, right? Why doesn't anybody in the church notice the minister's wife is being terrorized? Where's her husband during these times they break in to rape her and kidnap her?"

"I don't know," Tricia says.

"Give me the number, okay? And you say the FBI—at least she says the FBI is aware of what's going on? Where are they? This is too fishy." I'm irritated that this satanic business is always so vague, so elusive. If this woman's story is true, why hasn't somebody done something? Then I realize the point of our entire project; and guess that in all probability nobody believes her. I know I don't. Yet. I rattle on: "Why, for instance, would the FBI be in on it at all? They wouldn't deal with it unless it was a case of crossing state lines. That makes it all sound fishy."

"She says the cult does cross state lines; it's operating in Georgia too. And they phone to threaten her, and use of the telephone lines is FBI jurisdiction."

I take down the woman's number.

"What do you think?" asks Tricia.

"What do you think?" I say. "You've been listening to her for six months. Do you believe her?"

"I don't know," Tricia says with a catch in her throat. "I know I don't want to."

Just before the flight I call information for Orlando and ask who is listed under the phone number Tricia gave me.

It's the name of a minister.

Believing Too Much

On the first leg of my flight, I scan through a book I first read in high school. *The Screwtape Letters* is a fun, scary novel of demonic antics from the demons' perspective. In it, C.S. Lewis warns that the danger of thinking about the devil is either to disbelieve or to believe too much. It seems to me that disbelief leads to Edmunde Burke's quote at the beginning of this section; the result is that good men do nothing as evil triumphs. But the other extreme is just as dangerous, since believing too much leads inexorably to paranoia, to witch hunting.

Remember Arthur Miller's play, *The Crucible?* The riveting drama was written during the heyday of McCarthyism, when the US Senate was investigating the unAmerican activities of suspected communists. The play chronicled events of the Salem witch trials of 1692, but it holds lessons that desperately needed to be learned by those of the communist witch-hunters of the early 1950s McCarthy era. And it probably has much to say about possible responses to the threats of satanism in the 1990s.

Maybe we've learned something since December 5, 1484.

That was the year in which Pope Innocent VIII issued a Papal Bull sanctioning action against suspected witches. Those who took upon themselves this holy charge were called Inquisitors. And we all know how holy and just the Inquisition was.

In 1486 Jakob Sprenger and Prior Heinrich Kramer published their handy manual for witch hunters called *Malleus Maleficarum* or *The Hammer of Witches.*

Three hundred years of idiocy followed these events, years when paranoid citizens saw witches everywhere. As Miller brings out in his play and as demonstrated in the McCarthy hearings on suspected communists, witch hunting is easy. If, perhaps as a Godfearing citizen, you suspected anyone of being a satanic witch, you would ask if this were so. Of course, witches lie, so if a suspect responds, "No," you've probably got a witch. If the suspect answers, "Yes," then of course you've nailed a witch. So witch hunting through the centuries developed into a sporty game of accusation of anyone different/odd/irreligious/mentally ill/from other religions/psychically sensitive/unattractive/simply disliked.

For Christians, the Salem, Massachusetts, witch trials should serve as a dramatic example of what can happen when superstitious paranoia is coupled with misinterpretations of Scriptures. There is still conjecture that some of the 150 accused—out of only 100 or so households in the village—were actually practicing satanic witchcraft. But even verification of the practice of witchcraft does not constitute biblical grounds for execution. Highly regarded fundamentalist speaker and teacher Josh McDowell in *Demons, Witches and the Occult* points out on pages 77 and 78:

> It is unfortunate that much of the [witch hunting] persecution came from professing Christians doing it in the name of God. The passages which were used to justify the witch hunt were misread and taken totally out of context. The legal penalties of such Old Testament crimes were part of the then-operating theocracy in Israel.
>
> The Lord God was the King in Israel; He had the right to determine the crimes and punishments against His holy and sovereign state. One who participated in

witchcraft was aligning himself with Satan, the foe of God, the nation's Ruler. Such an alignment was treason against the government of Israel, a government directed personally by the Lord God.

Even today treason is often punished by death. However, since no nation today is a theocracy, a nation governed directly by God, the penalties instituted then are not applicable. Witchcraft is still evil and is still rebellion against God. It is not treason.

So even Bible-believing Christians have no justification for vigilante-style witch hunts, threatening harassment or abuse to those whose religion is satanism.

A proper response to the realities of thousands of kids dabbling in satanism, of thousands of suspected satanic cults operating throughout the U.S. and Canada isn't witch hunting. So a proper response isn't going to be easy.

In the name of law enforcement or in the name of public decency or in the name of the Lord Jesus Christ, we're not going to start slandering suspected satanists as if we're at a turkey shoot. We're not going to teach our children that rabid satanists are behind every tree, that growling demons will probably attack them one of these nights, that the devil is the source of their headache or fatigue or mischief. We're not going to treat every malady or abnormality or failure in others with a prescription for exorcism. Right?

Our response to this difficult issue can be rational and effective. Here are some basic suggestions on what a community, a school or a family can do about the dangers of faddish or deeply rooted satanism.

Community Response

Is satanism a factor in your community? Anyone who is concerned about such a question can with a little simple research find the answer. Remember that you're going for a consensus answer, since you can't believe 80 percent of what you hear. Right?

Check with your regional representatives of animal protection agencies such as the National Cattlemen's Association or the Society for the Prevention of Cruelty to Animals. Simply ask if your area is one in which ritualistic animal mutilations have been found.

Call area mental health professionals and simply ask if therapists are treating any number of child satanic abuse victims, adult ritual abuse survivors who were abused in the area, or teenagers coming out of satanic involvement. Don't get too nosy, since any further information is confidential.

Contact substance abuse, teenage crisis or teen treatment programs in your area and ask if satanism is a factor in the lives of the kids going through the programs.

Ask junior high, middle school, high school and college administrative representatives and school counselors in your area if any students seem to be involved in satanism.

Call a few churches that are particularly blatant about their stand on the Bible or their outspokenness about satanism. Ask if the church staff is aware of any satanic activity in the area.

Contact a few media representatives and ask if any occult crime or satanic activity is reported in your community.

Call the cops. Ask if teenagers in your area seem to be getting involved in satanic activity or occult crime.

Altogether, you'll have a fairly good idea if something's going on, if Satan is stalking your streets.

I've been traveling across America, talking in schools and in conferences with educators, teachers, principals, school administrators, and students. Some of them care—and they care a lot. Others care, but they don't seem to know how to help.

Teachers

What can a teacher do about kids who are playing along the edge of evil? Because of their unique positions, teachers can do plenty. As odd as it sounds, teachers have probably more of a chance simply to observe the faces of kids than does anyone else. As an instructor cares more about teaching students than about teaching lessons, he or she will see signs that even the kids' parents will miss—fear, anxiety, nervousness, illness, depression, aggression, sudden change of behavior. I've looked into the faces of about three million teenagers, and although a cursory look would suggest half of them are simply spaced out, I know that studying a teenage face reveals volumes about what's going on inside.

Of course, teachers as well as the rest of us can't start jumping to conclusions that every odd quirk they notice means a kid is conjuring Satan during lunchbreaks. But teachers, often the first line of defense against kids going over the edge, have a lot to offer teenagers with problems.

Here are some suggestions, based on recommendations from several teachers and school counselors I've talked with:

Make yourself available.

Be faithful to your students. Hold in confidence the things said in confidence.

Too often when I stand before school audiences and say "Talk to your teacher or counselor," some kids snicker and laugh. To them, the last person they would ever think of going to and talking to is a teacher or a counselor. Sometimes they have good reasons for that. Unless it becomes a matter of life and death—and, yes, sometimes it does—it is not professionally ethical to divulge counseling information.

Joan wrote:

I feel so alone and I feel like you're the only one in the whole world who I can talk to . . . . The counselor I'm going to now tells my parents everything, even if I ask her not to. I don't need someone to run to my parents every time I tell them something. So it always ends up that I don't tell her anything any more. Lately, I've been thinking about hanging myself. I don't want to but I can't go on like this anymore . . . .

Teachers, don't think of teaching as a job. I remember being told once as I considered the profession of teaching, if you want a job, work with computers or machinery, with things that don't feel anything. Teaching, as you well know, is demanding because you're dealing with the minds of delicate, snotty, impressionable, foulmouthed, curious, bored, innocent, decadent, fun, obnoxious, lovable, revolting kids who will be the adults in the next millennium. So, since you signed up for a challenging profession, live out your commitment to education by going the extra mile; *find out what's going on in the real world of the kids you teach.*

Don't try to become a teenager; adults who try too hard to be cool are either, as I've heard kids tell it, fools or spies. But care enough to know what their lives are like outside your classroom.

Here's another telling letter:

It's probably a waste of time writing to you because 1) you're just too darn busy to read letters from unimportant people, 2) you have thousands of letters like this one, and 3) I'm not special. For example, I'm not dying or contributing one million dollars. Sorry about that.

I've listened to you in person, and I've listened to your tapes. And quite frankly, I like you, sir. But I wonder about things. Are you sincere? Do you speak the truth? I'd like to say briefly that the last time I entrusted personal problems to an adult that very person turned out to be taking drugs—such as cocaine! I can't tell you how terribly betrayed I felt. I pray that you are different because we need someone we can really trust.

Love and respect, *Kelly*

When you decide an issue—drug use, suicide, occult dabbling—needs to be addressed, *give out effective material.*

Avoid material written for a Ph.D. in sociology. Naturally, materials must be accurate and contain information of value, but teenagers have got to be able to at least read the stuff.

Watch faces. Be alert. Look for trouble—especially in the case of dabblers, trouble around the satanic holidays.

Feel—and let them know you feel.

Listen; then refer your students to professionals if necessary. Particularly "listen" to their writing—many kids will express the level of their involvement in dabbling near the edge of evil in classroom essays and research papers.

Don't become a junior psychiatrist or a ghostbuster.

Particularly with the complex interplay of occult involvement, crime, drugs, sex and satanic group pressure, don't try to open wounds you cannot close. Once you show you care, you can listen. You can probe, but don't try to solve problems by using techniques you learned from a college psychology class. Stay in your field as a teacher who wants to be a friend. Listening and caring are two unbeatable techniques you have to offer.

If the school has a psychologist, a social worker, and/or a counselor, take advantage of their specialized skills. Refer kids to area mental health facilities. This doesn't mean you have to back out of the picture. You can say, "You have real problems and I wish you'd talk to Ms. Gannett, the school counselor. I'd still like to be available for you to talk to whenever you want. But your situation is beyond my depth."

If you show your willingness to be there, to be someone to talk to, and that you care, you are doing the best you can. Don't attempt to function as a psychiatric professional. In actual cases of satanic involvement, you *are* beyond your depth if you try to do more than listen and then make referrals.

In life and death or criminal matters, *contact proper authorities immediately*.

When a teenager talks about suicide, when there's no time to refer the student to a counselor, contact parents.

Communicate with the parents confidentially. Let the parents know of your concern and the reasons for it. Alert them. Occasionally a parent will resent this, but most are appreciative.

When you learn of criminal activity, immediately contact your superiors in the school who then will contact law enforcement. Rumors of adults recruiting minors into satanic groups need to be checked out by law enforcement since that recruitment often involves corruption of minors, drugs and sexual offenses. And remember the occult dabblers' use of illegal drugs, physical harassment of those getting out of a satanic group, mutilation of animals or exploitation of other minors are all crimes and should be seriously treated as such.

School Administrators

Administrators can back their teachers and counselors to prevent students from the dangers of overinvolvement in the occult. While there is always the consideration that satanism is claimed to be a religious question, nevertheless a school can take steps to stop kids from going over the edge.

For instance, Smoky Hill High School in Aurora, Colorado, has actually initiated a program offering counseling for young satanists. Other schools who've found themselves to be in a region of strong satanic activity have formed links with a community team to deal with severe problems. That is, the school counselor has a network of police contacts, clergy, therapists, medical personnel and child protection specialists who are knowledgeable in dealing with occult problems.

As part of its dress code, a Chicago school has banned all clothing and jewelry with satanic symbolism. Other schools have announced that religious proselytizing—even if the religion is satanic—is forbidden on school grounds. When rumors of adult satanic recruiters surfaced in a Tucson, Arizona, school, the administration without so much as a hint of paranoia simply increased its surveillance of adults loitering at or near the school.

Churches

What can a church do about teenagers—about any age group—getting involved in the occult, in satanism?

As odd as it sounds, apparently plenty of churches that doctrinally acknowledge all the standard biblical views on Satan and demonology never expect anything diabolical to happen.

Father LeBar, the occult consultant to the Archdiocese of New York, said that "churchleaders—without panicking—need to realize that the satanism fad is serious business. Young people's minds are being influenced and manipulated. Our society and sometimes even we in the church take great pains not to unduly indoctrinate children with godly influences for fear of pressuring them. But no spiritual guidance leaves only emptiness. What we must realize is that the empty spaces in them is being filled." They are filled, Father LeBar implied, with destructive belief systems such as satanism.

Some ministers I've talked with were shocked to discover their ministries were satanist targets. Many have met harassment and sometimes terror from satanic groups when their church began to speak out against the black arts.

In an Arvada, Colorado, church, a young lady in her mid-twenties was approached by ushers when she stood and began casting spells on the minister as he preached. She claimed to be a witch and said her local group had been instructed to attend church services—to purposely disrupt and intone curses. A similar incident took place in a Colorado Springs church, where the witch sent to desecrate the building was instead converted!

In Rebecca Brown's *He Came to Set the Captives Free*, Elaine, the ex-high priestess of The Brotherhood, claims she was taught by the cult to infiltrate and disrupt churches. In an eight-point strategy, Elaine says she was instructed to, among other ploys, make a public profession of faith and to volunteer for positions of responsibility. Elaine claims satanists will counterfeit believers in prayer, in reading Scriptures, in talking about Jesus, and in assenting to a belief in Christ.

But, Elaine points out, their devotion to the dark god prohibits them from meeting the biblical test of spiritual authenticity found in the New Testament passage, 1 John 4:1, 2: "Beloved, do not believe every spirit to see whether they are from God; for many false prophets have gone out into the world. By this you know the Spirit of God: every spirit that confesses that Jesus Christ has come in the flesh is from God." Elaine says that true satanists can agree to the elements of this simple spiritual "test," but cannot themselves state that Jesus of Nazareth is the Christ of God who came in the flesh as a human.

Even as I write what Elaine says, I have uneasy visions of paranoid "testings" inflicted on innocent churchgoers. I imagine them being branded satanists simply because they're not doctrinally convinced of Christ's deity or because they raise uncomfortable questions in the monthly church business meeting. Unfortunately, Christians who are to be the illuminating light of the world sometimes fall for sensationalized half-facts. Then some of them crusade to rabidly curse the darkness instead of letting their lights shine. Church members and pastors, please remember the Inquisition and Salem witch trials. Superstitious, hysterical witch hunting, itself diabolical, has no place in the house of God.

But while satanism grows as a fad or a long-range cultural phenomenon, expect to be harassed as Satan's enemy.

Bill Woods, a youth minister with Deer Valley Nazarene Church in Tucson, Arizona, told me that one Sunday their morning church service was disrupted by a woman who rolled on the floor and seemed to be offering up some sort of prayers or incantations.

Bill added that, of course, church youth workers are in prime spots to work with kids dabbling in the occult. In his youth work, he sets dress code policies to keep satanic items from being brought into youth activities, and has set up a videogame room to attract kids from the street, the strata of kids who're getting into satanism.

With the rise of satanism's new children, it seems to me that churches especially should be practically and spiritually prepared for "the fiery darts of the wicked one" with rational programs to educate families in preventing their kids from dabbling in the occult and with counseling programs and/or referral networks for satanic victims. And further, churches need to consider new forms of ministry to these children, teenagers and adults who with distorted Luciferian backgrounds are escaping from satanism into the church.

Child Protection Services

Ever wonder what it must feel like to be a child who's helpless before the horrors of ritual abuse—or any abuse, for that matter? Michelle Smith was subjected to unimaginable abuse in her "grooming" to become a bride of Satan. In *Michelle Remembers*, in a near hypnotic state she relives the hell of the abused child in a little-girl voice:

No one can hear me. My mouth won't move. No one will hear me. Please. Please. Everything's all right. Please. Please, someone know it's not all right. It's going slow; then it's going fast. Get away! Get that needle out of my hand. Quit doing that to me.

No. I won't make my head turn around. I won't! I won't do that! Oh, God, something's going to happen. Got to get back. No. I'm not going to go squish. No.

Mommy. Mommy! Mommy, please come. Mommy, where are you? Mommy! I want my mommy. I don't care what she's like. I want my mommy. I want my mommy! Please! Anybody! Please!

Everybody's walking away. I'll keep my mouth shut. I'll keep it shut. I promise I'll keep it shut. Please. No. Don't leave me here. Please don't leave me here. No, I don't want the bugs on my hands. No. Please. No. Don't go. Please. Come back. Come back. Please, I'll die . . . .

I'm evil. Is that right, sir? I'm all poisoned. I know. I know. I'm worse than everybody. I know. Yes, sir. I don't have a mother. No, sir. I wasn't born. I won't get upset anymore. I won't go near anybody. I'll keep my mouth shut. Don't hurt my mom. I don't know anything . . . .

It's written down. They wrote everything down in the book. They wrote my name. And all the bad things that would happen to me. They wrote it all down. They'd know who I was. They said I'd be all alone, all my life . . . .

I was the worst thing they'd ever met. All the people that have died, all the things that have happened—it's all my fault. I have to be taught a lesson. I'm going to be sorry. I'm going to be sorry. I am sorry. I already am sorry. I'm sorry to everybody . . . .

I don't want to be scared anymore. I can't take any more. I'm going to go away like I was told, because I'm going to be lost anyway. I'm so scared. I'm scared.

What is a proper response from the child protection profession to the satanic abuse of children and teenagers? Protection agencies, of course, come into the picture after the incidence of abuse, and so bear a demanding double burden—to coordinate care for the victim and preparation for prosecution. Attorney Andrew H. Vacchys, veteran advocate, lecturer and author on abuse, delinquency and the court system's responsibilities to child victims, offers the following recommendations in an undated Believe the Children article. Vacchys insists that in child ritual and sexual abuse, a team approach is necessary:

> Ritual abuse, which always includes sexual abuse, has profound consequences for its victims. An untreated child sexual abuse victim has a predictable range of fallout including delinquency, drug abuse, suicide and mental illness. Such fallout negatively impacts on the larger society, often when the former victim turns predator.
>
> Identification, treatment, and followup of cases of child ritual and/or sexual abuse cannot be limited to a single agency. Unless and until we establish a continuum of care for all children with the ongoing participation and cooperation of all agencies, public and private, victimized children will continue to fall through the cracks in the so-called "system."
>
> All agencies, from day care centers to schools to social services to probation to mental health, must participate jointly in a consortium model to provide services. Consideration of politics, ego and turf, while significant to individual agencies in terms of their own survival, are antithetical to the survival of children.

Vacchys then suggests the following reforms:

1. All child protective services agencies should have available the services of an on-staff validation team. This would include personnel specifically trained in diagnosing and treating intrafamilial child sexual abuse syndrome, occult ritual abuse and those trained in quasicriminal investigations. The training provided would be sufficient to qualify the validators as expert witnesses in court and to meet selected standards, preferably suitable for certification. Specifically barred as training would be the usual three-hour "sensitivity to the issues" briefings and the bizarre practice of rotating trained personnel to other divisions where newly acquired skills atrophy. It is not necessary to train all CPS workers in validation techniques, any more than it is necessary to subject all sexual abuse cases to validation. The validation process is psychologically intrusive, and is not indicated where there is sufficient other material (such as direct admissions, medical evidence, strong corroboration, eye-witnesses, or photographs) to substantiate the case.

2. The initial validation interview with the child should have both an investigative and therapeutic component, should utilize standard protocols, including anatomically correct dolls, nonverbal communication (such as drawings or pantomime), and play therapy, and should take place within a specially equipped Validation Suite.

3. The Validation Suite should be equipped with video and audio tape capability for preserving the child's statements. With the exception of actual testimony (if required) at trial, the trained validator should be the only individual conducting interviews with the child. This provision would avoid the "melt-down" effect on a child who is overinterviewed and elects adamant silence as his or her only weapon against painful psychic intrusion.

4. The child's video or audiotaped statements should be admissible at all nontrial proceedings, including those before a Grand Jury.

5. The validation should be counted as corroboration for trial purposes, if the validator is accorded expert witness status.

6. In those jurisdictions which fail to implement required training, an independent validation panel should be established whose members would be called on a rotating basis in all suspected cases. Such a panel would not be a party witness but would testify on its findings in each case.

7. Child protective services workers should be trained in the legal process, courtroom demeanor, and the basic rules of evidence.

8. Upon filing of a sexual abuse report, the child should be assigned an independent Law Guardian who should have authority to proceed with a case even if child protective services elects not to do so. They should be selected from an independent panel of lawyers, each of whom should be specifically trained, serve an apprenticeship with veteran practitioners, and be subject to at least annual evaluation of performance.

9. Law Guardians should be supervised by a qualified office or agency with the authority to remove if inadequate.

10. The confidentiality of child abuse records should be used only to protect the child, not the perpetrator (or the agency).

11. Similarly, a Law Guardian defending a child on acting out (e.g. delinquency) or acting in (e.g. runaway) charges should have full access to the child's family records if prior abuse or neglect cases had been reported to Child Protective Services.

12. Day care centers, camps, and other child care institutions should be subject to unannounced visits from specially trained investigative personnel.

13. Schools should be required to institute personal safety courses for all students, including those in kindergarten.

14. A massive program of public education must be undertaken—but not the usual narration of endless horror stories. It should be specifically aimed at refuting the ugly mythology that permeates too much of our societal consciousness: children fantasize, children have poor memories, children lie to manipulate, nice (translate, middle class and above) people do not sexually abuse their children, couldn't possibly perpetrate bizarre satanic abuse, etc.

Failure to implement these (and other) recommendations for specific change means business as usual. And business as usual in the child protective field means that the production lines will keep punching out the horribly impaired products of child ritual and sexual abuse: children who act out in delinquency and violence, children who act in with suicide, drug abuse, and kiddie prostitution, and children who act crazy by fleeing into the dark realm of insanity or multiple personality. Each undiagnosed and untreated child victim of ritual abuse is nothing more than a self-destruct mechanism masquerading as a human being. And when they implode or explode, they not only injure themselves and others, they pass judgment on us all.

Law Enforcement

I'm not one to advise law enforcement personnel on how to handle occult ritual crime. But representatives of law enforcement are in a good position to advise their own colleagues on the strange intricacies of satanism.

The occult isn't a popular topic among law enforcement personnel for all the reasons we've encountered: It's a religion, it's extremely secretive, it's elusive, it's incredibly dangerous.

"A 4-15 family fight call would be easy duty," writes Carole Allen and Pat Metoyer in their *Police Magazine* article of February 1987, "compared to conducting an occult crime investigation. While police can usually determine why drug dealers deal and petty thieves steal, the macabre aspect of occult crimes is a mystery to many officers."

It's easy to see why law enforcement is reluctant to mess with such cases on a satanic level. First, citizens will be alarmed if bizarre criminal activity is acknowledged in the community. Second, the satanic crime investigation itself is complex since it deals with unusual ritual elements and bizarre stories that are nearly impossible to substantiate. Third, bringing in satanism as motivation for a crime is practically a guarantee that the case will be thrown out of court. And finally, satanism is a religion.

Also, law enforcement personnel don't exactly like to appear foolish. Detective Pat Metoyer alludes to fruitless searches of the L.A. River bottom for ritually sacrificed bodies. Retired police captain Dale Griffis of Ohio shakes his head over the mishandled ballyhoo in Lucas County as law enforcement in the full glare of the media dug throughout a ceremonial site for alleged bodies of sacrifice victims. None were found. Michael Nelson, an Indiana deputy who was featured in the *Wall Street Journal* and *People* magazine for his investigations of grave desecration, was finally fired by Hendricks County Sheriff Waddell for his obsession with occult investigations.

Boise, Idaho, detective Larry Jones' File 18 newsletter carries cautionary tales about satanists purposely misleading police with strings of bizarre, conflicting stories until nothing can be believed about an incident. The newsletter also warns about storytellers out to ruin the credibility of local authorities who decide to take occult crime seriously. For instance, Jones reports a "Red Herring in Nebraska" in the January 1988 newsletter:

Detective W.E. Callister, McCook Police Department's Major Crimes Team, came across a case which tested his discernment and intuitive judgment. In September, a female runaway rolled into McCook on the bus and proceeded to tell a tale so bizarre that it could have been believable. After thorough background checking, Callister and his co-workers broke the story of Sandra Dawn Hilbert, WFA 23, 4-28-64.

She had posed as Anastasia Illyanna Novischik, 15, a runaway from Denver due to her pending initiation into a satanic ritual group. She had called the National Runaway Hotline from McCook, was picked up, and initially handled as an abandoned child, then an abused child. When the facts became known, Sandra AKA Anastasia was booked for felony criminal mischief, false reporting, and criminal impersonation.

Det. Callister wanted to warn other departments about this convincing prevaricator who, it seems, is an aspiring author. She had handwritten notes among her belongings which told a story in novel form about a character named Anastasia. Perhaps she was "living her story" in order to get a firsthand perspective. However, the chilling and detailed account she had told to investigators while pretending to be Anastasia was consistent with many of the reports we have printed about actual satanic and witchcraft rituals. She described grisly sacrifices of babies, cannibalism, sex with children, smearing and drinking blood, and anointing with urine and feces during adult-child satanic rituals. What investigator wouldn't prick up his ears when hearing statements such as these? But Callister finally saw through the charade and exposed the lies.

If you have been perplexed with a similar case, Det. Callister can supply more details and photos. Think of the "crow" he and his department would have had to eat if they had made premature public statements about this case. We do not know if this contrived story was Sandra's alone, or if she was a cleverly rehearsed plant to destroy the credibility of the local authorities. As in all cult/occult crime cases, it is better to err on the conservative side than to be too publicly liberal with information.

Law enforcement is concerned. They're concerned with overreaction to false reports, to exaggerated generalizations about the prevalence of the satanic crime problem, to their own uneasiness about dealing with such sticky cases. But they're doing something about that concern.

Law enforcement is educating its own. For instance, Robert J. Barry in the February/March issue of the National Sheriff's Association Magazine wrote in "Satanism: The Law Enforcement Response":

Law enforcement managers realize this renewed interest in satanism and the occult is a serious national problem. Authorities must meet the challenge by assuring these crimes are detected, reported, and prosecuted for what they are—satanic related.

This challenge is best addressed by a multifaceted approach:

—an increased awareness of the satanic trend by all law enforcement personnel,
—maintenance of special records on satanic type crimes,
—dissemination of information to appropriate organizations,
—cooperative intelligence gathering apparatus,
—county or state task forces to coordinate investigations of satanic-related crime,
—state and federal computer utilization for satanic-related crime,
—standardized report forms for satanic-related crime,
—the development of reliable sources of information and possible informants,
—allocation of adequate departmental resources,
—generalized training at recruit and in-service levels,
—in-depth training for specialized investigators,
—involvement of both community and private sector resources.

"This response," Barry concludes, "should lead to successful prosecution . . . and have important deterrent effects . . . . In addition, this effort should add to the strong existing paranoia of detection and prosecution present among most satanic cult members."

The establishment of a task force approach to occult crime has been tested in such diverse cities as Lenexa, Kansas, by Lee Craig—who includes even therapists and a media representative on the team—and Dallas/Fort Worth.

The Dallas/Fort Worth network is touted by many occult crime experts as the model for other developing task forces on deviant criminal cults. According to the *Dallas Morning News* of April, 1988, the task force was formed when "several agencies met in late 1986 to discuss an informant's claims of criminal cult activity.

"The network, which includes 30 area agencies, coordinates training and a computer data base at the Fort Worth Police Department's Gang Intelligence Unit. The unit also provides the services of their investigators . . . of ritual crime," writes Lee Hancock in the article "Crimes in the Name of Satan."

Self-Education

The key to law enforcement's response to occult crime, most experts say, is education. "You're darn right we need occult crime experts," said Deputy Harry Hatch, Conspiracy Section and Public Affairs Division of San Bernardino County Sheriff's department in California. "When we first started investigating occult crimes about a year ago, we didn't know what to look for evidence-wise. But after attending an occult crime seminar sponsored by the San Diego County Sheriff's Department, I learned we'd made a lot of mistakes and false assumptions along the way." Quoted on page 38 of the February

1987 *Police* magazine, Hatch says he recalls seeing occult crime evidence 20 years ago as a rookie cop; but neither he nor his colleagues knew what they were actually looking at in terms of evidence.

One of the resources available to law enforcement are reformed satanists and black witches such as Mary Ann Herold of Colorado. Dave Balsiger, another occult crime educator, quotes examples of the inside information ex-satanists like Mary Ann can provide:

Officers need to know that "often ceremonies are guarded by two and sometimes three rings of sentries. The outer guard will warn people away from the area, the second is usually armed and will stop you. The inner ring will kill to keep the group from being apprehended.

If a suicidal practitioner thinks you are a threat to their desire to die and reincarnate or resurrect, he/she might very well kill or hurt you, the police officer, in his "defense" of this sacrifice.

Remember covens and individual solitary practitioners are equipped with knives as ceremonial tools. Therefore, consider each group or individual as armed and potentially dangerous.

You might encounter an occultist who seems to possess "superhuman" strength. Be on guard.

Drug-induced satanism poses a double threat: the unpredictable effects of the drug mixed with the deviations of the practices.

Some agencies have instituted inhouse training programs on occult crime. Detective Harry Beltrane of Salt Lake County, Utah, Sheriff's Department says more than 300 of the county's deputies have been trained in occult crime.

Education is ongoing, and is often met with resistance. Occult crime is not only bizarre in its perpetration and motivation; it is also slippery in terms of providing hard evidence for prosecution while sidestepping the religious issue.

Passport Magazine's 1986 special issue on "America's Best Kept Secret" emphasizes the dilemma of police working on occult investigations on page 13: "'Police officers investigate crime,' Police Sergeant Randy Emon says, 'not religion. If an investigation leads an officer into the area of religious cults, then that officer runs the risk of having his case thrown right out of court unless he can prove without a doubt that a crime has been committed in connection with or as part of the cult.'"

The magazine quotes a Dr. Trostle: "Satanists are not stupid individuals. They know the political community, the criminal justice system and the academic community don't want anything to do with something having religious overtones."

But community law enforcement can, with networking task forces and education, handle the challenge of occult crime, according to Detective Larry Jones who heads the national Cult Crime Impact Network. His home base of Boise, Idaho, is an example. With trained officers speaking at various community organizations warning parents and teenagers about the criminal dangers of occult involvement, citizens began volunteering information on occult criminal activity in the area. When the local TV news programs picked up these stories and took pointers from occult-educated officers, their level-headed reports prompted even more intelligence calls to the police. Ex-satanic cultists found that "there were ears to hear what they had known but had kept to themselves for fear of ridicule," Larry writes in a recent issue of the organization's File 18 newsletter.

Local service organizations, now aware of the need for more training for local law enforcement, contributed funds for officers' advanced seminars on occult crime. The Northwest Passages Adolescent Hospital funded Larry's own trip to an advanced seminar in exchange for his training of the hospital staff and local therapists on satanic ritual abuse. A church-sponsored seminar on satanism resulted in the formation of a local ex-cultist's support group. This group then is providing informative materials to the community and serves as a referral agency, directing inquiries to a network of specialists knowledgeable in the occult.

The heightened community awareness of the problem—developed to this stage in just two years' time—is in turn helping Boise law enforcement as, according to Larry, "the level of incoming cult intelligence information is increasing. Sooner or later we will have enough pieces of the puzzle to take proactive steps to rescue potential victims and stop cult/occult criminal activity."

The major key to the ongoing success of Boise's battle against occult crimes, Larry concludes, "is willingness to share information outside our jurisdictional or professional 'kingdoms.'"

Now, at the crux of the battle—what can a parent do about teenagers edging near the evil of satanism?

▶ 24 ◀

Parent's Precautions

What can a parent do about kids getting head over heels into the occult?

First, find out if satanic dabbling is a part of your community's youth culture. How do you find out?

1. Check into what your community youth are reading.

Don't plan a witch-hunt book-burning. If you're alarmed at what you find being offered in reading materials in your community, alert the community to the problem and, as proper in a democratic society, allow the community in consensus to set boundaries for what is offered in bookshops and libraries.

With that in mind, since your purpose isn't censorship but education, your school librarians, public library officials and nearby university librarians will be glad to discuss their holdings of books on occult practices, how often they're checked out and by what age groups.

Check in your telephone book yellow pages for bookstores and occult paraphernalia shops. Call the bookstores to ask what occult holdings they have and how briskly these materials are selling to local teenagers. Visit the occult shops, in the pluralistic spirit that graces our society, and inquire what reading materials are ordered and bought by teenagers. You'll generally find occult bookstore proprietors knowledgeable and helpful in explaining questions on the occult—unless they perceive your inquiries as only prejudiced spying.

2. Find out if your community agencies have noticed teenagers dabbling in the occult in your area.

Contact local and regional mental health facilities. Simply ask an information official whether the facility handles teenage patients suffering from occultic or satanic trauma. If so, ask how pervasive such problems are among their adolescent clientele. Remember that many teenagers escape from satanism by committing themselves to alcohol or drug treatment programs.

Call several different denominational representatives—pastors, rabbis, priests—to ask if their religious group has noticed occultic practices among the youth of the community.

Check with city and county juvenile authorities and law enforcement personnel to again simply ask if teenage satanic dabbling is any kind of a problem in your area.

3. Check for telltale signs of satanic activity or crime near your community.

Call your Society for Prevention of Cruelty to Animals' local or regional office and ask about animal mutilations in the area.

Kindly, without the slightest tinge of hysteria in your voice, ask several local law enforcement personnel about any satanic group activity or occult crime in your region. Keep in mind one officer might be convinced there is no such thing occurring while another might be just as convinced there is something going on. Also remember that satanic activity itself is a religious issue; it doesn't become a law enforcement issue until a crime has unquestionably been committed.

Kindly, without the slightest tinge of hysteria in your voice, ask several media representatives in your area whether there seems to be any satanic activity or occult crime occurring. You may be surprised at the openness of the media to take on such a community evaluation themselves, providing your prompting is one of concern for local youth and not sensationalist witch hunting or religious persecution.

If you have some contact with a private mental health professional—a psychiatrist or psychologist—ask if anyone in the area is currently dealing with satanic abuse survivors or satanic terror victims from the local area. Expect no information beyond a yes or no since confidentiality and the safety of such patients are two of the therapist's primary considerations. An affirmative response suggests the possible presence of a hardcore traditional satanic cult in the region.

And what do you do with your satanic evaluation? Nothing beyond educating yourself with the information.

Stupidity might prompt some people's reactions to include religious discrimination, superstitious gossiping, unauthorized criminal investigation and law enforcement, book censorship, harassment of merchants, slander, breaching of confidences, exaggeration of facts, pronouncements of guilt by association, vigilante action, criticism of community agencies, misinformation—and I could go on listing the disgusting crimes often committed in the name of self-righteousness and sometimes even in the name of Christ. (I never forget that the more than a quarter million witches murdered during the Inquisition were indicted under the authority of a Pope named "Innocent.")

But I'm convinced better of you: You'll use the information to educate yourself on how you can help your children and your teenagers avoid selling their bodies, souls and spirits to Satan. If a responsible community agency wants to follow up on your findings because your research has exuded such rationality and charm, fine.

But don't plan a satanist tar and feathering. You're not The Exorcist.

Is satanic dabbling a part of your teenager's peer group? How do you find out?

1. You can rationally evaluate a group in which your teenager may be involved.

Please remember that scribbling "666," listening to Ozzy Osbourne, playing Dungeons and Dragons or buying earrings with a Nero's cross (the old peace sign/broken cross) or other symbols of the occult listed in Appendix A doesn't necessarily mean your kid's friends are avowed satanists. The satanic fad, like all fads, rubs off on all sorts of innocent bystanders. Don't jump to conclusions about your teenager's peer group—they might not be as diabolical as they look.

But does your teenager hang around with a group that has occult trappings and is actually cultlike? Remember dabbler and even self-styled covens may resemble not so much an organization as a club. For instance, a fantasy roleplaying group can devolve into an occult cult. Here are some marks of a destructive cult—occultic or otherwise—adapted from Cult Awareness Network materials:

• There is undue influence from group leadership, evidence of attempts at mind control.

• There is charismatic leadership, even a younger person who claims special knowledge and is given special power and privilege in the group.

• Deception pervades the group's activities. They claim to be one thing and are obviously something else. They present odd or inconsistent stories about what they do as a group, where they've been.

(The destructive, cultlike group as a concerted team emphasizes the typical teenage responses to "Where have you been?"

"Nowhere."

"Who were you with?"

"Nobody."

"What were you doing?"

"Nothing." Their deception and secrecy is conspiratorial.)

• The group exults in exclusivity, elitism and euphoria. Again, the group is guarded or vague about activities and purposes. Participants seem concerned about power and exhibit odd euphoric states—which can be results of or separate from drug-induced "highs."

• Alienation is encouraged by the group. Far beyond the normal teenage drive for independence, participants in these cultlike groups estrange themselves from family, old friends and society. There is a sudden display of changed values articulated in canned phrases repeated by other group members.

• There may be signs of exploitation in the group. A member may suggest he or she "owes" the group something such as money or a favor. Signs of exploitation can include physical abuse, demands for accomplishing certain dangerous tasks as payment or penance, blackmail and a period of ostracism from the group.

Remember that teenagers' lives are in transit. They're always going through something. And transition is the key period when teenagers are especially susceptible to the lure of cultlike groups—satanic or otherwise. Betty Naysmith, the volunteer researcher for the Cult Awareness Network in Chicago, suggests there are critical times when teenagers are especially open to the lures of cultlike groups:

after graduating from school, during the first year away from home;
when going through the stress of getting a new job;
any time the teenager is new to a school or group;
during periods of trauma—accidents, sickness, loss of a good friend, etc.;
whenever the family is undergoing a crisis—a divorce, a death, etc.

2. Talk with your teenager and your teenager's friends. Don't be one of those horrendous adult spies who tries to find out everything; if they told you everything they wouldn't be real teenagers any more.

As LAPD Detective Pat Metoyer says, "If your kid says, 'Aw, everybody's dabbling in this stuff; it's no big deal,' ask him to name five kids who are actually dabbling in it. If he can't, it'll suggest to him that it's not as casually common as he thinks. If he can name five others, you've got trouble!"

Ask your teenager and his or her group about satanic activity at school or in the community. Teenagers generally don't have the verbal skills of an adult, so don't expect lots of stimulating repartee. And don't expect any response if they get the idea you're playing FBI; so lighten up in your delivery. Actually, you might be surprised at what you can learn just by simply asking good questions such as:

Do you believe there's an actual devil?
Do kids still play much with Ouija boards?
If you sold your soul to the devil for something, what would it be?
Do you really think there are magic spells to make somebody fall in love with you?
Have you ever met a real witch?

If the group your kid runs with is particularly uncomfortable with such questions and if you notice cultlike tendencies in his or her occult interests, it's time to seriously evaluate your teenager's personal involvement in the black arts.

If your kid has no peer group, is a complete loner and shows interest in occult phenomena, it's also time to make that evaluation.

Is satanic dabbling a part of my teenager's life? How do I find out? What do I do about it?

1. Talk. Don't grill or badger the kid; but talk. Ask specific questions

about the occult and if you receive specific answers, ask how your teenager learned this information.

2. Watch for an overemphasized interest in the occult. Any normal teenager is curious about the unexplained, about the supernatural. But an obsession with occultic practices beyond the ninth grade suggests overinvolvement. Watch for:

• well-worn occult and satanic literature; also notice Bibles, Psalms or New Testaments kept by a teenager who is strongly anti-christian—the verses are needed for ritualistic backwards readings

• school essays about the occult or about fixations with death and violence

• occultic items such as a robe, a silver chalice or goblet, a sword, oddly shaped knives, black candles, bone collections (specifically skull, rib, upper right leg and the upper right arm bones), religious and/or occultic jewelry

• occultic symbols such as those listed in Appendix A drawn on or carved into your teenager's things; a large pentagram drawn on the floor

• an altar or something that could be used as an altar, sometimes camouflaged in a closet

• a "Book of Shadows," a satanic journal in a black covered book, a spiral or looseleaf binder, or a computerized journal

• writings in strange lettering—Egyptian glyphs, runes, backwards script or a homemade alphabet.

Detective Simandl suggests: "If these items are found it is preferable that the child not be confronted nor the items removed until a knowledgeable person can assist in interpreting the dabbler's level of involvement and the resources for proper intervention. A copy of the "Book of Shadows" diary made without the child's knowledge will prove useful in the evaluation.

NOTE: Somewhere along the line, our culture's parents seemed to be convinced en masse that teenagers' need for privacy was not a privilege but a divine commandment scratched into stone tablets. So how can a parent uncover these satanic items when Joe Sophomore has his room locked all the time?

Shock yourself. When you suspect satanic dabbling, look in the room. Search for and read the "Book of Shadows" journal. Take Los Angeles Police Detective Pat Metoyer's advice: "He won't let you in his room because it's private? He's got the door padlocked? Call a handyman and tear out the door." Take advice from Betty Naysmith, Cult Awareness Network researcher or Chicago Police Department's Jerry Simandl: "The goal is to prevent suicide and criminal acts. Search the room."

Take Jerry Johnston's advice: Respect a teenager's privacy as you would that of any adult, but when you suspect that privacy is misused, remember it's your house. Search your teenager's personal things if you think he or she is signing her or his life away to satanism. Yes, even if you made a deal that the room will be strictly off limits to you and other family members.

Try this analogy; it might make it easier: You give Joey $50 for this month's lunch money. You find Joey bought crack or PCP angel dust with most of the money. Now, crack or PCP is going to eat Joey's lunch; so it makes sense since Joey violated your trust to take back the rest of the money and refuse to give him more until he proves he can handle your trust again.

Perhaps you agreed never to look in your teenager's diary or search the bedroom. But some of the characteristics we're discussing make you strongly suspect that your kid is going to be physically, mentally, emotionally and spiritually warped by satanism. He's violated the privacy privilege you granted. Search the room; read the journal. Pull your kid back from the edge of evil.

3. Notice strong behavioral and personality changes. Watch for:
- a decided withdrawal from longtime friends and family
- a whole new set of friends
- any sign of self-mutilation such as occult symbols carved or tattooed into the skin; notice especially a design or satanic nickname written or tattooed on the web of skin between thumb and index finger—usually on the left hand
- a sudden and consistent switch to dark clothing
- a new interest—especially noticeable among guys—in buying jewelry with occult or religious designs
- remarkable increase in aggression and violent behavior
- chronic depression
- a distinct drop in grades and interest at school
- an obsessive interest in power/black/heavy metal bands that push satanic themes
- a preoccupation with death and destruction
- nightmares about demons
- (as outlandish as it sounds) missing pets in the family or neighborhood
- consistent inability to account for absences—usually episodes of sneaking out after the family is asleep—on satanic calendar holiday nights.

What do I do about a teenager who's dabbling or is even more heavily involved in satanism?

1. As noted above, make a copy of any writings and a list of any occult items belonging to your teenager.

2. Get an expert opinion on what these items suggest as to your teenager's level of involvement. Resources may be law enforcement, school counselors, clergy, mental health personnel or organizations such as those listed in Appendix B, "Resources."

3. With advice and referrals from these resources, arrange counseling for your teenager. Remember that in our culture, a commitment to the lord of death is, virtually, a signal that something is very wrong. Involve yourself in following and participating in the therapy prescribed.

4. With this mental-emotional facet of the problem addressed, consider the physical, practical aspects of your teenager's obsession with the occult.

Remove the satanic items and books. Destroy them if you wish; or put them in storage until the teenager can, once out on his own, decide what he wants to do with such items. You're not bound by any ethical, moral or civil law to allow anything in your home that you know is destructive. Don't allow any of these things back into your home since even small, innocent-seeming items have significant satanic meaning for your dabbler.

Gently insist to school officials that your concern for your teenager necessitates a search of his locker and/or desk to remove any occult paraphernalia or literature. If gentle insistence fails to allow you to search your own teenager's belongings at school, get some insistent clout from your dabbler's therapist and from law enforcement. Remember to search book lockers, gym lockers, storage bins in vocational shops, art lockers, etc.

Set specific and enforceable limits on your teenager's activities and whereabouts to preclude occult involvement. If your teenager is unmanageable, it's time you get help from parenting support groups such as Tough Love or others known to local mental health professionals.

The bottom line is: Get satanic influences physically away from your teenager and your teenager physically away from satanic influences.

5. Along with your concern about the mental-emotional and the physical-practical, don't minimize the spiritual aspect of teenage dabbling in satanism. Regardless of your own or your teenager's previous religious opinions, he or she apparently believes in the spiritual reality of either a powerful force or a powerful being called Satan, Lucifer, the devil. The dabbler believes in demons and demonic power, in the supernatural dimension of spirit. That's the dabbler's reality regardless of your own convictions.

You must acknowledge that perceived reality and arrange some kind of responsible spiritual ministry by legitimate clergy.

Perhaps you feel this spiritual business isn't important, isn't the crux of satanic dabbling. You're entitled to your opinion; but then so am I. And I'm convinced that the spirit of your teenager is just as vulnerable to the damages of satanism as are his emotions and mental state. If you're atheistic or agnostic, it may be tough to admit that your teenager began dabbling in evil as part of a search for spiritual reality.

If that thirst isn't satisfied by spiritual truth, no amount of protection or therapy is going to derail his or her search. Once away from therapy and away from your influence, he or she will be back on the track over the edge of evil in no time. Spiritual needs must be addressed.

Obviously this is touchy ground since charlatanism, foaming-at-the-mouth demonic exorcism services that resemble circus sideshows and unbiblical, irresponsible spiritual advice abound in religious circles.

So here's a deal. My address and phone number is listed in Appendix C as a resource. Call or write the Jerry Johnston Association. And regardless of where you live, I'll refer you to a contact who will, with compassion and integrity, minister to your teenager's very real spiritual needs. And if you'd like, to yours, too. Because you'll need some ministering to prepare you for the last step in what you can do about a kid who has drugged or meditated his or her way into altered states of consciousness, who has performed rituals to conjure demons, cast spells, who has considered or implemented plans to sacrificially torture a blood offering to Satan, who actually believes he or she has sold his or her soul for eternity in hell. So here's the sixth step:

6. Pray.

What do I do to prevent my teenager from ever becoming involved in satanism?

A. Be a parent. This isn't a book on parenting, but there are plenty of good books available from your public library, your doctor, your mental health services, community child protection services, churches, bookstores, etc. Get help, because unlike becoming a father or mother, becoming a *parent* doesn't come naturally.

I hope through our journey you've caught on to the fact that kids who get into satanism are kids who need help. They're looking for something, not finding it in their lives, and striking out for Hell to find it. A teenager who finds encouragement, love, understanding, responsibility, relationships to emulate, spiritual substance, consistent and loving discipline, training in critical thinking, openness to discuss tough issues such as sex, social training, wisdom, integrity, and attention at home, won't risk all that just to gut chickens and beg for demon possession.

Think through the opposites of those qualities. If those opposites characterize the Hell your teenager is already living in, there's little you can do as a quick-fix to prevent such a kid from being lured to the forbidden pleasures and thrills and power of evil.

A final word on preventing your teenager from self-destruction: Sometimes there's nothing you can do. In spite of the rampant, starkly scientific view of man as a victim in an uncaring universe, I need to remind you that your kid is more than a combination of chemicals and environment. Kids can and do climb out of the worst cesspools of "family life" to lead healthy, productive lives—if they choose to. They have a choice about what they do and who they become—no matter how much they want to foist the blame for wrong choices on their parents or their first-grade teachers or the cartoons they watched Saturday mornings.

So do what you can to prevent self-destructive behavior such as satanic involvement. But don't blame yourself for the rest of your life if your teenager chooses to love the god of the dunghill—"Beelzebub"—instead of responding to your love. Guide, love, listen, care about your kid—but remember you're not responsible for the choices he makes. If he is determined to sell his soul and live like the devil, there's frankly no way you can always be there to prevent him.

(There's a Hebrew word used in the Psalms, "selah," which means, "Pause and meditate on these things.")

So selah.

B. Be educated. This book is a general starter on understanding today's satanic cult. Check out the bibliography for other books specifically written to educate the reader in occult beliefs and practices. But stay sane: Don't overeducate yourself in satanism, okay?

C. If in your community satanic survey you discovered an unhealthy interest in the occult among local teenagers or adults, consider:

• filing a complaint with proper public officials about any satanic crime or misconduct

• writing a few nonsensationalist, rational letters to the editor of your local newspaper about the problems of mixing youth and Satan

• help arrange a program at your school, church, library or youth club about the dangers of satanic dabbling

• write appropriate local and state officials, including congressmen and senators, about investigating destructive satanic groups in your area. (Remind officials that the issue is not one of religion or human rights but of corruption of minors, illegalities, unethical practices, and mental health.)

D. Think through the advice suggested for teenagers at the end of Chapter 21 on what an individual can do about the lures, the ravages of satanism. Share your conclusions about that information with your children.

What can I do about preventing teenage suicide? Many people are hesitant to even discuss the subject of suicide. That attitude in itself indicates an unhealthy fear. Suicide is such a no-no topic in our society that many—perhaps thousands—of suicidal deaths are reported instead as accidents. But the issue needs to be addressed, so let's talk about suicide with our kids. Read up on the problem in books such as my *Why Suicide*, which outlines several commonly held myths such as:

Myth No. 1: People who talk about suicide don't commit suicide. Wrong. Dr. Edwin Shneidman, the country's leading suicide expert, blasts this idea. He says, "The notion that people who talk about suicide don't do it is the most dangerous myth in the world. Four out of five suicides have made previous attempts and in every single instance the person gives clues, warning signals, that he is about to do it."

Myth No. 2: Suicides usually happen without warning. No, suicides do not occur unpredictably. They are usually the result of long-term inner struggle expressed outwardly in some clearly recognizable actions and attitudes.

Myth No. 3: Suicidal people can't be talked out of it if they are really intent on dying. I quote again from Dr. Shneidman: "Nonsense! [A suicidal person] is in a state of confusion and irrational thinking; he wants to continue his life but can't see the way. We find so frequently that lethal drives last just a short time so that if you can get him through the period of severe stress, his entire outlook can change and the very next day he may no longer be the slightest bit suicidal."

Myth No. 4: An individual's improvement following a suicidal crisis means the suicide risk is over. Paul tried to hang himself because, as he put it in a terse note to his parents, "Nobody loves me. Nobody really talks to me. They just throw words at me."

Paul survived, however, and he seemed to be making improvement. "I thought he had solved his problem," said his father. But Paul made a second attempt four months after the first. Help arrived too late. His final note read, "Nobody listens. They say 'How are you?' and that's about as far as it goes. I don't want to live in a world where it hurts so bad inside all the time."

Myth No. 5: Suicide strikes more often among the rich. N. L. Farberow says: "Suicide is neither the rich man's disease nor the poor man's curse." In fact, suicide is very democratic and includes a proportionate number of victims from all levels of society. Another study says that "the average person who commits suicide is close to the average person."

Myth No. 6: Suicide is hereditary; it runs in families. There is absolutely no evidence to suggest that suicidal tendencies are hereditary. But there is unquestionably a powerfully negative influence on surviving families when a suicide occurs. One psychiatrist calls it survivor guilt—a curious belief that the "wrong person" died. A confused teenager told me, "My father was such a good man. He never hurt anybody and worked so hard for the family. Look at me. I'm a mess, and I keep screwing up in everything I do. Why am I the one still alive?"

When a family member takes his or her own life, it can prompt suicidal thoughts and even a suicide attempt among the survivors. This is especially true of a person already deeply troubled. But none of this has a thing to do with genetic factors. No one is doomed to act a certain way or destined to end it all because a family member made a fateful decision. A close relative's suicide may provide impetus for yet another fatal act, but I firmly believe it doesn't have to be that way.

Myth No. 7: Someone who commits suicide is mentally ill. Marcia attempted suicide when she was fifteen and again at seventeen. In her own words, "The agony and the confusion at the time seemed permanent. My main concern was that if the situation I was in was going to be permanent, I wanted no part of it. That death would be permanent was of no consideration to me. There is a great feeling of being hopeless and lost and your self-image is in pretty bad shape when you're thinking about suicide."

Marcia, I'm convinced, is not mentally ill. She is quite normal and, thankfully, quite alive today. But she does remind us how tough teenage life can be for some kids. It's a wonderful, terrible time, and there are plenty of obstacles along the way. Kids tell me about their pain, their feelings of rejection, and the ugly suspicion that no one really cares. But they aren't insane.

Myth No. 8: Only certain people are the suicidal type. There's no such thing as a suicidal personality type. This menace touches every point in a cross section of society and is not limited to certain individuals with a certain makeup. However, some people are greater risks than others—those who have attempted suicide before, recently bereaved persons, the seriously ill, alcoholics and drug abusers.

Myth No. 9: Most suicides are committed by older people with just a few years to live. False. Persons over 50 are, statistically, less likely to take their lives. The most endangered group are those in the 15- to 24-year-old age bracket.

Myth No. 10: Women threaten suicide, but men carry it out. This myth comes from a misinterpreted fact. Three times as many men as women commit suicide, but three times as many women as men attempt it. The explanation for this phenomenon lies in the suicide method. Women use less violent means such as pills or poison, increasing the chance of rescue. Men are more likely to kill themselves violently with a gun, a knife, or a rope.

Myth No. 11: Talking about suicide causes suicide by planting the idea in a person's head. Some critics claim that I inadvertently encourage teenagers to commit suicide. I think just the opposite is true. You see, I know many teens are already thinking about suicide, and they are often convinced no one has ever felt the way they feel. By talking about suicide and by identifying the feelings they are experiencing, we are bringing everything out into the open. Just knowing that others are struggling, too, helps immeasurably in a teenager's ability to cope.

No, talking about suicide will not cause suicide. But failing to talk about it may have disastrous consequences.

Warning Signs of Suicide

"I can't believe it. She just wasn't the kind of person you'd expect to commit suicide. There weren't any signs at all."

I've heard too many comments like this. There was no indication of anything wrong, they say. No clue as to a deep need. No sign of a serious problem. I have a hard time buying those comments, because seldom does a teenager commit suicide without giving some warning. My research has borne this out, and my conversations with many who have attempted suicide reinforce this conviction. A spokesperson for the Suicide and Crisis Center in Dallas says 80 percent of teenagers who commit suicide have given one or more signs of their intention beforehand. Some of these warning signs include:

1. Withdrawal—the teen who pulls away. To a certain extent, withdrawal is natural and good during the teenage years. Developing healthy independence equips a teen for successful adulthood. But when withdrawal is severe, when there is an obvious pulling away and into a shell, watch out.

2. Moodiness—the teen who's up and down. Everyone is moody from time to time. We're all influenced by the weather, our health, our circumstances. Teenagers are no different. But when there are chronic, wide shifts, up one day and on the bottom the next, there is cause for alarm. One expert observes that "sudden, inexplicable euphoria or whirlwind activity after a spell of gloom" means danger.

Moodiness is closely associated with the next two warning signs.

3. Depression—the teen who holds in. Self-pity can give way to suicidal thoughts: Nobody understands what I'm going through. There's no way I can get out of this situation.

4. Aggression—the teen who lashes out. Many suicide attempts are preceded by violent outbursts—fights, threats, cruel insults, even destruction of property. Frequently, acts of this nature are cries for help.

A less-obvious form of presuicidal aggression is risk-taking. This could include recklessness with vehicles or participation in dangerous activities.

5. Alcohol and drug abuse—the teen who turns on. Sudden indulgence by a young person who hadn't previously gotten drunk or done drugs is a definite red flag.

6. Sexual activity—the teen who lets go. Inappropriate sexual behavior sometimes reflects a desperate desire to relieve depression. By letting go completely with another person, the depressed teenager thinks satisfaction can finally be achieved. When there is no lasting satisfaction, suicidal thoughts can and often do intensify.

7. Eating disorders—the teen who punishes self. Anorexia and bulimia are words now well-known. These frightful diseases have a strong connection to self-destructive thoughts and should always be considered potentially suicidal.

8. Gift giving—the teen who gives up and gives away. Some teenagers who plan to take their lives will give away prized possessions to close friends or to others they wish were close friends.

9. Trauma—the teen who's been hit hard. Each person has an emotional threshold, an internal breaking point. A major traumatic event or series of circumstances can drive a teenager closer and closer to the edge.

10. Personality change—the teen who's not the same. Abrupt reversal is the thing to watch for.

11. Threat—the teen who speaks out. Any comment regarding the desire to die should be taken seriously. Some of the most common threats are "I wish I'd never been born" or "You're going to be sorry when I'm gone" or "I want to go to sleep and never wake up." These should be interpreted as seriously as "I'm going to kill myself."

What can I do about satanic influences in my kids' music?

Start at home, the Parents' Music Resource Center advises in their materials adapted for a July 1988 *Reader's Digest* article. "Start early and tune in to your children and their world. Instead of shouting, 'Cut down that noise!' listen to the lyrics and talk about them in light of your family's values. Watch some MTV together; then discuss what you've seen and heard. Pick up a teenage-level music magazine periodically; ask your kids about the groups reviewed. As a parent, you have every right to decide what kind of messages you want in your house."

PMRC also suggests a media watch. Ask kids what are the heavy rock stations and listen. If offensive material is aired, write down the objectionable words, time and date of the program and its commercial sponsors. Then fire off a letter of protest to the local station manager and the program's sponsors. Send a tape to the Federal Communications Commission and a transcript to your elected state and national representatives.

"There is another approach"—suggests the PMRC article—"the law. In two major decisions, the U.S. Supreme Court has held that 'obscene material is unprotected by the First Amendment.' The federal government has strict laws against the mailing, interstate transporting and importing of obscene materials, and a broadcasting law prohibiting obscene and indecent programming. Forty-three states have laws against the sale of obscene materials, and sellers can be arrested. If your state does not have such a law, ask your legislator to propose one."

As an example of what can be done, the article reports that "parents in San Antonio have shown just how effective community pressure can be. They were horrified to find thousands of preteens attending concerts by KISS, W.A.S.P. and other heavy-metal bands that exalted murder, sexual sadism, bestiality and drugs. So in 1985 parents persuaded the city council to design a first-of-its-kind ordinance requiring parents or legal guardians to accompany children under 14 to concerts featuring material deemed obscene to children.

"The impact of the ordinance," says Bobbie Mueller, head of Community Families in Action, "has been significant. Attendance by preteens has dropped substantially and performances are more restrained."

Remember that being labeled a "prude" by teenagers just may be a sort of compliment as you encourage the demise of satanic-oriented music. At least you're taking a stand as are many of the non-occultic superstars of rock. Just tell your kids you're in good company with The Boss, Bruce Springsteen, who says, "In many ways what's happening in music today is very corrupting. Let's help our children toss out the garbage."

What do I do about suspected ritual abuse of children?

Obviously this isn't the place for a thorough discussion of this horrendous problem. And, incidentally, it is horrendous. Before I got into this cursory investigation of what satanism may be doing in our culture, preschool/daycare and neighborhood satanic abuse of children was on my "least credible" list. It is no longer.

As in other complex areas of satanic evil and the dark occult, I must insist that you deal with professionals—with therapists, child protective specialists, medical personnel and law enforcement.

But the least I can do is provide a checklist of symptoms of ritual abuse in children. The list is not comprehensive, but it does seem to combine the highlights of several warning lists I've studied. This particular advice comes from Lauren Stratford, a courageous woman who, victimized by Satan's dupes throughout her childhood and adolescence, shares her story for our benefit in *Satan's Underground*. The following is adapted from the appendix to that story:

What Parents Should Watch for in Their Children:

Behavioral Changes

1. Talking to unseen persons, insisting they are real and not wanting to talk about that "imaginary friend." Children will often make up imaginary friends they'll talk and play with. But if the child is fearful when talking about the "friend" or fearful of the "imaginary friend," it is possible that the child is talking to a "spirit guide" or "spirit friend." Satanic cults brainwash victims that such a spirit will monitor their words and actions if they were to tell about any ritualistic abuse.

2. Playing out, acting out sexual situations. Often using new words for sexual activities or body parts.

3. Doing devil dances, spirit dances, or other heretofore-unfamiliar types of dances, songs, chants, and/or prayers. Ask your child what he is doing. This is a major warning sign if the child hasn't exhibited such behavior, seems totally preoccupied with doing it, and refuses to stop even under the warning of punishment.

4. Fear of or unusual preoccupation with the number "6" or multiples thereof. This is sometimes manifested by the child's terror of his sixth birthday. Such a fear might exist because a child has been told that he will die on his sixth birthday.

5. Verbal or written words that are strange or verbal or written words that are backwards. This is certainly not referring to children with dyslexia or other learning problems. These will be words or phrases that will suddenly become a vital and permanent part of the child's vocabulary. They will not be sporadically spoken on a whim, nor will the child leave these words and go on to other made-up words as children often do. The backward words may have a Christian meaning. If the child has been ritualistically abused, words of the Bible have been taught to the child in a backward manner so as to degrade or mock the Word of God.

6. Sudden, radically unexplainable mood change. For example, a child who has normally been rather reserved suddenly becomes hyperactive and starts tearing the house apart or having violent, unexplainable temper tantrums.

7. Sudden, irrational fear of being left alone for even a few minutes.

8. Fear of colors, especially red, black or purple.

9. Sudden, unexplainable fear of small spaces. Some children enjoy playing in small places. But if they suddenly become terrified of confined areas, it may be that they have been abused and/or shut in coffins, cemetery or field grave holes, closets, etc.

10. Sudden fear of bathing or extreme and heretofore-unexhibited preoccupation with cleanliness.

11. Sudden desire for frequent change of underwear.

12. Sudden change in normal toileting practices. Almost all ritualistically abused children have been forced to eat feces and drink urine as part of the degrading process. Be very concerned with a sudden fascination with or abhorrence to urine and feces by drinking the urine or putting feces into his or her mouth or spreading it over the body or the bathroom.

13. Sudden, violent, hostile aggressive behavior against parents or siblings. We are not talking about normal childhood anger that is to be expected among preschool-age children, but an obvious attempt to actually kill a family member with a weapon such as knife, or a violent threat to commit such an act.

14. Evaluate pictures or objects. If the child says that he or she brought these home from school or found them somewhere, watch for symbolisms or signs of satanism in pictures with pentagrams and/or a crescent moon with five stars in the curve of the moon and dominant colors of black, red and purple.

Watch for pictures with disproportionately large eyes or ears (The child may tell you, "The eyes are watching me," or "The ears are listening to me."); houses of construction paper with doors that open (Ask the child what happens when the door is opened); animals like rabbits, especially if a child is unusually adamant about the picture staying in a prominent location (It may represent mutilation or sacrifice, and the child was ordered to leave it on the refrigerator or other prominent place as a reminder of what could happen to a family member or pet if the child reveals his or her abuse).

15. Watch for a sudden fear of religious objects or persons. These would include crosses, statues, candles, communion bowls, cups, wine, bread, etc. Notice pronounced or sudden fears of clergymen, especially when dressed in clerical robes.

16. Notice sudden, irrational fear of certain places. These may be places where the ritualistic abuse was performed, or they may be places that are similar-looking that remind the child of the actual abuse site. They may also be places where the child was taken and shown bodies or parts of bodies of "people who didn't obey" or "people who talked." Such scare tactics frighten the child into obedience and silence. (Usually when a parent asks a child

why he is frightened, the nonabused child will tell why, or it will be obvious that this is simply the normal fear of a new setting. But if he has been ritualistically abused, the fear will not diminish, and he may be too scared to explain his fear to you.)

Teenagers, of course, are supposed to be rebellious, to be questioning the belief systems of their elders, to be selfish. Normal teenagers grow up through such mild forms of breaking away from parents. But if these characteristics are pronounced, if a teenager is preoccupied with suicidal thoughts, if he or she experiences unusually severe and recurring nightmares, and if several of the symptoms Lauren mentioned were part of that teenagers' preschool demeanor, be concerned. Search through memory, talk with your youth—keeping in mind the teenager may recall nothing of the experiences even if ritually abused.

But if there seem to be too many symptoms, seek some professional help. Check the resource directory in Appendix C.

Refuse to become hysterical about what may be no more than a teenager's headlong fall in a new love relationship; but consider the possibility that such pronounced symptoms could suggest early ritual abuse. No, your youth isn't too old to have been a victim. Don't forget that a therapist in Manhattan Beach, California, is currently treating a 31-year-old victim of satanic abuse in a local daycare center; this has been going on for at least decades.

It can happen.

Epilogue

Manhattan. I descend the greasy black steps below the Queens sidewalk to the subway. A blue-jeaned body snores under newspapers at the bottom of the stairs. Drug-emaciated beggars hold out gnarled palms. White and blue tile lines a far wall with chipped yellow paint below it as about 30 of us good citizens mill around the platform. I chat with a couple teenagers who are arguing about whether flattops are still in. "What do you think?" the short guy asks me. "What'd they do in LA? And I don't mean them honkies."

His flattop looks like a Moroccan fez; all it needs is a tassle. I shake my head. "Out," I say; and the other kid laughs till he nearly falls off the platform. The short kid flips me a finger but laughs.

I start talking with a fifty-ish Puerto Rican as if I didn't know that New Yorkers don't talk with strangers, much less each other on subways and streets. He tells me lurid tales of Brujeria among the Hispanic community.

The subway car is lined with drug helpline ads and posters of "Angelica: Mi Vida. Lunes a Viernes Telemundo 47." Out of 14 people in my end of the car, seven have their eyes closed—stoned, asleep or listening to headphones. The doors at the other end of the car open and a girl in her twenties wrapped tightly in gray sweatshirt and an orange scarf announces, "I'm a mother of two children, ladies and gentlemen, and I hate to beg. I have a college education—" And she goes on to enumerate the woes she's encountered in trying to keep a job and to find food. Now it's getting cold in her flat . . . . She then walks the length of the car holding out a chipped white enamel cup. Her eyes are clear; I unfortunately did enough drugs as a kid to know the signs, and I judge that she'll at least not buy drugs for herself. I put in ten bucks and it's instantly obvious that all the New Yorkers know I must be a sucker from out of town, from someplace like Farmsville, Iowa. She collects a few other coins. I glance her way as she goes to step out of the car and she looks, eyes wide, for four or five seconds. I wink; then she's gone.

I climb up into the cold wind bustling around 42nd Street and Fifth Avenue and find the 14-story old building after wandering around Times Square for a half hour. I pass a lady preacher who's yelling, "You better get right or get left 'cause Jesus is coming soon. The Antichrist is here already; he'll come to prominence with signs and wonders!" Her co-worker hands me a tract; they're with Gospel Sunrise in Dayton, Virginia. I pass stores from Perfumaria to 25-cent Live! Nude Reviews! to deli's with superb coffee. Bundled chess players match wits on card-table chessboards on a corner, gathering a crowd of observers including the distinguished and the derelict. The sidewalks rush with incredible faces and smells of old Hai Karate cologne, hot dogs, hot pretzels, of perfumes and wine fumes.

I step into the old brick building, ride the elevator to the fourteenth floor. Then I climb the stairs to the penthouse level and get buzzed through the security door into the white, friendly coffee-smell of the headquarters for the "Geraldo" show.

I talk with investigator Shirley Jonas to see if there's any information I can contribute to their upcoming special on satanism. There isn't. They've got more info than they can handle. Is there any info on teenagers' involvement in satanism I might use in *The Edge of Evil?* No; I've either bumbled across their information on my own or, since they're after the criminal element, their material is too heavy-duty for a book directed to communities, schools and parents.

As I leave, Christina at the front desk takes a call from Ken Wooden, the child advocate, author of *Child Lures;* and I'm reminded that one person can do something. One person can change things. I remember seeing Ken's warnings about ritual child abuse and child pornography in the Cult Crime Impact Network File 18 newsletters. I remember that he was instrumental in convincing the ritually abused Lauren Stratford to share her alarming story in the Harvest House book, *Satan's Underground.* A couple of weeks ago I ran across Ken guesting on a talk show called "Straight Talk" on which he'd said, "The average pedophile molests, according to a Duke University study, 265 children."

So people like Ken Wooden are getting the word out, warning parents, challenging professionals in child protective and law enforcement services with personal crusades against the exploitation of children.

One person can do something. Maybe it's not going to solve the problem; ten bucks isn't going to reverse the fortunes of a destitute mother. And one book and hundreds of talks to schools and community groups on the dangers of teenage satanic dabbling aren't going to pull our society's kids back from the edge of evil. But one person *can* do something.

You can do something. You've stuck with me through this whole adventure of tracing what satanism is doing to the generation that'll be taking over in the twenty-first century. And like me, you've learned about a problem most of us would rather not think about. With that knowledge comes responsibility. So do something. Don't go on some hysterical witch hunt to brand your neighbors as demonic satanists because they read horoscopes. Don't torch your local school library because you find books on paranormal experience. When your preschooler throws a tantrum don't launch into exorcism rituals. Don't bomb an identified satanist's house; satanism and witchcraft and paganism have all the civil protections afforded your religion. Use your head. Follow the recommendations compiled from the experts, the strategies outlined in the appendices. But for God's sake, do something to prevent even one more toddler or teenager from being literally or figuratively sacrificed to the god of death.

The reason we've got to do something now about so many of these social issues is that the problems multiply. Evil spreads exponentially. Ken Wooden pointed out the statistic on how many children are affected by the warped sexuality of one pedophile. And then each of those 265 molested kids grows to battle sexual problems, many becoming child molesters themselves—who each might in turn molest another 265 children.

In the same way, I'm convinced satanism is an exponential problem. Satanism is sexual perversion: ritual abuse of children is obviously perversion, but so is the sex-saturated ritual orgy that accompanies satanic worship. We didn't dwell on it, but you probably noticed that free-for-all sex is one of the hot attractions satanism has for teenagers. Whether ritually abused as children or sucked into satanism as teenagers, satanically tainted members of the upcoming generation are going to spread a warped sense of their sexuality. And I don't even want to think about the multiplication of sexual diseases that's inevitable in such worship as child molestation and helter-skelter sex.

Self-styled or traditional satanism is also violence. I know our trek through the dark side has seemed gruesome at times; let me assure you, I've spared you. In my years of speaking out about teenage suicide, I thought I'd have no problem handling satanic violence. Wrong. I've had trouble shaking images of teenagers' self-mutilation, torturing of animals, and witnessing of and participation in human torture. Satanists become ritually inured to violence. And violence begets violence, as we conclusively know from 20 years of studies in child abuse.

Dabbler and self-styled satanism is drugs. The news program I watched last night about the new spread of AIDS through infected needles in New York crack houses, the dope fiends lining the gutters of the streets I walked along this afternoon, the substance abuse crisis programs in every city in North America are evidence enough of the mind-warping dangers of drugs.

Satanism is psychic suicide. Yes, it's opinion time: I think anyone who dedicates his life to a force or god or lifestyle of evil is destroying himself spiritually. I noticed along a subway corridor this morning an Islamic display with a poster that read "Hell is in the chest of man." I think a true satanist is a walking spiritual Hell. Unless you're one of the influential but frankly few people who believe man is only a machine, you with me should be worried about the twisted spiritual belief structure of any satanist kid who'll be a parent in the next century.

With Satan as a god, the teenage dabbler is signing in blood for a body scarred with probable sexual disease and violence. He's asking for a mind warped by drugs and altered states that blur reality and illusion. Emotionally, any person living his formative teenage years in a combination of fear and repression of normal feelings such as compassion is going to be dangerous in personal and social relationships. Spiritually, anyone who believes his spirit is destined for Hell is going to live like it. We've got to do something before this new generation of Satan's children begets the next generation. I'm counting on you.

Is there a timing factor?

Let me read a couple of opinions: The first is religious, so if you're irreligious, prepare yourself. But it's a valid perspective to consider since, as many Christians believe the 1990s is, as writer Hal Lindsey put it, a "countdown to Armageddon," satanists also seem to believe these to be the "last days." And they'll act, as we've seen, according to their beliefs.

The 1986 *Passport* magazine article "America's Best Kept Secret" closes with:

As the return of Jesus Christ draws nearer, satanic activity and power is continually increasing, eventually to peak as never before in human history during the tribulation period. At the same time, a great apostasy or falling away from true Christian faith is to take place (1 Timothy 4:1). With many signs that both prophecies have already begun to happen, there is a tremendous need for all Christians, both young and old, to know and understand the ways and workings of Satan.

Another apocalyptic view I jotted down in our travels comes from the ex-cop psychologist Lyle Rapacki in Flagstaff, Arizona, who says, "North America is experiencing a dramatic rise in what was once a strictly secret, closed association of followers whose rites and rituals were known only to them. Satanism today is brazenly practiced across this country, and its brutal onslaught has caught nearly everyone by surprise.

"In the truest sense of the word, we are witnessing a spiritual war that has secular and temporal repercussions. To call this war anything else but what it is—spiritual—is to be guilty of aiding and abetting this demonic assault. We must be aware that not everything supernatural is of God."

Could this surge of diabolical business signal the end? Before we start panicking, we probably should realize that toward the end of every century, there seems to be an increase in end-of-time stories and a sense of an impending cosmic shift. But whenever the end looms, I think of the German astronomer and minister Stoeffler who predicted that the world would end in 1524 in a massive flood. His parishioners dutifully built rafts and arks. But when the deluge failed to appear, they simply threw Stoeffler into a pond and went about life. Or there was Winifred Barton, the Canadian psychic who in 1976 predicted the end would come at 9 p.m. June 13. At exactly that hour there were several loud peals of thunder and flashes of lightning over Toronto that prompted hundreds of terrified citizens to call the police. The police response? A spokesmen said, "We just told them to call back at 9:05."

So, even as a solid Bible-believing Christian, you need to be careful about date-setting and therefore undue concern about satanists taking over the world in the next few years.

But regardless of cosmic aspects in this rise of satanism in North America, we need to be concerned about what's happening in satanic circles these days. Maury Terry, author of *The Ultimate Evil*, the book I've been reading off and on through our quest, is eloquent in his closing remarks on the seriousness of this phenomenon:

I believe the satanic activity now being reported will increase. It will reach proportions heretofore unseen. From every indication and piece of evidence I'd gathered, the ominous signs point to a burgeoning cult movement in and around New York, Houston and Los Angeles, at the least.

These cities were part of the organized network [of The Process], and its membership ranks, I learned, were steadily growing—populated to a large extent by young and successful people from professional walks of life.

And beyond the umbrella, parent group, independent cults were springing to life in virtually every state in the U.S.A. In many instances, these groups would seek alliances with the old order, and some would do so successfully.

There is compelling evidence of the existence of a nationwide network of satanic cults, some aligned more closely than others. Some are purveying narcotics; others have branched into child pornography and violence, including murder. I am concerned that the toll of innocent victims will steadily mount unless law enforcement officials recognize the threat and face it.

The torch that was put into [Charles] Manson's hand in 1969 was never extinguished. It was instead passed to [Son of Sam] Berkowitz and others, and the violence and depravity continued. The evidence demonstrates that the force behind that carnage was in place both before and after the Manson and Son of Sam slayings. And, luring in various guises, it is still there.

There is no insulating Middle America. This time, it isn't an inner-city eruption that can be written off as the inevitable fallout from poverty and slums. No, this battleground is elsewhere: the list of the dead tells that story. The killer cults were born and nurtured in the comfort zone of America and are now victimizing it at will.

Manson's haunting testimony and a later warning from David Berkowitz echo loudly across the years. Two statements, made on opposite coasts nearly a decade apart. Yet the dire message is the same.

"What about your children?" Manson challenged a Los Angeles courtroom as the 1970s began. "You say there are just a few? There are many, many more, coming in the same direction. They are running in the streets—and they are coming right at you!"

In New York, Berkowitz would write: "There are other 'Sons' out there—God help the world."

Do Your Best

As I swing through the Marriott's gold revolving doors back onto the Broadway street of pinch-faced loiterers and beggars among the rushing crowds, I'm thinking about you, wondering just who you are. Make sure you introduce yourself when I get around to speak on suicide or drugs or satanism in your area.

It's getting windier, colder in the October early evening. And darker; a kid on the elevator had warned me about wandering around too much tonight: "Yeah, their idea of gun control in nighttime Manhattan is to hold a .38 with both hands." I push against the wind down Broadway and stumble into the middle of a strange menagerie of shouting young men in front of the Times Square Television Studios. A limousine is parked double, doors swung wide and shaved-headed men are trying to climb back into the car amid flying fists. The attackers are shouting something I can't catch. At the studio door is a young man I recognize from Geraldo Rivera's office earlier. "What's going on?" I yell.

"Ah, these are our guests for the show this evening." He points to the Neo-Nazi skinheads trying to clamber back into the car.

"And the other guys?"

"Jewish Defense League," he says. "I think."

I escape inside and ride the elevator to the fourth floor and find Geraldo apologizing to the audience that the taping is cancelled since the Neo-Nazi guests in the riot outside have deigned to return to their hotel.

After all the women in their forties and fifties have gotten their autographs and pictures, Geraldo in his dressing room/office is relaxed as I ask him to do a foreword for the book.

"Have to see the manuscript first," he says.

"So you've done, what? Three, four shows on satanism?" I ask. "What do we do about it?"

"Do your best," he says. "Like the media. They have to follow up everything, corroborate everything to get to the truth. Track down every lead on what this brand of satanism is doing to us. Send me the manuscript," he says as I leave.

I've got to do something about teenagers who are selling their souls for nothing more than Hell on earth.

Before I turn in for the night I call the lady who's been talking about being satanically terrorized to Tricia in Kansas City. Lynn is home.

"This is Jerry Johnston, Lynn. I wanted to call—"

Her voice is weary with the weight of evil. "She said you might. I called her just yesterday," says Lynn, "to tell her that they've said I won't live past Halloween. But my little grandson is safe. They won't bring him up in satanism now. He won't be beaten and driven crazy with evil." The voice lilts Southern, almost a whisper.

I nod into the phone. "I'm so glad. I was worried about the boy. I've been following your struggles and thinking of you. I'm glad you got him back."

"Oh," says Lynn. "I didn't get him back. They took him."

"I thought you said he's safe?"

"Oh, he's safe, Jerry. Safe in the arms of God."

Appendix A
Symbols

The "upside down" cross is an inverted Christian cross. This early-'60s peace symbol is now commonly thought of as the "Cross of Nero" by heavy metalheads and occultists.

The Inverted Cross

Cross of Nero

The "ankh" is an ancient magical Egyptian symbol for life. The top portion represents the female and the lower portion the male.

The Ankh

The "cross of confusion" is an ancient Roman symbol questioning the existence or validity of Christianity.

The Cross of Confusion

Four different ways which refer to the "mark of the beast: or Satan." Note that the letter "F" is the sixth letter of the alphabet.

666   **FFF**

Various Versions of the
Mark of the Beast

Here, the moon goddess "Diana" and the morning star of "Lucifer" are represented. This symbol is found in nearly all types of witchcraft and satanism. When the moon is turned to face the opposite direction, it is primarily satanic.

Diana and Lucifer

The Pentagram

The pentagram, or, without the circle, the pentacle is used in most forms of occult magic. A spirit conjured within the pentagram cannot supposedly leave the circle without permission. Witches generally conjure spirits from outside the pentagram while satanists can submit to possession by the spirit by standing within the pentagram while calling up a demon. Generally, the top point represents the spirit, and the other points represent wind, fire, earth, and water.

The Upside-down Pentagram

The upside down pentagram, often called the "baphomet," is strictly satanic in nature and represents the goat's head.

Hexagram "Seal of Solomon"

The hexagram, also referred to as the "Seal of Solomon," is said to be one of the most powerful symbols in the occult.

Double-bladed Ax

The Roman symbol of justice was a double bladed ax in the upright position. The representation of "anti-justice" is inverting the double bladed ax.

Triangle

The "triangle" may vary in size, but is generally inscribed or drawn on the ground and is the place where a demon would appear in conjuration rituals.

Circle

The "circle" has different meanings. One symbolizes eternity. Another implies protection from evil without and power within. When used for ritual, it is nine feet in diameter.

A "talisman" or "amulet" is an object with drawing or writing inscribed in it of a god's name or image of a supernatural power.

Talisman or Amulet

Trail Markers

There are many forms of directional trail markers which are employed by formal and casual occult groups alike. These markers indicate locations where occult activities may take place and how to get there. The markers depicted to the right show a small circle or starting place, then a direction to be taken. The rise or fall of the line shows hills and valleys type terrain.

Other marker types could be a pentagram on the right or left side of a road, trail, or even on a house or a building.

The inverted cross of satanic justice is often found carved into a traitor's chest. It is also used as a backdrop near a "baphomet" for curse and compassion rituals. The center vertical line indicates man's present. The horizontal line indicates eternity, past and future. The arch indicates the world. The inverted cross appearance symbolizes the defeat of Christianity.

The sexual ritual symbol is used to indicate the place and purpose. It is often carved into a stone or painted on the side of the road to show present use of the location.

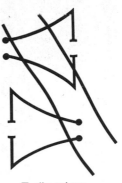

Trailmarkers

The blood ritual symbol represents human and animal sacrifices.

Blood Ritual Symbol

Black Mass indicators:

Black Mass Indicators

Sample Altar

Sample Altar

The altar may be any flat object where the implements of the ritual are placed. The altar will usually be placed within the nine foot circle. This diagram shows a marble or granite slab 48" × 22" × 2". The pentagram in the center is etched into the slab. Human or animal blood is then poured into the etching. Other symbols may be carved into the slab according to individual group traditions. Implements that would be placed on the altar would include: athame, chalice, candles, parchment, cauldron, Book of Shadows.

Swastika

The "swastika" or "broken cross" is of ancient origin. Originally, it represented the four winds, four seasons, and four points of the compass. At that time, its arms were at 90 degree angles turned the opposite way as depicted here. The "swastika" shown here shows the elements or forces turning against nature and out of harmony. Nazis and occult groups use it in this manner.

Anarchy

The symbol of "anarchy" represents the abolition of all law. Initially, those into "punk" music used this symbol, but it is now widely used by heavy metal followers and satanic dabblers.

Glossary

A.A.: The abbreviated form for Argenteum Astrum. This is a magickal order founded by Aleister Crowley in 1904. Several West Coast covens claim A.A. roots.

ATHAME: A dagger or sword, usually with a black handle and with magickal inscriptions on its blade.

BAPHOMET: A semi-human, semi-goat figure worshiped originally by the Knights Templar in the Middle Ages and now universally considered a focal insignia of satanism. The figure has a goat head, angelic wings, female breasts and a torch between its horns.

BEELZEBUB: The demon of decay in demonology, often thought to rank directly under Satan himself.

BELIAL: The demon of death and destruction in demonology.

BOOK OF SHADOWS: Also called a grimoire, this journal kept either by individual witches or satanists or by a coven or group, records the activities of the group and the incantations used.

CHALICE: A silver goblet used for blood communions.

CIRCLE: In every level of the occult, the circle represents wholeness. A ritual circle is used to protect conjurers as they stand outside the circle to summon demons; satanists sometimes proudly insist that they stand within the circle as the demon is summoned for complete possession. Often a group of witches, called by some a coven, is termed a circle.

CONE OF POWER: Imagining a vortex of energy directed toward a goal or person is a common ritual performed in witchcraft.

COVEN: Also called a clan, a coven is a group of satanists who gather to perform rites. Traditionally numbering thirteen, covens today can commonly number nine or any number within the self-styled groups.

CURSE: Invocation of an oath associated with black magic or sorcery intended to harm or destroy opponents or property; curses often require the invocation of evil spirits.

DAEMON: From the Greek daimon, a spirit, an evil spirit or demon.

DEVIL: The personification of evil called Lucifer or Satan. The word means accuser or slanderer. It is one of the names of Satan, also known as Lucifer.

DRUIDS: Celtic priests in pre-Christian Britain and Gaul. Skilled in astronomy and medicine, they worshiped the Sun, believed in immortality of the soul and reincarnation. Very powerful and very dangerous—still active today.

EQUINOX: The time at which the Sun crosses the equator. This takes place on March 21 and September 27, and on these days the length of day and night are the same.

GRIMOIRES: A medieval collection of magical spells, rituals and incantations. Also any coven or circle's Book of Shadows recording spells, ceremonies and histories of the group.

HALLOWEEN: Occult holiday, All Hallow's Eve, October 31, end and beginning of Celtic year.

HAND OF GLORY: The left hand of a person who has died. The hand is removed and a candle is positioned between the fingers. The ritual is used for protection against evil spirits.

HEAD: Central powerhouse of the body believed to contain all magical powers. For this reason, many human skulls are used on altars. Also the eating of the brain is believed to transfer power.

HEART: This is symbolic of the center of life. Symbol of eternity. By the eating of the heart, it is assumed that you will gain the characteristics and powers of the deceased.

HEXAGRAM: A six pointed star, also known as the Star of David. The hexagram is believed among occultists to protect and control demons.

HORNED GOD: Symbol of male sexuality in paganism and witchcraft. Part man, part goat.

INITIATE: One who has successfully passed through a ritual of initiation. Also, one who possesses secret knowledge.

INVERTED CROSS: Upside-down crucifix, often seen at occult sites.

LIGATURE: A spell which prevents a person from doing something.

LITHOMANCY: Magic using stones or semi-precious gems. Colors of stones are important to working.

LUCIFER: Means Morning Star; the archangel who protected the throne of God. Because of pride, he led a revolt against God, and was cast out of Heaven along with one-third of the angel population who later became demons. Also as the "lightbearer," considered a neutral being or force which man can use for good or evil in his attempts to attain godhood.

MAGIC: Technique of harnessing the secret powers of nature and seeking to influence events for one's own purposes. If the purpose is beneficial it is known as white magic. If its intention is to bring harm to others, or to destroy property, it is regarded as black magic.

MAGICK: Magic that employs ritual symbols and ceremony, including ceremonial costumes, dramatic invocations to the gods, potent incense and mystic sacraments.

MAGIC CIRCLE: A circle inscribed on the floor of a temple for ceremonial purposes. Often nine feet in diameter, believed to hold magical powers within and protect those involved in the ceremony from evil.

MAGISTER: Male leader of a coven.

MAGUS: A male witch.

NECROMANCY: A practice in which the "spirits of the dead" are summoned to provide omens relating to future events or to discover secrets of the past.

NECROPHILIA: The act of having sexual intercourse with the dead.

OCCULT: From the Latin word occultus, which means "secret" or "hidden," the occult refers to 1) secret or hidden knowledge available to initiates, 2) the supernatural, and 3) sometimes used of parapsychology and paranormal phenomena.

PENTACLE: A five-pointed star used as a magic symbol in rituals.

PENTAGRAM: A pentacle surrounded by a circle. It represents the four elements. When the star is inverted with two points up, it stands for black arts. When turned with a single point up, it symbolizes white magic. Pentagrams are also worn for "protection" and identification among members of The Craft.

RITUAL: A prescribed form of religious or magical ceremony.

RUNES: A northern European alphabet used by occult groups in secret writing. There are several forms of runeing.

SABBAT: A gathering of witches to commemorate a special date.

SANTERIA: Worship of the saints, a mingling of African tribal religions and Catholicism established by African slaves brought to the Americas and Caribbean.

SATAN: The angelic being created by the Christian God. He was an archangel who protected God's throne, rebelled and was cast out of heaven.

SHADOWS, BOOK OF: In witchcraft, the personal book of spells and rituals kept by individual witches and satanists and by covens as a whole. A Book of Shadows is traditionally destroyed when the witch dies.

SO MOTE IT BE: Words said at the end of an occult ceremony. Similar to "amen" in traditional religious services.

SOLSTICE: Summer and winter seasonal points at which the day is longest—usually June 21—and the night longest—generally December 21.

TALISMAN: Power object, usually an amulet or trinket.

VOODOO: An ancient religion combining Catholicism and sorcery. Those involved are extremely superstitious and are heavily involved in fetishism.

WARLOCK: Often used of a male witch; actually designates a traitor.

WICCA: The paganistic end of the witchcraft spectrum.

WITCH: A male or female practitioner of any sort of witchcraft.

WITCHCRAFT: A practice of occultic arts, from wiccan-nature worship to satanic worship.

YULE: Occult holiday, December 22, winter solstice, the shortest day of the year.

Appendix B
Resources

ACT—Affirming Children's Truth
Jackie McGauley
P. O. Box 417
Redondo Beach, CA 90277
213-376-5652
A child advocacy group for sexually and/or ritually abused children.

Adam Walsh Resource Center
1876 N. University, Suite 306
Fort Lauderdale, FL 33322
A clearinghouse for kidnapped children information.

B.A.D.D.—Bothered about Dungeons & Dragons
Patricia Pulling
Richmond, VA 23220
804-883-5616
An educational group on occult roleplaying games, teenage occult involvement and occult crime.

Believe the Children
Leslie Floberg
P. O. Box 1358
Manhattan Beach, CA 90266
National headquarters for association for parents and children of ritual abuse.

C.A.R.I.S.
Jack Roper
P. O. Box 1659
Milwaukee, WI 53201
414-771-7397/771-2940
Occult crime and satanic education organization.

Calvalcade Productions
Dale McCulley
7360 Potter Valley Road
Ukiah, CA 95482
702-743-1168
Company offering educational tools on satanic cults.

Childhelp
6463 Independence Avenue
Woodland Hills, CA 91367
1-800-422-4453
Agency offering assistance in child abuse and missing child cases.

Cult Awareness Network
P. O. Box 608370
Chicago, IL 60626
312-267-7777
Headquarters of organization monitoring destructive cult activity.

District Attorney Office/Victim Witness Service
Janet Fine
40 Thorndike
Cambridge, MA 02141
617-494-4232
An advocate in child abuse, ritual abuse cases.

Dolter, Steve
School Psychologist
9401 South Painter Ave.
Whittier, CA 90605
213-698-8121 Ext. 361
Counselor offering seminars on heavy metal and the occult.

EXODUS
Yvonne Peterson
San Antonio, TX
512-646-1222

FACES
71 Haynes Street
Manchester, CT 06040
203-646-1222

Incest Survivors Resource Network, Int.
15 Rutherford Place
New York, NY 10003
513-935-3031
Agency offering information on incest/ritual abuse.

Interfaith Council on Cults
Fr. James LeBar
2 Harvey Street
Hyde Park, NY 12538
Consultant on the occult.

Jerry Johnston Association
P. O. Box 12193
Overland Park, KS 66212-0193
Youth Specialist Organization.

Jewish Federation-Council
Task Force on Cults & Missionary Efforts
Raches Andres
6505 Wilshire Blvd.
Los Angeles, CA 90048
213-852-1234/818-990-8640
Organization offering updates on destructive cult activity.

Justice for Sexually Abused Children (J-SAC)
Andrea Landis
9703 S. Dixie Highway
Miami, FL 33156
305-284-0485
Activist group offering help in ritual abuse cases.

Michigan Protection and Advocacy Service
109 West Michigan Avenue, Suite 900
Lansing, MI 48933
517-487-1755
Child advocacy agency.

National Center on Child Abuse and Neglect
P. O. Box 1182
Washington, DC 20013
301-251-5157
Clearinghouse for child abuse information.

National Center for Missing & Exploited Children
1835 K Street, N.W., Suite 700
Washington, DC 20006
202-634-6795
Clearinghouse for missing and abused children.

National Child Abuse Coalition
1125 15th St., N.W., #300
Washington, DC 20006
202-293-7550
Resource group on child abuse problems.

National Coalition for Children's Justice
Mr. Ken Wooden
P. O. Box 4345
Shelburne, VT 05482
802-985-8458
Consultant and educator on all forms of child
exploitation.

National Commission for Prevention of Child
Abuse
332 S. Michigan Avenue, Suite 950
Chicago, IL 60604
Agency providing information and training materials.

Parents' Music Resource Center
1500 Arlington Blvd.
Arlington, VA 22209
Group monitoring rock music lyrics.

Sunny von Bulow Victim Advocacy Center
307 W. 7th Street, #1001
Fort Worth, TX 76102
917-877-3355
Agency advocating victims' rights.

UBC Rape Prevention & Education Program
Building T-9, Room 201
University of California
Berkeley, CA 94729
Office providing educational materials on occult
crime.

VOICES in Action, Inc.
P. O. Box 148309
Chicago, IL 60605

W.A.T.C.H.
Susan Joiner
P. O. Box 12638
El Paso, TX 79913
Group monitoring occult activity.

Writeway Literary Associates
David Balsiger
P. O. Box 10428
Costa Mesa, CA 92627
714-850-0349
Consultation and training on occult crime.

Law Enforcement/Investigators

Dale Griffis
P. O. Box 309
Tiffin, OH 44883
419-447-8611

Beaumont Police Department
Kurt Jackson, Officer
500 Grace
Beaumont, CA 92223
714-845-1161

Boise Police Department
Lt. Larry Jones
7200 Barrister Drive
Boise, ID 83704
208-377-6748

Denver Police Department
Detective William Wickersham
1331 Cherokee Street
Denver, CO 80204
303-575-3832

Denver Police Department
Detective Cleo Wilson
1331 Cherokee Street
Denver, CO 80204
303-575-3832

Sheriff's Department, Clallan County
Detective Larry Dunn
223 E. 4th Avenue
Port Angeles, WA 98362
206-452-7836

San Francisco Police Department
Detective Sandra Gallant
Intelligence Division 535
850 Bryant Street
San Francisco, CA 94103
415-553-1133

Main State Police, Criminal Investigations Division
Maurice Quellett
U. S. Route 1
Scarborough, MA 04074
207-883-3473

Detective Robert J. Simandl
Gang Crime Unit, Chicago Police Department
1121 S. State
Chicago, IL 60605
312-744-6328

Prosecutors/Attorneys/Legal Organizations

Jay Howell
2029 N. Third Street
Jacksonville Beach, FL 32050
904-247-1972

Children's Advocacy Center
Bob Jones
2202 Colice Road
Huntsville, AL 35801
205-830-3276

Office of the District Attorney
Laurence Hardoon
40 Thorndike Street
Cambridge, MA 02141
617-494-4050

National Legal Resource Center
Howard A. Davidson
Resource Director
1800 M Street, N.W., Suite 200
Washington, DC 20036
202-331-2250

National Center for Prosecution of Child Abuse
James C. Shrine, Director
1033 N. Fairfax Street, Suite 200
Alexandria, VA 22314
703-739-0321

Medical Examiners

William T. Terry, M.D.
P. O. Box 6179
Reno, NV 89613-6179
702-322-6462

Harbor–UCLA Medical Center
Carol Berkowitz, M.D.
1000 W. Carson
Carson, CA 90509
213-533-3091

Herman Jones Clinic
Daniel Higgins, M.D.
2699 Atlantic
Long Beach, CA 90807
213-435-1141

Mt. Sinai Hospital
Howard Levy, M.D.
2720 W. 15th
Chicago, IL 60608
312-650-6721

Dan Higgins, M.D.
St. Francis Medical Center
3630 East Imperial Hwy.
Lynwood, CA 90262
213-603-6060

Mental Health

Bennett Braun, M.D.
230 N. Michigan Avenue
Chicago, IL 60601

Lynda Detling
1901 Westcliff Drive, Suite 10
Newport Beach, CA 92660

Michael Durfee, M.D.
313 N. Figueroa
Los Angeles, CA 90012

Dr. Catherine Gould
16661 Ventura Blvd., Suite 303
Encino, CA 91436
213-650-0807

Pamela Hudson, L.C.S.W.
P. O. Box 807
Mendocino, CA 95460

The National Foundation for Children
Drs. Joseph & Laurie Braga
3120 Center Street
Coconut Grove, FL 33133
305-443-8625

Rapha
Box 580355
Houston, TX 77258
1-800-227-2657

South Bay Center for Counseling
Dr. Cheryl Kent
2617 Bell Avenue
Manhattan Beach, CA 90266

School of Social Science, University of Chicago
Dr. Jon Conte
969 E. 60th Street
Chicago, IL 60607

Susan Kelley, R.N., Ph.D.
Maternal Child Health Graduate Program
Boston College, School of Nursing
Chestnut Hill, MA 02167
617-552-4275

Helen Morrison, M.D.
919 N. Michigan Avenue
Chicago, IL 60611
312-944-1781

Noel Plourde, MA, MFCC
2810 Artesia Blvd.
Redondo Beach, CA 90278

Roberta G. Sachs, M.D.
660 LaSalle Place
Highland Park, IL 60035

Bethesda PsycHealth Institute
Wayne Van Kampen
4400 E. Iliff Avenue
Denver, CO 80222

Erikson Institute
James Garbarino, Ph.D.
25 West Chicago Avenue
Chicago, IL 60610
312-332-2792

Pathways
Martha Cockriel, L.C.S.W.
1050 Duncan, Suite H
Manhattan Beach, CA 90266
213-318-6658

Harbor/UCLA Medical Center
Dr. Roland Summit
1000 Carson Street, Building D-6
Carson, CA 90509
213-533-3129

Dr. Michelle Dugan
1050 Duncan, Suite H
Manhattan Beach, CA 90266
213-318-6658

Institute for Family Therapy
William Pinsof, Ph.D.
666 N. Lake Shore Drive
Chicago, IL 60611
312-908-7285

Harborview Sexual Assault Center
Lucy Berliner, MSW
325 9th Avenue
Seattle, WA 98101

Bibliography

Aquino, Michael. *The Crystal Tablet of Set.* 12th ed. (San Francisco: Temple of Set, 1987).

Adler, Margot. *Drawing Down the Moon* (New York: Beacon Press, 1986).

Allen-Baley, Carol, and David Balsiger. "Heavy Metal: A Weighty Police Problem." Writeway Literary Associates, 1986.

————, and Pat Metoyer. "Emerging Nightmare: Ritualistic Crime in America." *The Police and Firemen's Insurance Association Magazine* (August 1988): 4ff.

Angebert, Hean-Michel. *The Occult and the Third Reich* (New York: McGraw-Hill, 1976).

Aylesworth, Thomas. *The Story of Witches* (New York: McGraw-Hill, 1979).

Bainbridge, William S. *Satan's Power: A Deviant Psychotherapy Cult* (Berkeley and Los Angeles: University of California Press, 1978).

Balodis, Jacquie. "Soul Stealing: An Overview of Satanic and Black Witchcraft Ritual Abuse and Brainwashing." 1988.

Baskin, Wade. *The Sorcerer's Handbook* (New York: Philosophical Library, 1974).

Boar, Roger and Nigel Blundell. *The World's Most Infamous Murders* (New York: Exeter Books, 1984).

Bounds, E. M. *Satan: His Personality, Power and Overthrow* (Grand Rapids: Baker Book House, 1972).

Braun, Bennett G. *Multiplicity: Form, Function and Phenomena* (Chicago: Associated Mental Health Services, 1978).

Brown, Rebecca M.D. *Prepare for War* (Chino, CA: Chick Publications, 1987).

Brown, Rebecca M.D. *He Came to Set the Captives Free* (Chino, CA: Chick Publications, 1986).

Bubeck, Mark I. *The Adversary: The Christian Versus Demon Activity* (Chicago: Moody Press, 1975).

Bubeck, Mark I. *Overcoming the Adversary: Warfare Praying against Demon Activity* (Chicago: Moody Press, 1984).

Carr, Joseph J. *The Twisted Cross* (Shreveport: Huntington House, 1985).

————. *The Lucifer Connection* (Shreveport: Huntington House, 1987).

Cavendish, Richard. *A History of Magic* (New York: Taplinger Publishing Co., 1977).

————. *The Black Arts* (New York: G. P. Putnam's Sons, 1967).

Crowley, Aleister. *The Book of Thoth: A Short Essay on the Tarot of the Egyptians* (New York: Samuel Weiser, 1969).

————. *Confessions of Aleister Crowley* (New York: Bantam Books, 1971).

————. *Magick in Theory and Practice* (New York: Samuel Weiser, 1974).

Claire, Thomas C. *Occult Bibliography: An Annotated List, 1971–1975* (Metuchen, N.J.: Scarecrow Press, 1978).

Cox, H. G. *Seduction of the Spirit: The Use and Misuse of People's Religion* (New York: Simon & Schuster, 1977).

DiMaio, Debra, producer. "Satanic Worship" segment aired on the February 17, 1988, "Oprah Winfrey Show" (WLS-TV, Chicago).

DeHaan, Richard W. *Satan, Satanism and Witchcraft* (Grand Rapids: Zondervan, 1972).

Drury, Neville, and G. Tillet. *The Occult Sourcebook* (London: Routledge & Keegan Paul, 1985).

Ebon, Martin. *The Devil's Bride: Exorcism, Past and Present* (New York: Harper & Row, 1974).

Frattorola, John. "America's Best-Kept Secret." *Passport Magazine.* Special issue, 1986.

Green, Michael. *I Believe in Satan's Downfall* (Grand Rapids: William B. Eerdmans' Publishing Company, 1981).

Gurnall, William. *The Christian in Complete Armour*, Second Edition (Carlisle, PA: The Banner of Truth Trust, 1964).

Hammond, Frank and Ida Mae. *Pigs in the Parlor: A Practical Guide to Deliverance* (Kirkwood, MO: Impact Books, Inc., 1973).

Huegel, F. J. *The Mystery of Iniquity: How to Win in the War against Satan* (Minneapolis: Dimension Books, 1959).

Hunt, Dave, and T. A. McMahon. *America: The Sorcerer's New Apprentice: The Rise of New Age Shamanism* (Eugene, OR: Harvest House Publishers, 1988).

Johnston, Jerry. *Why Suicide?* (Nashville: Oliver Nelson, 1987).

Jones, Larry M., ed. *File 18 Newsletter*. Boise: Cult Crime Impact Network, 1986–

Jung, Carl G. *Psychology and the Occult* (Princeton: Princeton University Press, 1977).

Kahaner, Larry. *Cults That Kill: Probing the Underworld of Occult Crime* (New York: Warner Books, Inc., 1988).

Karman, Robert. *God, Satan, and the Mind* (Whittier, CA : Sunteleo Center, 1986).

King, Francis, and Stephen Skinner. *Techniques of High Magic: A Manual of Self-Initiation* (Rochester, VT.: Destiny Books, 1976).

Kirban, Salem. *Satan's Angels Exposed* (Huntington Valley, PA: Salem Kirban, Inc., 1980).

Kluft, Richard P., ed. *Childhood Antecedents of Multiple Personality* (Washington, D.C.: American Psychiatric Press, 1985).

Knight, Walker L. *The Weird World of the Occult* (Wheaton: Tyndale House Publishers, 1972).

Koch, Kurt. *Demonology: Past and Present* (Grand Rapids: Kregel Publications, 1973).

———. *Occult Bondage and Deliverance* (Grand Rapids: Kregel Publications, 1972).

LaVey, Anton S. *The Compleat Witch* (New York: Dodd, Mead, 1971).

———. *The Satanic Bible* (New York: Avon Books, 1969).

———. *The Satanic Rituals* (New York: Avon Books, 1972).

Leek, Sybil. *The Complete Art of Witchcraft* (New York: World Publishing, 1975).

Lewis, C. S. *The Screwtape Letters* (Chicago: Lord and King Associates, 1976).

Lindsey, Hal. *Satan Is Alive and Well on Planet Earth* (Grand Rapids: Zondervan, 1972).

Martin, Malachi. *Hostage to the Devil: The Possession and Exorcism of Five Living Americans* (New York: Harper and Row, 1976).

McDowell, Josh, and Don Stewart. *Demons, Witches and the Occult* (Wheaton: Tyndale House Publishers, 1986).

Montgomery, John W. *Demon Possession* (Minneapolis: Bethany Fellowship, 1976).

Moonstone, Amber K. *Pagan Kids' Activity Book* (Blue Mounds, WS : Amber K. Moonstone Publications, 1986).

Moore, Raymond S. *The Abaddon Conspiracy* (Minneapolis: Bethany Publishers, 1985).

Murrell, Conrad. *Practical Demonology: Tactics for Demon Warfare*, Second Edition (Bentley, LA: Saber Publications, 1973).

Nathan, Debbie. "Are These Women Child Molesters? The Making of a Modern Witch Trial." *The Village Voice.* 29 September 1987. 19ff.

Naysmith, Bette. *Ritualistic Abuse Inquiries Report* (Chicago: Cult Awareness Network, n.d.).

Penn-Lewis, Jessie. *War on the Saints: A Disclosure of the Deceptive Strategies Used by Evil Spirits against God's People* (Dorset, England: The Overcomer Literature Trust, 1977).

Pentecost, J. Dwight. *Your Adversary the Devil* (Grand Rapids: Zondervan, 1969).

Peterson, Robert. *Are Demons for Real?: Dramatic Incidents of Spirit Phenomena in Conflict with the Power of Christ* (Chicago: Moody Press, 1972).

Pittman, Howard O. *Demons: An Eyewitness Account* (Self Published).

Pratney, Winkie. *Devil Take the Youngest: The War on Childhood* (Shreveport, LA: Huntington House, Inc., 1985).

Rapacki, Lyle J. *Satanism: The Not So New Problem* (Flagstaff, AZ : INTEL, 1988).

Rivera, Geraldo, host. "Satanic Cults and Children" segment aired 19 November 1987, "Geraldo." New York, Investigative News Group.

Rockstad, Ernest B. *Counseling in the Demonic Crisis* (Andover, Kans.: Faith and Life Publications, n.d.).

Russell, Jeffrey Burton. *The Devil: Perceptions of Evil from Antiquity to Primitive Christianity*, (Ithaca, NY : Cornell University Press; 1977).

Russell, Jeffrey Burton. *A History of Witchcraft: Sorcery, Heretics, Pagans* (Ithaca, NY: Cornell University Press, 1980).

————. *Satan: The Early Christian Tradition* (Ithaca, N.Y.: Cornell University Press, 1981).

————. *Lucifer, the Devil in the Middle Ages* (Ithaca, N.Y.: Cornell University Press, 1984).

————. *Mephistopheles: the Devil in the Modern World* (Ithaca, N.Y.: Cornell University Press, 1986).

Ryrie, Charles C. *The Ryrie Study Bible* (Chicago: Moody Press, 1976).

St. Clair, David. *Say You Love Satan* (New York: Dell Publishing Co., Inc., 1987).

Schwarz, Ted, and Empey, Duane. *Satanism* (Grand Rapids: Zondervan, 1988).

Simandl, Robert J., and Bette Naysmith. "Dabbling Their Way to Ritual Crime." 1988.

Smith, Michelle, and Lawrence Pazder, M.D. *Michelle Remembers* (New York: Pocket Books, 1980).

Sparks, Beatrice. *Jay's Journal* (New York: Dell Publishing Co., Inc., 1979).

Starhawk. *The Spiral Dance: A Rebirth of the Ancient Religion of the Great Goddess* (San Francisco: Harper & Row, 1979).

Stone, Adrianne. "King Diamond: Swords and Sorcery." *Power Metal Magazine*. November 1988. 4ff.

Stratford, Lauren. *Satan's Underground: The Extraordinary Story of One Woman's Escape* (Eugene, OR: Harvest House Publishers, 1988).

Tatford, Fredk. A. *Satan: The Prince of Darkness* (Grand Rapids: Kregel Publications).

Taylor, Jack R. *Victory over the Devil* (Nashville: Broadman Press, 1973).

Terry, Maury. *The Ultimate Evil: An Investigation of America's Most Dangerous Satanic Occult* (Garden City, NY: Dolphin Books, 1987).

Thomas, F. W. *Kingdom of Darkness: A Penetrating Study of the Nethermost Realms of the Occult* (Plainfield, NJ: Logos International, 1973).

Unger, Merrill F. *Demons in the World Today* (Wheaton: Tyndale House Publishers, 1971).

————. *What Demons Can Do to Saints* (Chicago: Moody Press, 1977).

Vacchys, Andrew. "Crimes Against Children." Supplement provided by Believe the Children Organization, n.d.

Warnke, Mike. *The Satan Seller* (Plainfield, NJ: Logos International, 1972).

Warnke, Rose Hall. *The Great Pretender* (Lancaster, PA: Starburst Publications, 1985).

Webb, James. *The Occult Underground* (LaSalle, IL : Open Court Press, 1976).

————. *The Occult Establishment* (LaSalle, IL : Open Court Press, 1976).

Wedge, Thomas W. *The Satan Hunter* (Canton, OH: Daring Books, 1988).

White, John Wesley. *The Devil: What the Scriptures Teach about Him* (Wheaton: Tyndale House Publishers, Inc., 1977).

Wiersbe, Warren W. *The Strategy of Satan: How to Detect and Defeat Him* (Wheaton: Tyndale House Publishers, Inc. 1979).

Wooden, Kenneth, and Peter W. Kunhardt, producers. "The Devil Worshipers," on "20/20." 16 May 1985.

X, Tim and Betsy. *The Enemy: Satan's Struggle for Two Boys' Souls* (Wheaton: Tyndale House Publishers, 1973).